Explorers, Traders, and Slavers

Explorers, Traders, and Slavers
Forging the Old Spanish Trail
1678–1850

~

JOSEPH P. SÁNCHEZ

UNIVERSITY OF UTAH PRESS ~ SALT LAKE CITY

LIBRARY OF CONGRESS CATALOGING-IN-PUBLICATION DATA

Sánchez, Joseph P.
   Explorers, traders, and slavers : forging the old Spanish Trail, 1678–1850 /
Joseph P. Sánchez.
      p.   cm.
   Includes bibliographical references and index.
   ISBN 0-87480-526-0 (alk. paper)
   1. Old Spanish Trail—History. 2. Southwest, New—Discovery and
exploration—Spanish. 3. Indian traders—Southwest, New—History. 4. Slave
traders—Southwest, New—History.   I. Title.
F799.S26   1996   96-39357

For my wife, Clara,
and my sons, Joseph and Paul,
who accompanied me on several segments
of the Old Spanish Trail

Contents

Preface

THIS BOOK IS by no means a definitive history of the efforts of Hispanic frontiersmen to develop trade routes to the Great Basin between 1678 and 1850. Nor is the book an attempt to present a comprehensive study of the Hispanic dream to found a direct emigration route from New Mexico to California between 1776 and 1850. Rather, this book endeavors to identify salient themes and historical personages in the early history of the Old Spanish Trail and its many variants. A definitive history would be impossible, for the origins of the Old Spanish Trail begin in an unspecified antiquity when Native Americans first blazed a rough trail from an unknown geographic point. It was they who conceived a route running from the Great Salt Lake to the pueblos on the Río Grande and later to the Spanish settlements of New Mexico. Also, it was they who traveled southwest to California's San Joaquin Valley for trade or war with tribes in those remote areas. Like all trails throughout the Western Hemisphere that evolved into modern highways, the Old Spanish Trail developed from a series of Indian trails that ran from the upper Río Grande to the Great Basin via the Great Salt Lake.

When Ute traders first realized that a "new" people—the Spanish— had settled among the Pueblo Indians of the Río Grande in 1598, the various routes they had used to the Pueblo lands took on added significance. Later, in the 1670s, when Spanish colonials in New Mexico became more aware of the presence of "Yutas" among them, the historical trail began to evolve, but its origins were from the northwest in Utah, not from New Mexico.

A definitive history also cannot be written about the Hispanic efforts to learn about the route or blaze new variants of it. History begins with a written word, and few frontiersmen who could write left accounts about their exploits along the many routes that came to be known as the Old Spanish Trail. In the beginning, contact between Utes and Spaniards, unless officially sanctioned, went unrecorded. Later, when Spanish officials prohibited trade with Utes in their country, Hispanic frontiersmen wisely chose not to leave a paper trail which could implicate them in disobeying Spanish law. Only when some were caught and the legal process generated a historical record was knowledge about the Yuta country recorded.

In 1765 Juan María Antonio Rivera led the first two recorded expeditions to the Yuta country. To date little is known about the enigmatic Rivera, who seems to have faded from history as quickly as he appeared. Perhaps Spanish or Mexican archives will one day reveal biographical data about the life of this explorer who recorded the first known indigenous and European place-names in the area of western Colorado and eastern Utah. Indeed, more is known about some of the men who accompanied him, for they had served on earlier and later expeditions as guides and translators and, as local frontiersmen, some became involved in land disputes and other legal matters, leaving traces about themselves in the historical record. The Rivera expeditions, although significant, were predated by trips by New Mexicans as far north as the Gunnison River and as far west as the Colorado River. Rivera's expeditions were limited in their objectives to certain geographic areas, but they did pique the imaginations of his contemporaries. By 1776, the year of the Domínguez-Escalante expedition, some of the objectives and the arenas of exploration had changed. By then, California had been occupied by the Spanish and explorers had blazed new trails from the Pacific coast to the Colorado River and beyond to Oraibe, then part of New Mexico's northwestern claim.

From 1776 to 1850, several historical themes intertwined to help account for how the Old Spanish Trail with its variants came into being. The themes of this study include the legendary origins of the Old Spanish Trail; the cartographic development of the Old Spanish Trail; early Spanish policies and exploration efforts to connect New Mexico and California; the desire of New Mexican frontiersmen to trade as far west as the Great Basin; and the development of an immigration route from New Mexico to California by New Mexican frontiersmen and, later, Anglo-American mountain men, late comers in a longstanding history that was over a century old. Because data is scarce, the triangular trade between powerful tribes in the area that took Indian slaves from weaker tribes, Hispanics from New Mexico who traded horses for Indian slaves, and some Mormons who became a third party in the slave trade, is mentioned but left for future researchers. Similarly, available documentation reveals relatively few details about the *rescates,* or trade fairs, at certain annual rendezvous, wherein Hispanics rescued kinsmen who were taken in raids by various tribes upon their settlements.

This book endeavors to fill a gap briefly addressed by Leroy R. Hafen and Ann W. Hafen in their celebrated book *Old Spanish Trail: Santa Fé to Los Angeles,* published in 1954. The present volume leaves off at the point that the Hafens pick up the story of the later history of the Old Spanish Trail. Other scholars also have studied Hispanic efforts to establish trade routes to the Great Basin or immigration routes to California from New Mexico. But their works, many of them referenced in the present study, have been isolated to scholarly journals which have been perused by relatively few readers and researchers. The present study brings into view a history of the Hispanic participation in the development of a route, a land, and a country—for long before there was a Jamestown, our national story had begun in New Mexico.

A word about the use of the word *Yuta.* Its historical spelling found in Spanish colonial and Mexican period documents is usually "Yuta" (phonetically "Lluta," the double "ll" in Spanish pronounced as a "y"). The modern spelling, Ute, for the general tribal affiliation, and Utah for the state, derive from the Spanish. Early Spanish colonials tended to spell words as they heard them. Usually the phonetic spellings they gave to indigenous words are those that have emerged in modern vocabularies throughout the Americas. Although the author in this work tended to favor Yuta for its historical value, Ute and Yuta are interchangeably used herein.

The author gratefully acknowledges the assistance of Bruce Erickson, a doctoral student in history at the University of New Mexico, for "chasing down facts and references" and for his critical reading of Chapter VII. Don Garate, Historian at Tumacacori National Monument for the National Park Service generously shared his information about Juan Bautista de Anza with me. New Mexico State Historian Robert Torres generously shared references from the New Mexico State Archives and Records Center in Santa Fe. And Lou Ann Jacobson, Director of the Anasazi Research Center, Dolores, Colorado, deserves special mention for her efforts in bringing the present volume to it published form. A very special debt of gratitude is owed Dr. Juan Maura of the University of Vermont for assisting me in the Archivo del Servicio Histórico Militar in Madrid.

Joseph P. Sánchez
Director
Spanish Colonial Research Center

Map 1   Juan de la Cosa's Map of 1500. Museo Naval, Madrid, Spain.

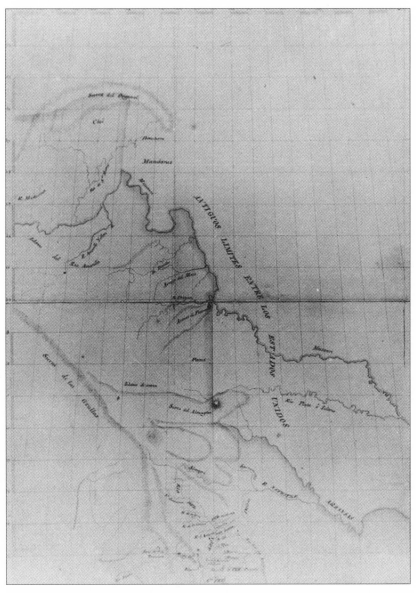

Map 2 Map of 1819 featuring the Rocky Mountains and the Yellowstone River.
Archivo General de Indias, Sevilla, Spain.

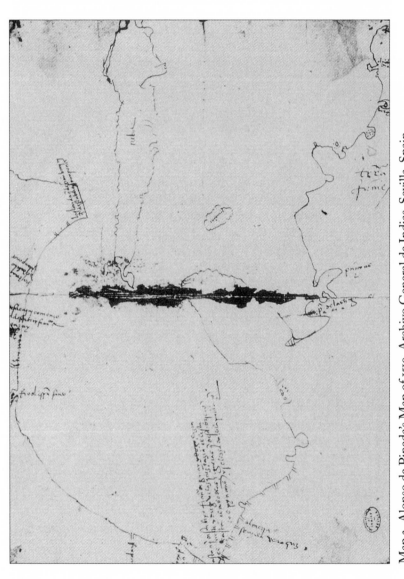

Map 3　Alonso de Pineda's Map of 1519. Archivo General de Indias, Sevilla, Spain.

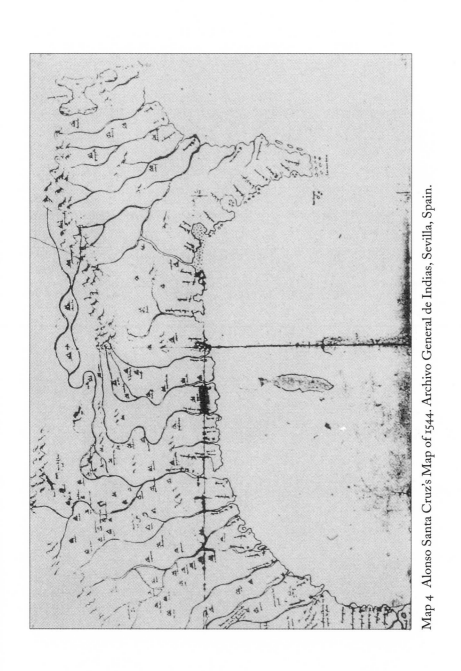

Map 4 Alonso Santa Cruz's Map of 1544. Archivo General de Indias, Sevilla, Spain.

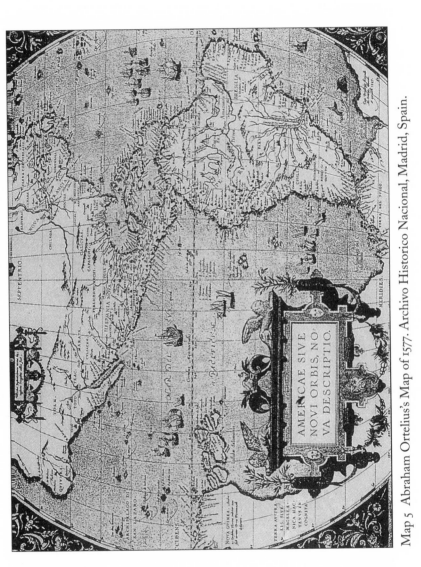

Map 5 Abraham Ortelius's Map of 1577. Archivo Historico Nacional, Madrid, Spain.

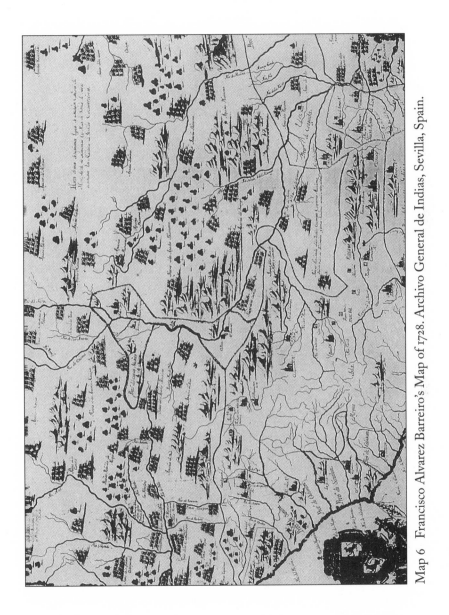

Map 6 Francisco Alvarez Barreiro's Map of 1728. Archivo General de Indias, Sevilla, Spain.

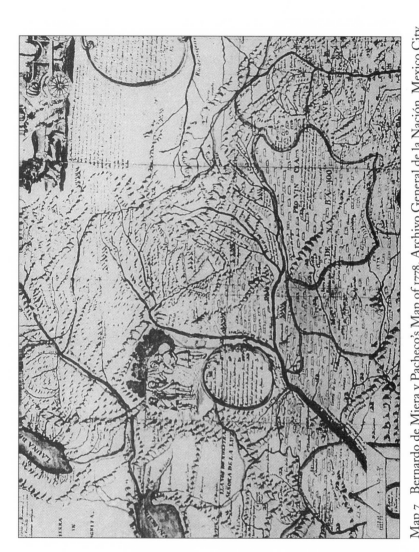

Map 7   Bernardo de Miera y Pacheco's Map of 1778. Archivo General de la Nación, Mexico City.

Map 8 Nicolas Lafora's Map of 1771. Archivo General de Indias, Sevilla, Spain.

Map 9 Antonio de Alzate's Map of 1760. Archivo General de Indias, Sevilla, Spain.

Map 10 Manuel Mascaro's Map of 1779. Archivo General de Indias, Sevilla, Spain.

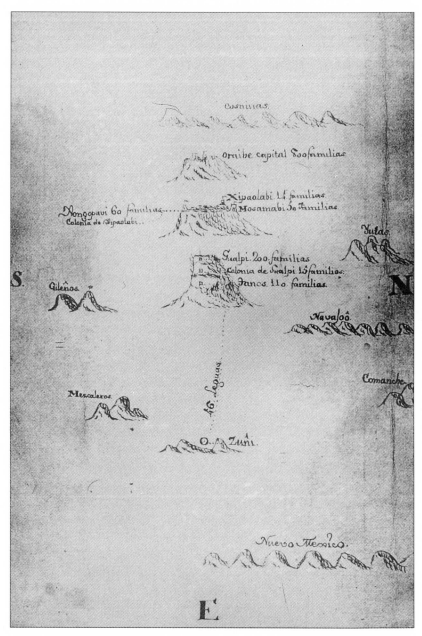

Map 11 Bernardo Miera y Pacheco's Map showing the "Province of Moqui."
Biblioteca Nacional, Mexico City.

Explorers, Traders, and Slavers

CHAPTER I

Cartographical Pathways to the Old Spanish Trail

The Road to Mythical Teguayo

LIKE ALMOST EVERY colonial road in North America, the Old Spanish Trail, with all of its variations, was forged from Indian pathways similar to those that crisscrossed the entire Western Hemisphere. From that standpoint, the origins of the Old Spanish Trail are obscure, although it first came into the historical limelight when Yuta guides led Spanish colonial frontiersmen in New Mexico northwestward from Santa Fe beyond Abiquiú through the Utah canyonlands to the vicinity of the Great Salt Lake. Only then, at its historical debut, did the Yuta country become part of the Spanish claim to New Mexico.

The Spanish claim to New Mexico developed quickly in the sixteenth century. Significantly, not quite forty-eight years had passed since Christopher Columbus's first voyage, when, in 1540, Spanish explorers under Francisco Vázquez de Coronado camped on the west side of present Albuquerque,[1] on their way to traversing much of the interior of the continent and reaching the Great Plains of central Kansas. They had, indeed, taken a major step north from Mexico. Spain's fascination with North America grew throughout the colonial period. Maps drawn between 1500 when Juan de la Cosa, having sailed with Columbus, printed his chart featuring the Caribbean Islands (Map 1) and 1819 when Facundo Melgares, governor of New Mexico, sent a map to the viceroy in Mexico City showing Santa Fe in relation to the southern Rockies as far north as South Pass (Map 2) sharpened the European view of North

America. Among other natural landmarks, the 1819 map featured the Yellowstone River and the Missouri River drainage.

The historical road leading to Santa Fe (founded in 1610), the capital of New Mexico and the jumping-off point of the Old Spanish Trail, began far away in the Caribbean when Spanish officials sent exploring expeditions first to Florida and then towards Yucatan and other points along the Gulf of Mexico. By 1519 Alonso de Pineda had reconnoitered the entire gulf from the Yucatan Peninsula northward along the Texas coastline to Florida, sailing past mouths of rivers, among them the Río Panuco, the Río Grande, and the Río del Espíritu Santo, today's Mississippi River (Map 3). Pineda's map appears as a sketchy line drawing, but its contribution pointing the way to Santa Fe became more evident in the following two decades. In 1544 Alonzo de Santa Cruz, chief cartographer of the Casa de Contratación in Sevilla, incorporated information from the Hernando de Soto expedition (1539–43) and produced what historians have referred to as the "so-called de Soto Map" (Map 4). Santa Cruz's map is the first to show the interior of North America south of the Appalachian Mountains as well as the coastal highlands between Texas and Florida.

The map by Santa Cruz is also the first to indicate the historical corridor of a Spanish colonial route that has long since faded from memory. Simultaneous with Soto's march were two other expeditions. One was led by Francisco Vázquez de Coronado (1540–42) and the other led by Juan Rodríguez Cabrillo (1542–43). Vázquez de Coronado's route is also sketchy, except that known points where he visited such as Compostela in Mexico, Zuñí Pueblo, Acoma Pueblo, and Pecos Pueblo in New Mexico as well as the Río Grande Valley of Albuquerque can be identified in the twentieth century. His route covered nearly 2,000 miles from Compostela to central Kansas by way of present-day Arizona, New Mexico, Texas, and Oklahoma.

From Zuñí Pueblo, one wing of the expedition pointed the way north toward Utah. In summer 1540, Pedro de Tovar, led by Indian guides, visited the Hopi villages of northeastern Arizona and García López de Cárdenas and his small scouting party, also led by Indian guides, became the first Europeans to see the Grand Canyon. There, on its southern edge, they peered north across the Grand Canyon toward the Yuta country which they glimpsed at a distance. Immense and deep, the Grand Canyon was a barrier which could not, at the time, be overcome by the explorers, who were impressed with its breathtaking view. A few months later and hundreds of miles away, they were also the first

Europeans to see the Great Plains and the seemingly limitless buffalo herds of North America.

Meanwhile, Juan Rodríguez Cabrillo explored the California coastline from La Paz to Oregon's Rogue River beyond Cabo Blanco. Both Vázquez de Coronado and Rodríguez Cabrillo left detailed descriptions of what they had seen and accomplished. Together with the Soto expedition, the exploring parties of Vázquez de Coronado and Rodríguez Cabrillo accumulated enough information to give Spanish officials their first understanding of the vastness of North America. In time, the lands explored by Vázquez de Coronado and Rodríguez Cabrillo would become the focal points of the Old Spanish Trail.

In 1577 Abraham Ortelius, the famous Dutch cartographer, published his hemispheric map of the Americas (Map 5) based on his interpretation of New World exploration and discovery. Although filled with errors regarding his placement of the area that would soon be called New Mexico, his map nonetheless had publicized its approximate location. Indeed, Ortelius had misplaced the Río Grande and showed it flowing into the Pacific Ocean. Cicuic (Pecos) and Tiguex (the large Indian district in the valley surrounding old Albuquerque) were placed along the Pacific coast, and Chucho (Acoma) and other places known to Coronado and his contemporaries were similarly incorrectly located. Also significant was his misplacement of Gran Quivira in the northwest corner of his map.

Nearly a century later, a new word appeared that would add perspective to Ortelius's cartographical error and place Gran Quivira on the Great Plains to the east where it belonged and where every Spanish frontiersmen in New Mexico knew it to be. That word was *Teguayo,* a large area near a great salt lake associated with the mythical origins of the Aztecs and other indigenous legendary place-names such as *Copala, Sierra Azul,* and *Siete Cuevas.* In their writings about the origins of the people of Mexico and Central America, early Spanish writers recorded their belief that American Indians came from seven caves near the Lake of Copala, which was later associated with *Gran Teguayo,* northwest of New Mexico.[2]

Long before *Teguayo* became known to Europeans, however, the road to New Mexico was slowly being defined. The sixteenth century ended with the establishment of a Spanish base of operations at the confluence of the Río Grande and Río Chama in northern New Mexico when, in 1598, Juan de Oñate led a large party of settlers there. Opening a new stretch of road from Nueva Vizcaya (present Chihuahua) to New

Mexico, the settlers reached San Juan de los Caballeros near present San Juan Pueblo in July after a six-month trek northward from Santa Barbara, hitherto the last outpost on the Mexican frontier.

In 1601 cartographer Enrico Martínez produced a map of New Mexico showing all of the Indian pueblos along the Río Grande and the route from Mexico City, known as the *Camino Real de Tierra Adentro,* to the Río Conchos and beyond to the area of present El Paso, Texas. There the trail crossed into New Mexico, wending northward toward the confluence of the Río Grande and the Río Chama. Avoiding the meandering Río Grande for nearly 100 miles, Spanish colonial settlers took a more level route, later known as the *Jornada del Muerto,* away from the river east of the Organ Mountains to a point near present San Marcial south of Socorro, New Mexico, where the route rejoined the Río Grande. The settlers followed the river until they reached San Juan de los Caballeros. Once established, they explored New Mexico in all directions, visiting every Indian pueblo and the Great Plains several times over the next few years. One detail on Martínez's map revealed that Oñate's men were cognizant that the Río Grande emanated from the north far above Taos Pueblo. While no one yet knew its origins, later generations would note that the *nacimiento* of the Río Grande was in the mountains just beyond the present San Luis Valley in southern Colorado. Perhaps the most salient feature of Martínez's map is the dotted line showing the route that came to be known as the *Camino Real de Tierra Adentro,* which ran from Mexico City to New Mexico, ultimately terminating at Santa Fe, east of the Río Grande at the southern base of the Sangre de Cristo Mountains. By the end of the decade, in 1610, Santa Fe was established under the direction of Governor Pedro de Peralta.

Except for vague glimpses, the region north of New Mexico was little known to Spanish frontiersmen. The earliest known cartographic reference to *Teguayo,* or *Tatago,* appears in Diego de Peñalosa's proposal to explore the area in 1678.[3] In his report of 1686, Fray Alonso de Posada, who had served as the Franciscan custodian of the New Mexico missions during the period 1661–65, acknowledged a relationship between *Teguayo* and the Utes. He wrote, "Beyond the pueblos of Moqui (Hopi), looking westerly at a distance of 26 leagues, one arrives at the nation which are called Yutas, which is the one formerly called *Teguayo,* it is one nation of the Yutas which reaches close to the South Sea."[4] Knowledge of the Yutas, however, may have been acquired much earlier. In 1601, after his expedition to the Great Plains, Juan de Oñate met with a delegation from Quivira seeking an alliance against the Escanjaques, a

Plains tribe in their region. One Quiviran leader told Oñate that if he sought gold he had gone the wrong way. According to Fray Zarate Salmeron, the Quiviran said that the "Spaniards had traveled a great deal out of their way on the route that they took, that if they had gone directly north, they would have arrived quickly; and so, according to what they said, one should go by way of Taos and through the lands of the great Captain Quima."[5] The Quiviran even offered to take Oñate there; however, although the Spaniard considered sending twelve soldiers, he changed his mind, thus missing an opportunity to make the first contact with the Utes.

Slowly Spaniards learned about the land to the northwest of their settlements. Almost two decades after his comments about Captain Quima, Friar Salmeron wrote about the route to the northwest: "If one goes from New Mexico on this exploration, one ought to go by way of the Río Zama [Chama] traveling to the northwest. That is what the Indians of New Mexico told me when I questioned them."[6] In his report of 1686, Fray Alonso de Posada stated that on his expedition to the Colorado River from New Mexico in 1605 Juan de Oñate met with Indians from "many nations," among them two men "who said they were from the Kingdoms of *Teguayo,* and seeing him eat from a silver vessel, they told him that in their land there was much of the same metal."[7] Whether Oñate took an interest in the men is unknown, but he did not plan to go to *Teguayo.* Although Spanish expeditions in the early decades of the seventeenth century may have picked up clues regarding the Yuta country, the land north and northwest of New Mexico would wait another half-century before Spanish frontiersmen ventured in that direction.

Mysterious and mythical, *Teguayo* marked the way to the Yuta country to the northwest in the same way Quivira drew Spanish explorers to the Great Plains. Once knowledge was gained, cartographers would correct Ortelius's map in regard to his placement of Gran Quivira and add Teguayo to the toponyms on their maps. In 1686, Alonso de Posada, offered a first view of *Teguayo* to Spanish officials when he wrote:

> Many cosmographers and astrologers confuse this kingdom of *Teguayo* with that of *Gran Quivira,* but the facts are that *Gran Quivira* is to the east and borders on the North Sea [Atlantic Ocean], while *Teguayo* is north and borders on the Sea of the West [Pacific Ocean]. The many islands, gulfs and bays which are in the direction of the south they belong to *La Quivira.* It is not surprising that they do so because these lands are unknown.[8]

The cartographical issue served only to create more interest in the Yuta country among Hispanic frontiersmen in New Mexico who wished to trade in the area.

Throughout most of the seventeenth century, however, little was learned about what lay beyond Taos Pueblo because most Spanish interest was directed toward the Great Plains and the buffalo herds and many native tribes who lived there. It was during this period, nevertheless, that the birth of the Old Spanish Trail took place. By the middle of the century, Yuta tribesmen had ventured south to trade with Puebloans and Spaniards alike. Knowledge of the Yuta country was slowly coming into historical focus. By the end of the century, the word Yuta had become part of the common New Mexico frontier vocabulary. In his report of 1686, Friar Posada had placed the Yuta country in geographic perspective from Santa Fe when he wrote:

> It remains only for us to tell of the location and direction of the kingdom and provinces which they call *Teguayo*. To provide some understanding of this land, let us recall again the location of the villa of *Santa Fe*, the capital of New Mexico which is as stated at thirty-seven degrees. Taking from this villa a straight line to the northwest between north and south and crossing the *sierras* called *Casafuerte* or *Nabajo*, one reaches the large river which runs directly west for a distance of sixty leagues which are possessed by the *Apacha* nation. Crossing this river, one enters the nation called the *Yuta*, a warlike people.
>
> Beyond this nation some seventy leagues in the same northwest direction one enters afterwards between some hills at a distance of fifty leagues more or less, the land which the Indians of the North call *Teguayo*, and the Mexican Indians by an old tradition call *Copala*.[9]

Like the Holy Grail, its attendant crown of thorns, the lance used to pierce the crucified Christ, the piece of the One True Cross, and the cape used by Pontius Pilate to drape Christ, the search for *Copala* had its litany of associations. The Spaniards' fascination with *Copala* led them to look for the legendary caves from which the Aztecs were said to have originated out of the ground and the mythical *Sierra Azul*, rich in minerals— both of which were associated with the *Siete Cuevas* and *Teguayo*. Some Spaniards believed them to be one and the same as *Copala*. None of these was associated with Gran Quivira, only with *Teguayo*. Posada wrote:

> By the same ancient traditions, it is said that from Teguayo comes not only the Mexican Indians, which were the last, but all the other nations

which in different times were inhabiting these lands and kingdoms of New Spain. They say that Guatemala and all the other kingdoms and provinces of Peru and those close by have their beginnings there.[10]

Apparently, Posada's knowledge about *Teguayo* was learned just prior to the Pueblo Revolt of 1680, when contact was made between Ute traders who, crossing the Río San Juan, had ventured southward to New Mexico and Spanish frontiersmen who dared to meet them at certain northern rendezvous points for trade. Early Spanish contact with the Utes most likely occurred uneventfully at the yearly trade fairs in Taos, Picuris, or even Pecos. New Mexican frontiersmen easily could have met Ute traders when they came to trade with the Río Grande pueblos—these included San Juan, Santa Clara, San Ildefonso, and Pojoaque. In the same way that Spanish frontiersmen had learned about the Yuta country, the Utes were keenly aware that all roads led to Santa Fe, one of them connecting with the Yuta country. Posada reiterated this fact when he wrote:

> Looking from the said villa [Santa Fe] to the northwest, we will have at seventy leagues the *Yuta* nation. Beyond at a distance of some one hundred and eighty leagues from the villa are the kingdom and provinces of *Teguayo*. Looking directly west are the South Sea [Pacific Ocean] and California at two hundred leagues. Looking to the southwest at a hundred leagues we find *El Cuartelejo* of the *Apacha* nation and *Sierra Azul*. At seventy leagues from there are the provinces of Sonora and Sinaloa.[11]

It would not be until the beginning of the next century, sometime around 1711, however, that a more sustained interest in the land of the Yutas would develop among New Mexicans. The trade between New Mexicans and Utes was still unofficial, but contact between them had been established in the seventeenth century and reestablished soon after the reconquest of New Mexico following the Pueblo Revolt of 1680.

Trade, largely clandestine, with the Utes took place over a vast area covering much of present-day Utah and southern Colorado as far east as Walsenburg. Throughout this extensive area, that reached to the Platte River, the Spaniards formed varied relationships with as many tribes as could be identified within it. The more important tribes between Utah and the southeastern edge of present Colorado included Comanches, Apaches, Cuartelejos, Faraones, Jicarillas, Pananas (Pawnees), Yutas (Utes), and Kansa. They ranged within an area covered by many river valleys such as the Arkansas (the Río Napestle), the Colorado (Río Colorado), the Red (Río Rojo), the North Platte (the Río San Lorenzo), the South Platte (Río de Jesús María), the Platte (Río Chato), the Purgatoire (Río de las Animas), and a long list of lesser streams.[12]

The complexities involving geography and the many cultures that lived within the broad area made it virtually impossible for Spanish policy to be administered with any degree of consistency. From the headwaters of the Canadian River to the Colorado River there had occurred a long history between Spanish colonial frontiersmen and various tribes wrought by trial and error that included friendships, animosities, and hostilities. The relationships between Spanish frontiersmen and their Indian counterparts had been forged through years of unofficial trading encounters along river valleys in the land north of New Mexico.

In the seventeenth century some New Mexicans sought official permission for expeditions to the Yuta country. Interest among Spanish frontiersmen in Santa Fe ran high, but officials continued to deny licenses for expeditions to the northwest. Posada recounted an occasion in which one such petition was made and denied. When he was minister in New Mexico an Indian called don Juanillo from the Pueblo of Jemez told him of the many people and different nations in the kingdom of *Teguayo*. Don Juanillo had been a captive for two years in the provinces of *Teguayo*, and he described the area. Posada wrote:

> . . . they have in them a very large number of people of different languages some of which were spoken in New Mexico and also a large lake with its entire circumference populated. On different occasions he told the governors of New Mexico they should make a journey to those provinces and that he would go as a guide for the Spaniards. Although Captain Francisco Luján petitioned once and again a second time for this journey, he was unable to secure permission. This is the most that can be said and is known at present of the river and provinces of *Teguayo*.[13]

Juanillo's brief description offered a glimpse of *Teguayo* and the distinct possibility that *Teguayo* was a real place connected with a longstanding indigenous slave trade of which Juanillo himself had been a victim.

Interest in *Teguayo* was not exclusive to New Mexican frontiersmen. Far to the southwest of New Mexico, Sonoran frontiersmen also marveled at what lay beyond the Grand Canyon and the Hopi Indians. They also were attracted by the mystery of *Teguayo*, of which they had learned by word of mouth from New Mexicans and by reading reports that had mentioned it. In the 1690s the Jesuit Eusebio Francisco Kino and his

soldier escort Captain Juan Mateo Mange took a keen interest in
Teguayo from a geographical viewpoint. In their writings, they indicated
a scholarly curiosity about the Seven Caves, linked with the genesis
story of the Aztecs, which was also associated with *Copala* and *Teguayo*.[14]
Indeed, they expressed the hope that *Teguayo* was not far from the *Sierra
Azul*, another geographical legend which was thought to exist beyond
the tribal lands of the Sobaipuris in Sonora's Pimería Alta. Kino and
Mange believed that cartographers were correct in placing *Teguayo* in a
region adjoining the *Sierra Azul*.[15] Despite their hopes and beliefs, the
impetus for exploring the Yuta country would come from New Mexico.

In the eighteenth century, raids by Comanches, Apaches, and Utes
into New Mexico hampered official decisions to explore northward as
well as expansion of settlements beyond Santa Fe and Santa Cruz de la
Cañada. In his inspection of presidios in 1724–26, Pedro de Rivera took
scant note of the land northwest from New Mexico. As he passed from
Chihuahua to El Paso, however, he came across some ruins northwest of
the mission San Antonio de Casas Grandes. Of the ruins he noted with
an air of authority, albeit in error, that he had seen "the ruins of a palace
which the Emperor Moctezuma constructed when, from the area
northwest of New Mexico, about 300 leagues from a place called *El
Teguayo*, he and 6,000 people left there to inhabit the City of Mexico."[16]
His use of the word *Teguayo* indicates that even at that late date in Spanish colonial history the legendary and geographic dimensions of that
place-name persisted as far south as Chihuahua and, as lore would have
it, *Teguayo* was still associated with the origin of the Aztecs. Rivera's cartographer, Francisco Alvarez Barreiro, moreover, indicated the location
of the "Río Azul" and the "Laguna de Teguaio" on the top left-hand side
of his map, indicating the far northwest and annotating on it the origins
of the Mexican people (Map 6). Although Rivera was not the least bit
interested in *Teguayo*, he did contribute to its cartographical longevity.
Rivera, a military man, was more concerned with real, not the imagined,
threats to New Mexico. His hope was to consolidate the frontier, not expand it.

Despite lukewarm official support, intrepid frontiersmen continued
to expand the frontier, starting new settlements in out-of-the-way areas
in defiance of the danger presented by warlike tribes. Expansion into
fertile river valleys motivated Hispanic settlers to establish towns north
of Santa Fe as well as south of Albuquerque, which was founded in 1706.
In the 1730s two towns were settled northwest of Santa Fe which would
become significant outposts of trade with the Yutas. Abiquiú was settled

by 1734, although by the 1720s settlers had begun to move into the area, and Ojo Caliente was established by 1735.[17] A century later, by 1830, Tierra Amarilla, with its large grant stretching northward to Chama, became an offshoot of the settlement pattern started by the establishment of Abiquiú. The route from Abiquiú to the Yuta country crossed through the heart of present Tierra Amarilla near Los Ojos and the ridges of Tecolote Mesa.

Although *Teguayo* appeared to be a mythical place in official Spanish thinking, Franciscans dreamed of creating a mission field there before Spanish settlers, miners, traders, or soldiers could get there. One such Franciscan was Fray Carlos Delgado, the missionary at Isleta Pueblo in New Mexico. In 1744, sixty-seven-year-old Fray Carlos proposed to work among the Hopi, Navajo, and the people of Gran Teguayo, if another missionary could be sent to replace him in his absence.[18] His proposal was based on information he had learned from the Navajos, who were ever so eager to conjure up stories to satisfy the Spanish quest for new discoveries. To that end, he gave the following account of Teguayo:

> Information which I Fray Carlos Delgado give to your Reverence Fray Pedro Navarrete of El Gran Teguayo, which is between west and north. It is distant about two hundred leagues more or less from this custodia. On this entry that I made to Nabajoa, I heard some of the natives tell how this Teguayo, so renowned, is made up of various nations, for in it are found people from all of them, both civilized from among those whom we are governing as well as others who are heathen. One division, or city, is so large that, after their manner of expressing themselves, they say that one cannot walk around it within eight days. In it lives a king of much dignity and ostentation, who, as they say, neither looks nor speaks to anyone, except very briefly, such is his severity. He rules all the nations in those regions, and I am sure they desire to be acquainted with our holy habit, for they say that in former times a religious went there and contracted a fatal illness. After his death they kept him in a box, which they give one to understand is of silver. The said religious merited this honor because of his having catechized the king. All his successors regard as relics a shrine of gold, and the articles used in saying mass, as well as other things that he used.[19]

Father Delgado's proposal would come to naught, however, and he never undertook his proposed expedition. Missionary work among the Yutas in their country, moreover, would never be fully realized by the Franciscans.

Decades passed before a government-sanctioned expedition took place, and with official interest came a historical documentary record. In 1765 Juan María Antonio Rivera led a small party guided by Utes from Santa Fe to Abiquiú and beyond to the Dolores River. Some of the men in the party had hitherto enjoyed a trading interest with the Utes. The expedition went beyond the Dolores River and meandered to the Gunnison River, reaching a point on the Colorado River, before returning to Santa Fe. Although Rivera provided Spanish officials with a report, he does not seem to have produced a map to accompany it. Rivera's expedition nevertheless created an interest in what lay beyond the land of the Yutas. Eleven years later another official expedition would probe the Yuta country and provide a better understanding of its people, flora, and fauna.

In 1776 two Franciscan priests, Francisco Atanasio Domínguez and Francisco Silvestre Vélez de Escalante, proposed to establish a route between Santa Fe and Monterey in California. Their proposal resulted in a major expedition which failed in its objective to reach the Pacific coast because of bad weather in the mountains west of Utah but succeeded in providing more information about the land. It also produced maps that would enhance the Spanish claim to the interior. With Domínguez and Escalante was the cartographer and astronomer Bernardo de Miera y Pacheco. The maps drawn by Miera y Pacheco featured rivers, salt lakes, place-names, and mountains seen on the expedition (Map 7). Of *Teguayo* Escalante wrote:

> It is nothing but the land by which the Tihuas, Tehuas and other Indians transmigrated to this kingdom; which is clearly shown by the ruins of the pueblos which I have seen in it, whose form was the same that they afterwards gave to theirs in New Mexico; and the fragments of clay and pottery which I also saw in the said country are much like that which the said Tehuas make today. To which is added the prevailing tradition with them, which proves the same; and that I have gone on foot more than three hundred leagues in the said direction up to 41 degrees and 19 minutes latitude and have found no information whatever among the Indians who today are occupying that country of others who live in pueblos.[20]

And so, some understanding of mythical *Teguayo* had been reached. For the small Spanish expedition, myth and reality met on the edge of a place the Yutas called Timpanogos.

Escalante's description of the valley and lake of Timpanogos (present Utah Lake), and of the people he observed living along it, called the

Timpanogotzis or *Timpanocuitzis,* was the first reliable eye-witness account of it.[21] Because the people there ate a great amount of fish, he said they were called Fish Eaters *(Come Pescado)* by a neighboring tribe, the Sabuagana Utes.[22] He wrote of the sierra along the northern side of the Río de San Buenaventura, which extended from northeast to southwest for more than "seventy leagues" and had a width of approximately "forty leagues" (a league equalled 2.5 miles). Four medium-sized rivers flowed into the lake from the sierras that surrounded it.[23] The first river (probably present Spanish Fork River), which they did not name, flowed toward the south. It was characterized as having "hot waters upon spreading meadows." The second river, shown as *Río de San Nicolás* (present Hobble Creek or Dry Creek) on Miera y Pacheco's map, ran northward; and the third was "three leagues and a half northwest" from the second and noted on the map as *Río de San Antonio de Padua* (present Provo River). The expedition did not report on the fourth river because they did not travel to it. They named it, nevertheless, *Río de Santa Ana* (present American Fork River). The valley floor, observed Escalante, measured from northeast to southwest sixteen leagues long and ten or twelve leagues wide. His estimation of forty-two miles long by twenty-six to thirty-two miles wide, was too large.[24] The lake itself appeared to be six leagues wide and fifteen leagues long, making it approximately sixteen miles wide and forty miles long. The actual measurements are thirteen miles wide and twenty-five miles long. Given the grandeur of the area with its high mountains, Escalante's eyes must have been impressed with the panoramic view that distorted his ability to grasp its size accurately.

The land with its adjoining valleys, wrote Escalante, contained very abundant pasturages, some of which produced flax and hemp. Escalante thought some of it had been planted purposely by the natives. One of the first things the Spaniards noticed about the climate surrounding the valley and lake was its warm air. Even in a cool September, Escalante thought the air felt warm by day and night in the valley, for they had come through much cooler temperatures to the east.[25] Lake Timpanogos abounded in several species of fish, geese, beavers, and other animals. The entire area was surrounded by timber, providing plenty of firewood. Seeds were gathered from the bountiful wild plants in the valley and a gruel was made from them. Their diet was supplemented with jackrabbits, coney rabbits, and fowl. On occasion, when hunting parties could avoid Comanches, the Indians hunted buffalo to the north and northwest. One of the lakes that the Spaniards had heard about was quite large (obviously the Great Salt Lake) and was considered harmful by the Timpanois because of its extremely saturated salt content. Escalante noted that "the Timpanois assured us that anyone who wet some part of the body with them immediately felt a lot of itching in the part moistened."[26]

Escalante said that the people feared the Comanches, who attacked them infrequently from the north through the gap in the mountains. Generally, however, the *Lagunas* (Lake Dwellers), whom Escalante also sometimes called the *Timpanogotzis*, lived in peace with their neighbors. Their dwellings appeared as "little wattle huts of osier, out of which they have interestingly crafted baskets an[d] other utensils for ordinary use." They dressed poorly, thought Escalante; some wore deerskin jackets and long leggings, or, in cold weather, they wore robes from rabbit pelts. He noted the people possessed good features and most of the men were fully bearded, an uncommon trait among indigenous peoples they had met throughout the Americas. The Spaniards even took note of the Indians' language with its variations in pronunciation and vocabulary.[27] Although no figures were given, Escalante noted that the population in the valley was quite large.

The view provided by Escalante's writings and Miera y Pacheco's map helped establish the northern extent of what was known about the Yuta country, its southern extremity bordered by the Grand Canyon, as well as its westernmost extent, lined by the mountains and ridges of the Great Basin. In many ways the Domínguez-Escalante expedition defined the Yuta country, for Miera y Pacheco had depicted it graphically, thus influencing colonial cartographers of the period.

The subsequent cartography of the eighteenth century added little new information regarding the Yuta country; in fact, it appears to have relied on Miera y Pacheco's work. Nicolas Lafora's map of 1771 (Map 8), Antonio de Alzate's map of 1768 (Map 9), and Manuel Mascaró's map of 1779 (Map 10) in which the Yuta country is shown are based on knowledge gained by the Rivera expedition of 1765 and the Domínguez-Escalante expedition of 1776. Other than the informal trade that took place between Santa Fe frontiersmen and Yuta traders, Spanish official interest in establishing a route that would connect New Mexico with California appears to have waned. The development of the Old Spanish Trail occurred naturally, as Spanish traders from Santa Fe taught each other about the Yuta country and the different ways to get to Yuta rendezvous trading points. That knowledge contributed to the development of the many variations of the Old Spanish Trail.

By the nineteenth century, traders from Santa Fe had developed their own route to get to California. Certainly, by the 1830s a route had been established that ran from Abiquiú, past Tierra Amarilla, to the Río San Juan, to a place near present Kanab north of the Grand Canyon, to an oasis at a stopping place called Las Vegas, and thence westward to Los Angeles. Just prior to the Anglo-American occupation of the land between Texas and California, the Old Spanish Trail had been established with many variants leading to the Yuta country; but only one of those variants led to California. Unfortunately, Spanish and Mexican maps did not depict all of the variations of the Old Spanish Trail; but historical documentation described its varied routes prior to 1850. By then, the word *Teguayo*, which had inspired Hispanic frontiersmen from New Mexico to go to the Yuta country, had long been forgotten.

Mythical Teguayo and historical New Mexico came together in the many variants of the Old Spanish Trail. The land with its many rivers, valleys, ridges, and mountains became the geographic stage for a historical pageant that ran its course throughout the Spanish and Mexican periods, based upon the Hispanic desire for trade in the Great Basin and a route from New Mexico to California. Indeed, the New Mexican penchant for trade formed the driving force paving the way to the Yuta country. A resisting force delaying the development of the Old Spanish Trail was the implementation of an Indian policy by Spanish officials prohibiting New Mexican frontiersmen from going to the Yuta country. Despite the official policy, New Mexicans persisted in a clandestine trade that ran from the 1670s to the 1850s.

Chapter II

Spanish Colonial Indian Policy and the Origins of the Historical Route to the Yuta Country

The First Expedition of Juan Maria Antonio Rivera, June 1765

Official Spanish interest in the Yuta country came, in part, as a result of Spanish colonial policies regarding relationships with semi-nomadic tribes. Spanish Indian policies dealing with sedentary tribes, which were largely considered peaceful, and semi-nomadic tribes, which were thought to be warlike, influenced the nature of trade with the two types of tribes. Identification of Indian groups along the Río Grande and in the Great Plains was made early in the period of exploration between 1539 and 1598.[28] Nevertheless, the administration of the dual Indian policies would never be simple. Early Spanish explorers in New Mexico first encountered Indians of the Río Grande pueblos regularly trading agricultural products for buffalo hides, meat, and fat with tribes from the Great Plains.

Indeed, Spanish explorers noted that certain pueblos bordering on the eastern New Mexico plains, such as Taos, Picuris, Pecos, the Galisteo Basin pueblos, and Las Humanas, were sites where Plains Indians and people from the Río Grande pueblos came to trade their products.[29] The Indians often met on a seasonal or annual basis, and doubtless Utes occasionally attended these fairs. Shortly after the establishment of New

Mexico by Juan de Oñate in 1598, New Mexican settlers became involved in this lucrative trade. Between 1598 and 1680 the Spanish colonials assumed control of these trade centers, much to the chagrin of the puebloans who resented the Spanish presence.

In 1680 the longstanding frustrations among the Pueblos with Spanish colonial policies, attitudes, and abuses exploded in a widespread rebellion in which Spanish occupation of New Mexico was interrupted for twelve years.[30] In the revolt, Utes and Apache warriors allied with those from the Pueblos to drive out the Spaniards. With the reconquest of New Mexico twelve years later, Spanish officials quickly realized that Spain's hold on New Mexico was tenuous at best and that Spanish control of trade centers was not what it had been in the past. Since the days of Oñate, Spanish colonials in Santa Fe had been hesitant about relations with Plains Indians because New Mexico could easily be overrun in an extended war with those tribes to the east. Wisely, Oñate had prohibited colonists from trading with them without special permission.[31] After the Pueblo Revolt, New Mexicans were even more concerned about the warlike tribes. In the eighteenth century, trade with Plains Indians played a significant role in maintaining peaceful relations as well as avoiding the destruction of the *provincia de Nuevo México* at their hands, although at times it did seem as if Ute, Apache, and Comanche warriors were on the verge of such destruction.[32]

Throughout the eighteenth century, New Mexican governors attempted to limit trading activities to fairs by prohibiting trade with Plains Indians at all other times. Governors required that anyone wishing to trade with semi-nomadic tribes acquire a license to do so. Unlicensed trading was forbidden because officials feared their lack of control over individuals who could commit irregularities such as cheating or stealing, which could result in violence and thus endanger the entire province. Licensing could not guarantee honesty, but it offered the advantage that the applicant could be scrutinized with reference to his character and somewhat controlled by officials who could recommend or deny the license.[33] Yet, despite licensing, disturbances and unlawful trading continued to plague officials.

To strengthen the conviction that regulation and control of trade was a sound policy preferable to military intervention, Governor Francisco Cuervo y Valdes issued a *bando* (proclamation) on 25 August 1705 providing that no one could trade without a license from the governor under penalty of forfeiture of goods to be traded or received in trade and a fine, half of which would be paid to the local war fund and the rest to the Real Hacienda (treasury). Cuervo y Valdes, furthermore, prohibited any acts of deception in trade, particularly at Taos, Pecos, and Picuris.[34] Nearly seven years later, on 16 December 1712, Governor Juan Ignacio Flores Mogollón published a similar *bando* directing Spanish settlers and Pueblo Indians to cease trading with the Jicarilla and Cuartelejo Apaches as well as the Utes because fraudulent trading practiced by Pueblo Indians and Spanish colonists was harmful to the security of the province. Aside from the usual fines and penalties for unauthorized and unlicensed trading, Mogollón added a jail term of several months for those violating his proclamation.[35] Thus, control of trade and trading practices—not military intimidation—was the method practiced by certain Spanish officials who believed that a lasting peace with their enemies could never be achieved solely through military force.

A system of barter was used for virtually all commercial activities in New Mexico. Colonial traders bartered with their Plains Indian counterparts for corn, tobacco, awls, buffalo hides and fat, piñon, salt, beads, pelts, jerky, blankets, and other items. Trading activities with Plains Indians were known as *rescates*—trade fairs in which captives also were traded or rescued through bartering.

In the eighteenth century, *rescates* were held throughout New Mexico in such places as Taos, Picuris, Pecos, San Juan, Santa Clara, Abiquiú, Tierra Amarilla, and Santa Cruz de la Canada. There, Spanish or Indian captives taken in war or merely kidnapped were ransomed by kinsmen. Usually alms were collected or royal funds were allocated to ransom captives in life-threatening situations. Ransomed native captives, referred to as *piezas de indios,* were baptized and reared as Catholic Christians; commonly, they were used as domestic servants by their Spanish liberators, some of whom were Franciscan missionaries.[36] Plains Indians tended to keep non-tribal captives as their slaves; like the Spaniards, Plains Indians returned their own to their kinsmen after ransoming them at the *rescates.*

By mid-eighteenth century, Comanche raiders had increased their activities throughout New Mexico. In 1749 Governor Tomás Vélez Cachupín strove to achieve peace and stability in New Mexico by permitting Comanches to trade in the province, but warned them that trading privileges would be curtailed if their raiding continued.[37] As part of his policy to control the Comanches, Vélez moved to cultivate peaceful relations with the Yutas. His goal was to form an alliance with the Yutas in case hostilities with the Comanches were to resume. Luck favored him in this endeavor, for the Yutas made contact with him on one of their trading trips to San Juan.[38] Later, Vélez visited their rancherias that were a day's ride from San Juan and negotiated a self-monitoring plan whereby the Yuta chiefs, not the Spaniards, would punish warriors who stole Spanish livestock. The policy seemed to work well, because the Yutas, who resented Spanish authority, preferred to punish individuals for their crimes rather than let the Spaniards find the entire tribe culpable for the acts of a few.[39]

Aside from the peace brought between Spaniards and Utes, Vélez was keenly aware of the importance of the Ute trade with the settlers of the Española Valley, including those in Abiquiú, Santa Cruz de la Cañada, and other nearby villages. During Vélez's first term as governor (1749–54), official inroads into the New Mexico Indian trade were made, but did not supplant, unlicensed trading activities between New Mexicans, Pueblo Indians, Plains Indians, and Utes. There were some setbacks to Vélez's efforts during his first term. After he had encouraged peace and alliances with the Utes against the Comanches, there occurred a major breach. After some Utes had raided southward toward Santa Fe, New Mexican frontiersmen organized a force and moved against Ute camps. In one incident, they destroyed a camp of a hundred tepees, capturing or killing many Utes. The Ute retaliation against the Spaniards, however, devastated much of the frontier in New Mexico. New Mexicans were forced to seek peace. By 1750, Vélez had managed to pacify the Indians, promising to treat them fairly. If Utes raided New Mexico, Vélez, instead of carrying out a punitive expedition against them, notified Ute leaders, who would return stolen property and punish the culprits themselves.[40]

Between 1754 and 1762, the intervening governors weakened much of what Vélez had accomplished.[41] During those years, Comanches reverted to raiding and taking Spanish property and trading it at local fairs. In 1762 Vélez returned for a second term and, once again, commenced to restore the peace with the Comanches. Turning his attention to the Yutas, Vélez assured them that they could count on fairness from the Spaniards. To prove his point, Vélez took an interest in a case involving a *genízaro* named Juan de la Cruz Valdéz who was charged with stealing a horse from a Ute who had been trading at San Juan. With impunity, Valdéz sold the horse to a settler of the area. Knowing the eyes of the Yutas were upon him, Vélez sentenced Valdéz to four years at the *obraje* at Encinillas and ordered that he receive fifty lashes at the pillory in the presence of Utes.[42]

The peace Vélez had worked to establish was virtually dismantled by Governor Pedro Fermín de Mendinueta. Upon assuming office in 1767, he encouraged open warfare against *indios barbaros,* especially the Comanches. Retaliating against Mendinueta's military actions, Comanches penetrated the Sangre de Cristo Mountains north of Taos Pueblo and directed their attacks westward toward the San Luis Valley and southward toward Santa Fe. The Utes, who had expanded into New Mexico earlier, were pushed westward to the San Juan Mountains along the present New Mexico-Colorado border. To combat Comanche depredations, Mendinueta enlisted the aid of Pueblo, Apache, and Ute warriors as auxiliaries in 1768, without apparent success.[43]

Ironically, despite their disparate approaches in dealing with the various Ute tribes, the development of the Old Spanish Trail took its greatest strides during the administrations of governors Vélez Capuchín and Mendinueta. Ordered by Governor Vélez Cachupín, the first two official expeditions to the Yuta country as far north as the Colorado River were led by Juan María Antonio Rivera in June and October of 1765. Under orders from Governor Pedro Fermín de Mendinueta, the first Spanish expedition to reach Utah Lake, near Provo, and learn of the Great Salt Lake was led by Domínguez and Escalante in 1776. Despite intervening years of warfare, and through trade and peace, the stage had been set for Spanish efforts to cross into Yuta territory.

Governor Cachupín's keen interest in keeping his word to the Yutas may have led directly to the two official expeditions led by Rivera he authorized in 1765 to the Yuta country. The first Rivera expedition stemmed from news that had spread throughout New Mexico of a Yuta warrior who had traded a piece of silver ore to a blacksmith in Abiquiú. The expedition undertaken in June 1765 left Abiquiú shortly thereafter.[44] The first expedition led by Rivera to determine the source of the silver ore was short and offered little to recommend its success. One peculiar detail adds historical interest to the expedition: it appears that Rivera was ordered not to describe portions of his march over well-known territory. The detail suggests that Vélez hoped to keep the route a secret, at least for the time being.[45] However, judging from the personnel of the expedition who obviously knew a route to the Yuta country, it was clear that unofficial trade had been carried on for a number of years.

In the first expedition, the small party departed from Santo Tomás y Santa Rosa de Abiquiu, their point of assembly, in late June 1765. Aside from its leader, Rivera, were Gregorio Sandoval, Antonio Martín, Joseph Martín, Andrés Sandoval, and Joaquin or Juachinillo, the interpreter, probably a *genízaro* of Ute origin.[46] Other members mentioned by Rivera in his diary entry for 19 July were Andrés Chama and Miguel Abeita. Following a familiar trade route to the Yuta country, the expedition made its way along the Chama River Valley toward *Piedra Parada* (literally "Standing Rock," present Chimney Rock in northwestern New Mexico) a well-known landmark. By the end of June, Rivera and his men had crossed much rocky terrain; just before meeting the meandering *Río Chama,* they came to a small river called *Las Cebollas* which lay near excellent meadows, with much pasturage. Rivera wrote that it was not a permanent river every year. "During dry years," he commented, "the river dries up, but it opens up near another river two leagues hence."[47] They camped along it for the night. A few leagues later, leaving the *Río de las Cebollas,* they came to the *Río Chama.* Of the occasion, Rivera wrote:

> June 28th . . . We left the said place following the same direction bearing a little to the northwest. We traveled about five and a half to six leagues until we reached the *Río Chama,* leaving behind us another river which is permanent called *Las Nutrias.* The said route is along gentle land without any rock. It is somewhat uneven with some chamiso but well-provided with much pasturage as well as sufficient and good water. We rested along this river in a large meadow adjoining it. About three o'clock in the afternoon, we departed in the same direction. Traveling through level, but rocky land, we came to a small river which runs all year long through a meadow. It is about a league and a half from the *Río Chama.* Embellished by many flowers, we named it the *Río Señor San Joseph.* There, we stopped for the night.[48]

Traveling northwesterly, they left the *Río Chama* and proceeded through flat, rockless land. They passed by a large lake "half a league long. . . . We named this place *Laguna de San Pedro* because it was his feast day. Along the way are many meadowlands, the principle one is called *El Coyote* by the Yutas because it has forty pools filled with water."[49] Wending their way through a small canyon on 29 June, they reached a brackish spring the Yutas called *Agua del Berrendo.* Not far from there they came to another spring they called *Tierra Amarilla.* Descending a small narrow canyon, they camped near its exit for the night. Rivera called it *Embudo* because it was so narrow. On 30 June they continued northwesterly, reaching the Río de Navajo, where they stopped to rest. They then traveled in the same direction passing a steep hill until they reached a river they named *San Juan.*[50]

For the next two days they continued northwesterly through a spring-filled canyon the Yutas called *Lobo Amarillo*. On 1 July 1765 Rivera wrote: "There, we stopped to rest for the afternoon. There must be from the said river [San Juan] to the cienega [in the small narrow canyon] five leagues. Afterwards we continued in the same direction, traveling about two leagues through good land until arriving at the river the Yutas call *Piedra Parada* [Standing Rock] where we camped for the night. There is much pasturage, good meadowlands, and sufficient water."[51]

Near there, Rivera probably crossed the Río Navajó. He reported that on 3 July 1765, after crossing two rivers they named the San Xavier and the Nuestra Señora de Guadalupe, they reached the river they called *Río de los Pinos*, still so called because pine trees grow along its banks.[52] Nearby, they found some ruins of burnt adobe construction and took samples to show Governor Vélez as evidence for future exploration.

Traveling west and slightly north from there on 4 July, the expedition came to present day *Río Flórido*, smaller than *Río de los Pinos*, where they again discovered ruins of adobes and burned metals. From there they continued to another river, which they named *Río de las Animas*, a designation still used.[53] In 1776, Domínguez and Escalante, relying on Rivera's guides, said that they were near the western point of *La Sierra de la Plata* where the Animas River originates.[54] Along the river, Rivera encountered a ranchería, or Indian settlement, its principal chief, Coraque, and his three subordinate captains, Joso, El Cabezón, and Picado. Hoping to gather information about the Ute who had taken the silver ore to Abiquiú, Rivera and his men distributed gifts of maize, pinole, and tobacco. When they communicated to Coraque that they sought the Yuta named *Cuero de Lobo* (Wolfskin), they were told that he was not there and that he had gone to a Payuchi settlement about five leagues hence to visit his mother-in-law.[55] They also learned about another ranchería downstream on the Animas whose principal chief was *Caballo Rosillo* (Red Horse). There, they understood, lived an old woman who knew of another silver deposit. It appears that her father had, at one time, taken silver ore to trade in Abiquiú. As the story went, he traded the ore to a Spaniard named Joseph Manuel Trujillo Herrera, who had "made two rosaries and a cross from it." Rivera and a small party went to find the woman while the rest of the expedition continued to the *Río Dolores*. The experience proved to be quite disagreeable, as Rivera wrote:

> On July 6 . . . After we had discussed the new information among ourselves, all in agreement resolved that Gregorio de Sandoval, Antonio

Martín, the interpreter, and I should go to the Payuchi settlement. Having finished our business, we went to see whether the said Yuta woman would give us new information about the Yuta we sought. When we got there, we presented her with gifts as we did with other Yutas. We visited with her hoping to get a better understanding from her. When we told her our business, she put on such a mean face that she had nothing over the devil.[56]

Thus, the visit to the aged, reluctant informant proved fruitless.

Disappointed by her attitude, the Spaniards went to Chief Asigare, a Payuchi war captain, and complained about her treatment of them. Demonstrating his friendship through signs, he summoned the old woman. She explained that she, like others, had just come down from a mountain, *Sierra del Datil,* with a load of red clay. She became abusive after she had explained to them that she would not go to show them the silver deposits. Then, with a sympathetic tone in her voice, she agreed to give them directions to see the silver outcroppings. Rivera, his small escort, and their Yuta guides left, running their horses first at a quick trot, then at a full gallop. By the end of the first day, they stopped along a stream to rest themselves and their jaded horses. On 8 July wrote Rivera,

> We continued the route, and after traveling a little way we came upon the hogan of a Navajo and the dry arroyo which seemed to be what the Yuta woman had told us about. Leaving the route on the right side, we went up the arroyo to the part where a small hill begins which faces north. We climbed and moved from one to another part for about six leagues through forest and flat land. We surveyed different places trying to find the land the Yuta woman had told us about and as the Yuta chieftain had shown us. So angry were we at the Yuta woman, that we returned where she was as thoughts to kill her for lying to us and costing us so much hardship crossed our minds. By the time we got to the settlement, however, we had calmed down. At a fast trot and gallop, we got to a camp where our men were taking their siesta along one of the rivers which we had crossed previously. We called it Río del Luzero. . . . There, we encountered and rejoined our men after three days of absence without anything to eat. . . . In the end, what mattered most was to find the said Yuta Cuero de Lobo.[57]

When Rivera rejoined his men, they were accompanied by Payuchis. On 16 July 1765 Andrés Sandoval and Rivera met with Chief Chino and gave him gifts of tobacco, pinole, flour, corn, "and whatever else it took to win them over."[58] Chief Chino asked what the Spaniards were doing in such forbidding country so far from home. Rivera told him that they sought a Yuta called *Cuero de Lobo* who was said to be living among the Payuchi. He also asked Chief Chino about the large river known as the Río del Tisón. The chief responded that it was true that *Cuero de Lobo* had been living among them but that he had returned to his land. Hoping to dissuade the Spaniards from traveling any farther, Chief Chino told them that the river was too far away and that the only way there was through rough, waterless country with little forage for their animals. The route was so winding that their horses would quickly fatigue and the men would get dizzy from the sun's heat, which was severe and insufferable along that route. He reminded Rivera that, as the Spaniards did not know the way, they would suffer many hardships or they would die from hunger, that is, if hostile tribes on either side of the river did not kill them first. He advised them that they should return to their own land and said that if Rivera wanted to proceed, the best time to go was "when the leaves of the trees start to fall," sometime around the month of October on the Spanish calendar. The chief then counseled them that "we could go along the entire river where we were presently which flows into the Río del Tizón."[59] The travel time from where they were would take six days; there were numerous tribes along the way.

Chief Chino told them that they would encounter a tribe called *Orejas Agujeradas* (Pierced Ears). He told them, as did Chief Asigare, that there was one tribe that "kills people solely with the smoke that they make without one being aware that they had done so." He explained that once the smoke reached the olfactory senses, the victim died quickly. He also told them about a particular creature who would tear apart anyone who passed his domain and did not pay him a pelt as homage. He further told Rivera that "on the other side of the river there is a large trench which is so broad that trade is made without crossing it. The people throw what they want to trade across it: bridles and knives which the Spaniards trade with the Yutas and other tribes. Those from the other side throw their chamois across in exchange."[60]

The linguistic variety was so great along the river that some tribes could not intelligently communicate with one another. On the other hand, the river could be crossed. "The manner of crossing the river is on a vessel called a *jícara* which carries only two people. They sit back to back, with one facing where they have left, and the other where they are going. Those on this bank of the river cannot cross until the river is low as it is so big. On the other side are some bearded white men dressed in armor with metal hats. Even their women adorn both their arms with iron armlets called *brazaletes*. Their hair is styled with braids as do Spanish women. Among them is one they call *Castira*, which means *Castilla*. That is what is known about the said river."[61]

On 17 July, Rivera resumed his search for *Cuero de Lobo*. Along the way, the Spaniards traded with the Payuchis. That night, they camped along the *Río de el Luzero*. The next day, they left the river and proceeded to the "part of the Sierra de la Plata called *La Grulla* where there is a river with abundant water. We called it the Río de San Joaquín. There we found about twenty Yuta camps. Among them was *Cuero de Lobo*. We gave gifts to everyone in a way that would be possible to have enough. Afterwards we began to communicate. *Cuero de Lobo* said that if we gave him a horse for the next day, we would go see the silver."[62] Rivera observed that they spent the rest of the day in conversation with the Yutas but learned nothing new.

The next day they prepared to go see the silver. Rivera wrote:

> July 19 . . . We got the horses ready. One of the Yutas named Chief Largo seeing that we prepared to leave asked us for a horse so that he could accompany us. One was given to him. Then *Cuero de Lobo* said that not all of us should go, only Gregorio Sandoval, Joseph Martín, Miguel Abeita, Andrés Chama, the interpreter, and myself. That done, we traveled along the upper river through the water instead of the land route as both banks were formed by an escarpment which appeared eminent. We went about eight leagues until we arrived at a bend which the mountain makes. There is a short piece of flat terrain. . . . There, we left the horses and we climbed to its summit where we saw a great variety of veins of various colors which are countless. It can be said without exaggeration that the entire mountain is made of pure metal. All around could be seen *pamino* which is red and yellow; in other parts there is caliche of small white gravel. The stone throughout manifested great richness of metals. We particularly found some veins of black lead and others of red lead, *punta de ahuja* [needle point] and other dark or whitish metals which look like quicksilver. In order to see better if various types of silver could be found as the Yutas had told us, we camped on that mountain for two days. We could not learn more because the Yutas explained that what they thought was silver was actually lead. . . . On July 22 . . . Realizing we could not accomplish our objective, we descended the mountain carrying some loose metal ore as we did not have the proper equipment to dig for more other than a chisel for cutting silver.[63]

Eleven years later, Domínguez and Escalante corroborated Rivera's story somewhat, probably adding a bit more hopeful information than actually existed. Describing the Sierra de la Plata, Domínguez and Escalante remarked about one of its canyons "in which there are said to be veins and outcropping of metallic ore." In the same entry, Escalante made reference to the Rivera expedition's sojourn through the same country, writing:

> However, although years ago certain individuals from New Mexico came to inspect them by order of the governor, who at the time was Don Tomás Vélez Cachupín, and carried back metal-bearing rocks, it was not ascertained for sure what kind of metal they consisted of. The opinion which some formed previously, from the accounts of various Indians, and from some citizens of the kingdom, that they were silver ore, furnished the sierra with this name.[64]

Domínguez and Escalante perhaps were somewhat exuberant in their description, for Rivera never claimed to have found silver. In fact, once Rivera and his men reached the *Río Dolores,* they were disappointed in their hope to find the silver deposit they sought.[65] Having learned of a large river further on, probably the *Río del Tizón* (present Colorado River), the explorers returned to New Mexico with the idea that they would undertake another expedition. After they arrived in Santa Fe, Rivera reported to Governor Vélez about what he had learned. He told about the many tribes they had met, about his encounter with *Cuero de Lobo,* the many ruins of ancient pueblos he had seen, and the mountain of lead. The report made Vélez all the more interested in sponsoring a second expedition in the fall of 1765.

Chapter III

The Search for the Río del Tizón

Rivera's Second Expedition to the Yutas,

October 1765

IT WAS AUTUMN 1765 when Governor Tomas Vélez Cachupín ordered Juan María Antonio Rivera to carry out a second expedition to the little-known area he had previously explored in order to determine the location of the large river they had heard about and to see if silver could be found within the environs. Rivera's instructions from the governor prescribed that he find the Payuchis who had offered to lead them to the *Río del Tizón* and learn about the land and its people. The governor instructed Rivera's party to "incorporate themselves immediately with the Payuchi settlement that had offered to show them the way to the Río del Tizón by winning them over by smoking tobacco with them."[66] In particular, Rivera was to learn whether there were large towns in the area, what nations lived along its banks, and the truth of the twice-told tale that flitted throughout Abiquiú that white, bearded men "dressed in a European manner" lived there.

The expedition's members carried trade goods with them in case they met up with other European traders in the area; they would claim to be trading rather than exploring. Should it be safe to do so, Vélez instructed Rivera to let some of his men, accompanied by Payuchis, cross the river and trade. Curiously, Vélez wanted to know whether the Río del Tizón "originates from the Gran Laguna Copala which the Pueblo Indians call Teguayo that they say is where they come from." One other request stood out in the governor's instructions: on his return from the

Río del Tizón, Rivera was to survey the Sierra de la Plata or La Grulla to see whether rich metal could be found there, as he had seen what appeared to be virgin silver.[67] The second expedition departed Abiquiú in late September 1765.

In the second expedition, Rivera was accompanied by traders who had been to the Yuta country previously and were familiar with the route. Among them were Gregorio Sandoval, Antonio Martín, and the *genízaro* interpreter Joaquín from Abiquiú. Three names not mentioned in Rivera's diary of apparent participants in the expedition were Andrés Muñiz, his brother Antonio Lucrecio Muñiz, and Pedro Mora, who served as guides for the Domínguez-Escalante expedition eleven years later.

Rivera's second diary, which he completed on 20 November 1765, nearly a month after he returned from the second expedition, picks up miles away from Abiquiú at the Payuchi settlement on the Río Nuestra Señora de Dolores, which they had reached on the first expedition. Given that at the end of the second expedition it took Rivera fifteen days to return to New Mexico, it is likely that he left Abiquiú in late September. It was sometime in the first five days of October that Rivera met the Yutas once again. "We met two captains of the adjoining settlements," wrote Rivera, "who were Asigare, who guided us on our first expedition, and the other named Cabezón of the Mauchi nation. We gave them gifts in the best possible way so as to make it possible to converse with them about our desire for them to show us as friends to the other people and nations ahead so that we could trade with them without revealing our real purpose."[68] Aside from finding silver, their "real purpose" was to learn as much about the land as possible for future exploration. It seems that the Yutas were aware of possible Spanish intrigue and demurred from taking them anywhere. Chief Cabezón told them that "the Mauchi determined not to let us pass saying that we were going to reconnoiter their lands and could ruin their trade."[69]

The Yutas deliberated once again, however, and in the midst of their discussions, a disturbance occurred. It seems that, unbeknownst to the Mauchi, Chief Asigare had recommended a certain Payuchi tribesman to guide the Spaniards. The Payuchi man unexpectedly made an appearance in the Mauchi camp offering himself as a guide and saying he had no fear of the Spaniards. Suddenly a scuffle broke out when a Mauchi warrior jumped out from the gathering and struck the Payuchi. Just then, Chief Asigare arrived and, seeing the attack on the Payuchi, announced that he would give the Spaniards guides and "that although he was too ill to go, he did not support the immediate disturbance."[70] The next day, Chief Asigare sent Rivera the grandson of Chief Chino Payuchi to serve as a guide. The Spaniards paid him, probably by giving him a horse, and shortly departed, descending the Río Nuestra Señora de los Dolores.

On 6 October 1765 they left the Dolores River and meandered first to the northwest and then veered toward the northeast as they made their way beyond the river for twelve leagues. Finally, they reached the settlement of Chief Chino Payuchi, grandfather of their guide. The Spaniards observed five campsites and noted that most of the warriors were out hunting deer. Chief Chino Payuchi accepted their gifts and told them that his grandson would take them any place within his territory they wanted to go. He advised them that, as they were not far from the end of his land, the Spaniards should get another guide to take them beyond. Chief Chino Payuchi then departed. The Spaniards named the settlement La Soledad, as the grey sky appeared somewhat gloomy to them.

Leaving La Soledad, they traveled over the ridge of a mountain and descended into a canyon. Rivera noted that the terrain was not hard on the animals, as it was well provided with pasturage and good shelter. The next day they crossed a series of "beautiful valleys, with many basins and ridges that were easily traveled with no delays. One had a layer of small rock as far as the stream we reached."[71] Along the stream were five Payuchi settlements. Upon seeing the Spaniards, the natives, sounding alarms, fled into the forest. Gregorio Sandoval and the Payuchi guide went to bring them back. They "attempted to talk to their guards and calm them by explaining that we were Spaniards of Peace who came to trade with them." There they arranged for another guide to take them where they wanted to go. Before letting their former guide depart, the Spaniards gave him a horse, and "we bade him take care of it like no other."[72]

On 8 October, their new guide took them eastward about two leagues before winding around a very steep ridge and then going northward for three leagues. From there they went northwest about a league and a half before reaching a stream. Stopping to rest on the ridge of a mountain they called San Cristóbal, they took in a panoramic view of the country with all its valleys and four branching streams. The next day they traveled northwest, following a wide path to a canyon. Continuing in a northwestly direction, they reached three Mauchi settlements. Meeting the inhabitants, Rivera wrote, "We asked them if there was water ahead. They said there was not much more than a small spring which was around the hill from where they stood. From there, it would take one day to reach the Tabehuachi nation. On the way, there is a very full river in which one cannot stand, for its canyon-like banks are too steep and narrow. There is no meadow there for one to walk on or to make camp unless one ascends the ridge. Thanking them, we decided to stay there and camp rather than suffer ahead."[73]

Traveling through a very narrow trail on 10 October, Rivera described their ordeal:

> We went west about three leagues through level terrain with little rock. It had some small oak along the route to a short canyon which was very rocky. Getting on the trail which was so narrow that a horse barely fit on it, as from its trailhead to the end was three musket shots long. It cost us much work to get through it, having to lift much of our cargo which was made more difficult by the cold and furious winds from the north that blew through there. It was so strong that the horses and mules balked at it; we had to turn their heads away from the wind. The wind blew for more than a half hour. Had it been longer, we might have frozen to death. Descending a ridge, we looked for a place to get out through another canyon which was between two mountains, but it turned out impossible, for the only way out was the canyon through which ran the river. This was so difficult that the only way out was to stay in the river which reached the chests of the horses. It was that way until we ascended the next ridge of the mountain on the other side which was also steep and narrow like the previous one. In one, we had to remove the cargo from the animals to get through; in the other, we had to wend our way by pulling the animals through (some by the ears), and in another by their tails. Having ascended the ridge, we could see a very pleasant valley as far as the eye could see.[74]

In one of the mountainous areas, later identified by the Domínguez and Escalante expedition as the *Sierra de los Tabehuachis* (present Uncompaghre Plateau), Rivera and his men met a Tabehuachi hunter who sat and talked with them and he told them that they were close to his people. He warned them that the Tabehuachi had recently taken horses from the Comanche in a battle that had occurred a few days before. Traveling six to seven leagues through a canyon, the Spaniards reached a Tabehuachi settlement called *Passochi*, which was named after three boys of their tribe who had burned to death there. The settlement was that of Chief Tonampechi. The Spaniards were greeted by a number of Tabehuachi who came out to receive them and show them a good camping spot near their settlement. The Tabehuachi shared some of their deer meat with the Spaniards, who responded in kind, giving them some of their provisions. The Tabehuachi were about to celebrate their victory against the Comanches, but Chief Tonampechi told his people to cancel their dances that night so that they could gather and talk with the Spaniards.

At twilight, the Tabehuachi, forming a circle, sat to converse with their guests. They smoked tobacco and shared their food as a sign of peace. Rivera reported in his diary that "they told us that Spaniards had never passed through the country where we were going, and the people would be agitated. They asked us not to cross where we planned, for the people on the other side would cause us harm. The chief told us to beware those who called themselves friends. They already knew that we were going to the big river to see where there might be other Spaniards."[75]

Hoping to dissuade Rivera, the Tabehuachi told them that they did not know the way to where the Spaniards wanted to go because it was too far north from where they were. There was, they said, too much risk due to their war with the Comanche. Therefore, they said, it would be better for them not to go there. Boldly, Rivera responded that the words of the Tabehuachi were "nothing more than pretenses not to let us go there." The Spaniards said that they would still go there even though they might be killed. He wrote, "we still wanted to go forward" and insisted that the Tabehuachi who "knew the land and the way should tell us." Finally, the Tabehuachi relented, saying that they were indeed friends of the Spaniards and that if they were properly paid they would be happy to show them the way "to the Río Grande del Tizón by way of the north end where many go to trade with the people on the other side."[76] The Spaniards stayed with the Tabehuachi three days, during which time they celebrated and traded. Although Rivera thought it a good idea to stay and reinforce his friendship with the Tabehuachi, he complained that "We did not wish to make them unhappy, we accepted their invitation, but to the point, we did not like wasting two days in the same place participating in their style of trade, which we thought badly done, for our maintenance of food and tobacco was not useful. On the third day, they gave us a celebration with a dance which began at sunrise, wasting in it much food. Nevertheless, we reciprocated with a good meal which left them very pleased." Although the Tabehuachi were somewhat loath to guide the Spaniards, saying no one knew the way, "that night they drew us a plan of the Río Tizón showing us the many watering places everywhere on the west side."[77]

With a Tabehuachi guide, the Spaniards departed on 14 October, traveling in a northwestly direction. After two leagues of march, the guide took them off the path they were on because there was little water along it and too much rock which would fatigue their horses and mules. He suggested they cross a mountain, as this was a shorter way with little rock and much water. He convinced the Spaniards that the Tabehuachi often went that way to the big river; they shrugged their shoulders and acquiesced. "We followed his judgement," wrote Rivera, "and we traveled over the mountain about fourteen leagues making certain of what he told us. We continued going to the said watering place which is in the most conspicuous place, but it had such little water that it lasted for only half of our herd; it also had little pasturage, poor shelter, but much firewood. That night occurred such a furious storm of wind and rain that given what had gone on before we named this place Purgatory."[78]

The next day they traveled northward five leagues through an area filled with small cactus plants. That area, wrote Rivera, "stretched for three leagues with such great abundance [of cacti] that the horses and mules could not go through it except over a trail until we descended to a very mountainous valley with no pasturage, and no shelter. . . . I agreed with the guide . . . to go to the watering place that was in a canyon which had a stream . . . we traveled . . . a little more than ten leagues. After the horses and mules had been watered, our guide told us that we would climb to the top of a hill which was on the other side of the stream and we would see the Río Grande del Tizón which we sought."[79]

On 16 October they reached the large river. There, the Tabehuachi guide called over some boys who had accompanied the expedition and sent them to invite the people on the other side of the river to come and trade with the Spaniards. Gregorio Sandoval and Rivera went with them to scout along the river. "We crossed the only ford it has," wrote Rivera; "the high water reached the saddles of our horses. . . . The width of the ford is 60 to 70 varas,[80] the rest of the river is boxed with steep banks. It is very enclosed at its deepest part which is three estados. Three streams flow into it up river to the east. When it floods, it fills the entire meadow which is more than a league. It reaches the bottom of a hill where it leaves debris."[81]

Somehow the river did not meet Rivera's expectations and he questioned whether it was the Río del Tizón. Meeting with his guide, he commented that he felt something was amiss. Rivera could not believe the large river he saw was the river he sought. Finally, after meeting other Yutas who seemed to confirm to him that it was the large river he sought, he changed his mind and felt he had reached the Río del Tizón. Still, his doubt persisted. Of the situation, he wrote:

> Once again, we communicated with our guide telling him that this was not the Río del Tizón which we sought and that he had failed us. To that he responded sadly that there was no other major river in the area than that one. He would never have brought us here had he not heard the people down at the ranchería say that the high river was not passable for it was now reaching the meadow. At the confluence of all the large rivers we had crossed, we met some people and asked them, and we now felt certain about the river: here was the crossing to go to the Spaniards on the other side who were five or six *jornadas* [days] march. It could be done at great risk owing to hostile tribes in the area.[82]

The Tabehuachi guide and other Yutas warned Rivera about crossing the Río del Tizón. They told him he would do so at great risk owing to the hostile tribes on the other side. About a day's march after crossing the river, they told Rivera that he would encounter a tribe who ate their children because the hunting in their area was so poor. Another day beyond them, the Spaniards would meet other people, very white with hair the color of straw who were the most warlike of all the tribes in the area. Their land was so large it would take two days to cross it. Given the peril, they recommended that the Spaniards cross it only at night. After that, Rivera and his men should reach the foot of a small mountain with a bountiful lake. That area was inhabited by a people who were like rocks.[83] Beyond there, they would head toward the skirt of a mountain in which direction they would encounter the Spaniards they sought. "They live on the banks of a small stream with plenty of water," wrote Rivera, "These are the first people one reaches who have houses. They are Spaniards, we are told, because they speak just like us, they are very fair, with heavy beards, and they dress in buckskin, for they do not have clothes like us in our land."[84]

Rivera told his guide that if he took them there he would be paid more; but the Tabehuachi and another man who claimed to be his father said that the expedition was too small in number to go any further. They said, "Upon reaching a ruddy-colored people, they would take each of us by the hand in peace, and we would never again return to our land or ever be seen again. They would kill our guides for having taken us there. As captain, I should go back and bring more people, only that way would it be possible to enter that land."[85]

On 17 October, Rivera was greeted by five Seguagana messengers who seemed to try to persuade them not to go any farther. They told Rivera that there were no people in the area because they were scattered throughout the mountains hunting. Rivera, still in doubt, asked them whether this was the large river he sought. Their response seemed to convince him that it was. He wrote, "We asked them about what had occurred with our guide in relation to the river. . . . They confirmed the same, and we were then persuaded that it was the river we sought, although we did not feel we were at the right part of it." They told him that their leader was Chief Cuchara, who apparently had been involved in a battle with the Spaniards they sought. They explained that they had stayed away from Rivera because they thought he was angry at them as they too had killed Spaniards. They said all the Spaniards had been killed in battle. Oddly, Rivera noted, "With that, the talking stopped."[86]

The next day, Rivera stayed long enough to trade with the Sabuagana. At that time, they were invited to trade with another chieftain beyond there. They went to his settlement and stayed two days because their horses were jaded and their hooves need to be pared. Rivera called a council of his men to discuss whether they should go on. Given their condition and provisions, they doubted the wisdom of going any farther.

On 20 October, Rivera turned around, guided by Sabuaganas. Going eastward, the party traveled through large valleys that had numerous cactus plants. Finally, after twelve leagues they reached a large spring and camped for the night. The next day, traveling in the same direction as the previous day, they arrived at another Sabuagana settlement. The chief was too ill to accompany them, but he told them that when he recovered he would take them to where there was silver, which they called *cuchillo*. At that time, however, he felt it was too risky to go because Comanches in the area had recently attacked them. Although Rivera still wished to go to the part of the *Río del Tizón* where the Spaniards they sought were said to be, he decided to stay and trade with the Sabuaganas. Not long after, he returned to the *Río del Tizón*, and, at that point, Rivera decided to return to New Mexico. In the last entry of his second diary, he wrote: "In the meadow of the Great Río Tizón, on a tree with white bark, I carved a large cross with the words 'Long Live Jesus' at the top and my name. At the foot of the tree, I carved the year so that it could be verified at a future time that we had gotten that far."[87]

It took Rivera and his men fifteen days to return to Santa Fe. He ended his diary by concluding that "The return trip took fourteen and a half days by the most direct route with regular marches. It is estimated that the distance from the Villa de Santa Fe to the Río del Tizón is one hundred fifty leagues. I judge that the referenced river empties into the Gulf of California."[88] Rivera was correct about the Río del Tizón flowing into the Gulf of California. Also, he had contributed much knowledge about western Colorado and eastern Utah. His diary identified Yuta groups not previously known to the Spaniards. And he contributed to the mythology of the area, for the stories he heard from the Tabehuachis seemed to conjure up legends of lost civilizations that had puzzled Spanish explorers since the sixteenth century.

Reflecting on the Tabehuachi's stories, Rivera and his men crossed the Colorado River but did not go far beyond it. To Rivera, some elements of what the Tabehuachi had said sounded plausible, yet there was room for skepticism. The persistence of such stories about cannibalistic native groups in North America and other curiosities upon which European lore fed surfaced again in the 1770s. In 1775–76, the Franciscan explorer Fray Francisco Hermenegildo Garcés, blazing a trail from Mission San Gabriel in the Los Angeles area eastward across the Mojave Desert to the Colorado River, seemed to have investigated the possible practice of cannibalism in that area. He wrote: Regarding "the Chidumas, who I persuade myself are the Yumas, up to the present time have I not heard that they eat human flesh."[89] It seems that Spanish colonials always kept one ear cocked in expectation that they would hear about cannibalism among the tribes of North America.

Rivera had led the first official Spanish expedition in the exploration of the San Miguel, Dolores, Uncompahgre, Gunnison, and Colorado rivers. Eleven years later, the Domínguez-Escalante expedition passed through much of the same area as it meandered through western Colorado. Reflecting on the Rivera expedition of 1765, Escalante, camped on the east bank of the Uncompaghre River on 28 August 1776, wrote:

> Farther down, and about four leagues to the north of this Vega de San Agustín, this river joins another, larger one, named San Xavier [today's Gunnison River] by our own, and river of the Tomichi by the Yutas. To these two rivers, already joined together, there came Don Juan María de Ribera in the year of '65, crossing the same Sierra de los Tabehuachis, on the top of which is the site he named El Purgatorio, according to the indications he gives in his itinerary.
>
> The meadow where he halted in order to ford the river—and where they say he carved on a poplar sapling a cross, the letters spelling his name and the expedition's year—is situated almost near the same junc-

ture on the southern side, as we were assured by our interpreter, Andrés Muñiz, who came with the said Don Juan María in the year mentioned as far as La Sierra de los Tabehuachis. He said that although he had stayed three days' marches behind on this side of the river at that time when he came along its edge this past year of '75 with Pedro Mora and Gregorio Sandoval—who had accompanied Don Juan María throughout the entire expedition mentioned—they said that they had reached it then and from it had started their return, they alone having crossed it when they were sent by the said Don Juan María to look for Yutas on the side opposite the meadow where they stopped and from where they came back—and so, that this was the one which they then judged to be the great Río del Tizón [Colorado River].⁹⁰

In any event, Rivera's men did go upstream and eastward of the Colorado River, hoping to find any information regarding silver deposits. This eluded them. In the end, the explorers had explored over 150 leagues (approximately 375 miles) from Santa Fe, farther than any hitherto-recorded Spanish penetration of the Yuta country. It was clear even to Rivera and his men, however, that other traders from New Mexico had seen much of that country before them and that they were not the first Hispanics into that little-known wilderness. Still, Rivera left important documentation about southwestern Colorado and eastern Utah, for he followed on his outward-bound trip a route "suggestively identical to the Old Spanish Trail."⁹¹

Rivera's expedition was, from the point of view that it failed to find any mineral wealth, unsuccessful. From a historical view, however, it resulted in a documented description of a route that would become one of the variations of the Old Spanish Trail. Above all, Rivera's expedition served as an impetus for the next major official expedition to the Yuta country, that led by the friars Domínguez and Escalante. For Spanish officials, there were other factors besides the challenge of religious conversion of the Hopis and the Yutas motivating them to pursue Domínguez's and Escalante's proposal for an expedition to the Yuta country. In the intervening eleven years between the two expeditions, California had been opened to settlement in 1769. With the rediscovery of Monterey Bay and the discovery of San Francisco Bay, California's importance grew in the minds of Spanish officials. By 1775 the interest created by the Rivera expedition in a possible westward route resulted in a plan to establish a trade trail between Santa Fe, New Mexico, and Monterey, California. Rivera's expedition established a line of march to be followed by Domínguez and Escalante in their quest to reach California. Domínguez and Escalante would later provide a clearer explanation of where Rivera and his men had been, for not only would they use some of Rivera's guides but also they would better describe the route to the Uncompaghre Plateau and the Colorado River. In 1765 Rivera and his men had pointed to the first leg of the Old Spanish Trail.

CHAPTER IV

Fages, Garcés, Moraga and Muñoz

Early California and the Southern Route of the

Old Spanish Trail, 1769–1806

LITTLE WAS KNOWN about California during Juan María Antonio Rivera's exploration of the Yuta country, as it had not yet been established by Spain. For a long time California was all but totally ignored by Spanish officials. From 1540 to 1768 the California coast was visited mainly by mariners either exploring New Spain's northwestern littoral or stopping there to recuperate from the ravages of scurvy suffered during trans-Pacific voyages from the Philippines. While it does seem that little was accomplished in occupying California during this period, these years represent a silent unfolding of Spanish planning. Much of the data reported by seagoing Spaniards regarding the land, coupled with intelligence concerning the danger of Russian encroachment on Spanish claims in the northwest, generated forces leading to the eventual settlement of California.

Although Spanish fears regarding the possible loss of territory to Russia prompted a newly found vigilance concerning California and the interior colonies, other factors were present in 1768 for Spain's consideration of a California colony. The fear that Englishmen would eventually discover the Strait of Anian, the Spanish version of the "Northwest Passage," also stimulated Spanish interest in the north. Stories about bearded white men dressed in buckskin clothing living in the interior reinforced such fears. Heretofore-ignored missionary petitions to evangelize Indians in northern New Spain and its frontiers thus received renewed consideration. Finally, the appointment of José de Gálvez as *visitador general,* a high-ranking official position, resulted in the Spanish occupation of New Spain's Pacific northwest. Gálvez favored the establishment of California.

In 1769, a two-pronged effort to establish a base at San Diego was launched by order of Gálvez, who had chosen Governor Gaspar de Portolá to lead an expedition from La Paz overland through the Baja California peninsula to San Diego. Simultaneously, the second prong left by sea; it arrived in San Diego Bay and established a base camp before Portolá reached the area. Shortly after his arrival, Portolá led the first Spanish overland march along the coast, following closely the present coastal highway, from San Diego to Monterey, discovering San Francisco Bay. In the next decade, Monterey, the capital of Spanish Alta California, grew in prominence—so much so that by 1775 Spanish officials began to consider an overland connection between New Mexico and California. The Old Spanish Trail, however, would have to wait until 1781 when Los Angeles, its terminus, came into existence. Slowly, the wheels of history turned, creating a purpose for the route from New Mexico to California that would romantically be called the Old Spanish Trail.

Meanwhile, much information was being gathered about California's interior by a contemporary of Rivera, Pedro Fages. Fages (1754–1794) was an intrepid military officer of the *Compañía Franca de Voluntarios de Cataluña,*[92] known to English-speaking writers as the Catalonian Volunteers. He was from Guisona, Catalonia, in northeastern Spain and had arrived in Mexico as part of the reorganization of the colonial army in 1767. Dressed in the typical officer uniform of the day, Fages wore blue breeches, white stockings, black shoes, white cotton shirt, a yellow waistcoat with white buttons, and a black cravat. His cockaded officer's hat was large and gallooned with silver silk thread. His long blue overcoat with yellow collar and yellow stitching added to his official presence. In contrast, his men wore short blue cloaks with sleeves, white cotton shirts, blue breeches, white stockings, and black shoes. Their headwear was a small, blue woolen cap.[93] Despite Fages's efforts to keep discipline among his troops, his men were frequently unkempt and often traded the buttons of their clothing to Indians for food or other items.

During the Sonora campaign of 1767, Fages and twenty-five Catalonian Volunteers were called to participate in the founding California expedition of 1769. As members of the sea wing of the expedition, which preceded that of Governor Portolá who went by land, the Catalonian

Volunteers arrived with crews and personnel, most of them deathly ill from scurvy, on the *San Carlos* and the *San Antonio* and established a base camp at San Diego Bay. Soon after the arrival of Portolá, Fages and several others participated in the expedition to Monterey during which San Francisco Bay was discovered.

On 21 November 1770 Fages left Monterey with six soldiers and a muleteer. His objective was to find a way to Point Reyes on the northern arm of San Francisco Bay by traveling inland. Until then, the only way to Point Reyes was by sea, for the large bay and the rivers flowing into it had frustrated a direct land route to the northern arm of the bay. After fourteen days, Fages and his men failed to get to Point Reyes by land.[94]

The search for a route to Point Reyes challenged Fages. Undaunted, in 1772, he again led an expedition from Monterey, passing south through the Santa Clara Valley, a great plain which the Spaniards called Robles del Puerto de San Francisco. Moving northwesterly, the expedition headed toward present Oakland, and then traveled around the bay, reaching the inner San Pablo Bay. There they were stalled by an impassable channel that eventually came to be called Carquinez Strait. Hoping to ford this, they followed the channel northeasterly until they made an amazing discovery. Far upstream, they crossed arroyos and hills leading to a high pass where they espied a plain teeming with wildlife. Ascending the pass, Fages and his men were the first Europeans to see the Great Central Valley on one side and San Francisco Bay on the other. Of the event, the Franciscan, Fray Juan Crespí, a member of the expedition, wrote:

> We saw that the land opened into a great plain as level as the palm of the hand, the valley opening about half the quadrant, sixteen quarters from northwest to southeast, all level land as far as the eye could reach. Below the pass we beheld the estuary that we were following and saw that it was formed by two large rivers.[95]

They surmised that a feasible, practical route to Point Reyes was not possible, as the waterways could not be easily circumvented. The two rivers they saw were the Sacramento and the San Joaquin. Thus the Spaniards had made a most significant discovery, for they were the first Europeans to understand the strategic importance of the Monterey-San Francisco Bay area.

Later that year, Fages, leading a small detachment of soldiers in search of deserters, left San Diego en route to San Luis Obispo. Following an established route which would have led through Mission San

Gabriel, Fages changed the line of march toward the east through El Cajon Pass, thus avoiding a visit to the mission and its priest, Father Paterna, who detested him. Instead, Fages traveled northeasterly and then cut back toward the northwest along the San Gabriel Mountain Range; he followed the edge of the Mojave Desert via Palmdale to Antelope Valley, passed present-day Grapevine, and finally reached Buena Vista Hills and village, which he named. Fages and his men then became the first Europeans to enter the San Joaquin Valley. He described the area as follows:

> From the village of Buena Vista, the plain continues toward the south for seven leagues more, over good lands with some water. And at the end of these seven leagues one goes toward the south through a pass, partly of valleys and arroyos, very thickly grown with groves of live oaks, as are also all the hills and sierras which form these valleys. Going now three leagues more in the same direction, one comes to a very large plain, which keeps getting wider and wider, both toward the east and toward the south, leaving to the north and northwest many sierras.[96]

Peering into the distance beyond the plains to its surrounding sierras, Fages and his men must have fought off a great temptation to continue toward the northeast. For now, however, they merely reported on what they had seen.

The connection between the great Central Valley in the north and the San Joaquin Valley and the Tulares in the south was not lost on Fages and his men, who understood the significance of the fertility of both places and the important natural resources they had discovered. In his exploration of the San Joaquin Valley, Fages and his men saw the immense plain covered with vegetation and a large lake. The Tulares was a large marshy area in which grew tule, the common bulrush from which the area took its name. As a result of Fages's explorations, the Tulares became commonly noted on Spanish colonial maps of California. In promoting his discoveries in 1774, Fages wrote *A Historical, Political and Natural Description of California*, pointing out the importance of the resources in the interior.[97] After the establishment of missions, presidios, and farmlands, California's importance grew rapidly in the eyes of Spanish officials. Similarly, New Mexico's governors took notice of California as a possible trading partner.

Although Fages and his men at the time were ignorant of Teguayo and the Yuta country, they had contributed information which would extend the myth of Gran Teguayo to the San Francisco Bay area. Indeed, a later Mexican-period map showed a Río Timpanogos flowing from the Great Salt Lake to San Francisco Bay, where Fages's Río San Joaquín and Río Sacramento were located. Perhaps hope sprang eternal that an easy route from Timpanogos to the Monterey-San Francisco Bay area existed. Fages's exploration of California's interior opened the way for further Spanish interest in the hinterland.

The development of a segment of the Old Spanish Trail from the California side resulted from the efforts of and indefatigable Franciscan missionary, Francisco Hermenegildo Garcés (1738–1781). Between 1774 and 1776, Garcés explored from southern Arizona to Mission San Gabriel, California, near Los Angeles. He also went beyond the Mojave Desert, crossing the Colorado River south of the Grand Canyon, and moving eastward to the Hopi villages of northeastern Arizona. In his explorations, he often noted where Fages had been before him, sometimes noting horse tracks left by the Catalonian and his men.

Born in Aragón, Spain, on 12 April 1738, Garcés entered the Francisan order at age fifteen, studied theology in the monastery of Calatayud, and, at age twenty-five, was ordained. In 1766 he was accepted into the college of Santa Cruz de Querétaro, Mexico, where he served as a confessor. A year later, with the expulsion of the Jesuits, Garcés took the opportunity to become a missionary in Sonora. Once at Horcasitas, Sonora, Garcés was assigned to the northernmost mission in Pimería Alta—Mission San Xavier del Bac, south of present Tucson, Arizona. Despite his youthful thirty years of age, the natives called him "El Viejo" (the Old Man),[98] and later, because he limped, "El Cojo" (the Lame One).

Within a short period as missionary among the Pimas and Papagos, Garcés proved himself an energetic explorer. In August 1768 he made his first trip to the Gila River. The following year he entered Apache territory in the same region. In 1770 he returned to baptize dying natives who were struck by a severe epidemic in the Gila area. And, in 1771, after an absence of three months from San Xavier del Bac, Garcés reached the mouth of the Colorado River, south of its confluence with the Gila River.[99]

Garcés's reputation as an explorer grew rapidly. After California was established, Fray Junípero Serra, custodian of the California missions, proposed to Viceroy Antonio María de Bucaréli the idea of developing a land route from Sonora to the Pacific coast. Bucaréli ordered Captain Juan Bautista de Anza, the legendary soldier from Sonora then stationed at Tubac in present southern Arizona, to lead the expedition, provided that Garcés and Fray Juan Díaz accompany him. The expedition set out on 2 January 1774 from Tubac, crossing the Colorado River near Yuma, with its destination at Mission San Gabriel in the Los Angeles area. From San Gabriel, Garcés visited San Diego where he met with Father Junipero Serra.[100] The two had known each other since 1767 when they met in Tepic during the Jesuit expulsion, waiting to replace the ousted Jesuits in the missions to the north as well as those in Baja California. At San Diego they made plans to return to San Gabriel, which they reached on 11 April 1774 after five days of travel.[101]

Upon arriving at San Gabriel, Garcés was disappointed at having missed the opportunity to join Anza on his expedition to Monterey, for he had been specially charged "by high authority to investigate the feasibility of opening communication between Monterey and New Mexico."[102] It had been his desire to return to San Xavier del Bac from Monterey through a northern route, perhaps following the eastern slope of the sierras and reaching the Mojave Desert, familiar ground to him.[103] Of his feelings on the matter, Garcés wrote: "I have been very sorry that advantage has not been taken of this occasion, so opportune for discovering the course of the San Francisco River, which I believe is connected with the Colorado, and both with some very large lakes, or a water which is still and is very large, as the Gileños have told me."[104] The San Francisco River was the San Joaquín, which had been discovered in 1772 by Fages and Crespi. It is possible that Garcés's comment may have been the origin of the notion that the Great Salt Lake was connected to San Francisco Bay through the mythical Río de Teguayo.

On his return to southern Arizona, Garcés traveled south to the Santa Ana River then swung southeast to the Cahuilla Valley, moving directly to the Imperial Valley and from there toward Yuma. All the while, Garcés thought about a more northerly route to Monterey.[105] At Yuma, the natives under Chief Salvador Palma treated him well and helped him raft across the Colorado River.

Garcés was convinced in his belief that a route could be found from California to New Mexico. Writing in 1776 he opined that "As regards that of New Mexico, it is possible to proceed through the Yutas and seek the Río de San Felipe, and down the banks of this will be found my road. I doubt not that there may open another, better, and shorter than that which I traced from Oriabe to the Jalchedunes, for inasmuch as I was at the mercy of the Indians, I went where they took me."[106] Indeed, Garcés was interested in the explorations from New Mexico to the land of the Yutas. In 1775, he received a copy of Escalante's letter regarding a route from New Mexico to the Hopi villages and the proposed route from Santa Fe to Monterey. Garcés strongly recommended its possibilities:

> . . . the transit has itself to seek (i.e., must be sought) through the Yutas who live at the confluence of the rivers to the north of Moqui, of whom I learned that they were friends of New Mexico, and that, having here passed the Río Colorado, they roam southwest, descending to the Chemeguet Cajuala who live on the other side, and seeking the Río de San Felipe, they follow it to where I was. If from the said Yutas be taken the direction westnorthwest, as says the reverend padre, it is certain one could go to Monte-Rey and also to the Puerto de San Francisco, if there did not intervene the broad Tulares which have now been discovered, and through which only will it be possible to pass by means of boats (en caso de disponer embarcaciones). But even proceeding on this course it appears to me possible to traverse the large river of which I had information among the Noches and which is that which discharges (desagua) in the Tulares united with the Río de San Felipe or very close thereto; yet this seems to me a great circuit for the transit to Monte Rey, and in any event there is required the descent to head said Tulares. For this would be very useful, in spite of the greater distance, the discovery of the cited large river which according to reports comes from the northwest and may be the one which they called (Río) del Tizon on the expedition that in the year 1604 Don Juan de Oñate made from New Mexico.[107]

Doubtless, Garcés already realized that he had indeed blazed the last leg of the route to California from New Mexico and felt its feasibility lay through the Yuta country. If an exploratory party, such as the one Escalante had proposed, could get through from New Mexico, it would prove Garcés's contention.

Garcés's knowledge of the land between San Gabriel and Oraibe was learned slowly. In 1775, for example, he had participated in the second Anza expedition which left from Santa Eulalia in Sonora, retracing the route to the Colorado River near Yuma. In that expedition, he learned more about the land. After returning to San Xavier del Bac, Garcés, challenged by what lay beyond what he had seen, set out on his longest journey through the region bordering California along the Colorado River. In his explorations, he hoped to found a route from California to New Mexico. He had a plan he believed would work.

Leaving San Xavier del Bac south of Tucson on 3 January 1776, Garcés and two Indian companions set out northwesterly on the long jaunt along the Colorado River to present Needles. From there, they turned

westward into the Mojave Desert, where he discovered the Mojave
River. Continuing across the desert, he followed El Cajon Pass into the
San Diego area, thence north to San Gabriel. Leaving San Gabriel,
Garcés traveled through the San Fernando Valley, the Antelope Valley,
and the Tehachapi Range into the San Joaquin Valley to present Bakers-
field, reaching the present Kern and White rivers.

Once in the San Joaquin Valley, Garcés, heading northward on 24
April 1776, wrote in his diary, "I departed west, and at a little distance
took a course north, on which I surmounted the great sierra."[108] Proceeding northeast the following day, Garcés approached the Tulares and
stopped at an Indian ranchería where Pedro Fages had been in 1773. Proceeding northeasterly, Garcés skirted the southern end of the Sierra Nevada. His diary entry for 25–26 April 1776 described his route into the
Tehachapi Range:

> Apr. 25. I completed the passage of the sierra, crossed a valley, and came
> upon another large sierra which makes off the from the Sierra Nevada
> and extends northeastward; to which I gave the name of (Sierra de)
> San Marcos. We made the ascent *(hizimos alto)* near an arroyo, having
> traveled thus far four leagues north. In the evening I went a league in
> the same direction, and halted in the cited arroyo. There are on this
> sierra large pines, oaks, and other trees.
>
> Apr. 26. I surmounted the Sierra de San Marcos, having traveled two
> leagues and a half north; thereupon I saw large sierras, and caxones very
> leafy and grassy, and in three leagues and a half further, on courses west
> and southwest, I arrived at some rancherias of the Cuabajay na-
> tion. . . . I named [it] the Rancheria de San Pasqual.[109]

By 1 May 1776 Garcés had reached the present-day Kern River. De-
siring to cross the river, which he wrote "made much noise at the outlet
(al salir) of the Sierra de San Marcos," he found it to be too high and too
fast. He asked the natives to make him a raft, but they demurred, saying
they did not know how. So they persuaded Garcés to disrobe to his
underclothes, whereupon four swimmers convoyed "El Viejo" across the
river. The next day, having traveled four leagues farther north, Garcés
made contact with "some bearded Indians, and among them one old
man who had it (the beard) so grown *(poblada)* long and gray that he re-
sembled an anchorite much to be revered."[110]

On 3 May 1776 Garcés reached the northernmost point of his advance, the White River, southwest of present-day Sequoia National

Park. At one rancheria Garcés met an Indian from the Noches Pagni-noas tribe, located farther north, who offered to take him to his land. The tribe was apparently a small group of Yokuts, belonging to the Mariposan linguistic stock, although Elliot Coues, Garcés's biographer, speculated that the Indian could possibly have been a member of the Palligawanap tribe, a Paiute group who lived along the Kern River.[111] The man told Garcés that in his land they had killed two Spanish sol-diers. Of the two soldiers, Garcés (who presumed they were deserters) wrote that they had been killed because "they were very wicked with the women; adding they had cut off the [deserters] hands, had laid open the breast and all the body, had torn them asunder, and scattered the re-mains."[112] The Indians also told Garcés of other tribes to the north of there as well as about another great river, which later Spaniards called the San Joaquin, that ran from the northeast. Garcés noted that the Si-erra de San Marcos was at the southern end of the Tulares, writing that "this Sierra de San Marcos is that which they [earlier expeditions] saw snowy about 40 leagues of distance on the east of the Tulares; for though here there is no such distance, I saw clearly how the sierras go widening or disparting (from each other) in such a manner that at the last only is seen that of San Marcos."[113]

Returning to the rancheria he had visited on 1 May, Garcés received fresh supplies. After traveling in the area for a few days, he followed his route back to the Kern River, which he called Río de San Felipe, in the vicinity of present Bakersfield.[114] By 17 May, Garcés had reached the Mojave River. From there he meandered in an easterly direction—sometimes southeasterly, but mainly northeasterly—toward present Piute Springs in the Mojave Desert.[115]

The hot June sun found Garcés near the Colorado River. Backtrack-ing to the Mojave Desert, Garcés and his companions struck eastward toward the Hopi pueblos of northeastern Arizona. Having crossed the Colorado near present Fort Mojave, Garcés moved in an east-northeast direction.[116] His route from the environs of Fort Mojave to Cataract Canyon (where he visited the Yavasupai) was a well-known Indian trail. Near present Kingman, Garcés visited the Hualapai.

By 9 June, Garcés was at the foot of the Sierra Morena, present Cer-bat Range, where he followed a line of march up the Hualapai Valley on the western flank of the Peacock Range. From there he moved to the Ar-royo de San Bernabe, present Truxton Wash, then to present Hackberry. Leaving the land of the Mojave tribes, Garcés entered the land of the Yavapais. On 15 June, Garcés reached the *Pozos de San Basilio*, present

Peach Springs, about fourteen miles from Truxton Station. Following a line of march close to the present railroad line, he headed toward present Aubrey Cliffs, which run in a north to south direction. He crossed the cliffs as he went toward Pine Spring on his way to Cataract Canyon.[117]

The entrance to Cataract Canyon proved important in the establishment of a route south of the Grand Canyon to the Hopi pueblos which seemed to connect California to New Mexico. Of the event, Garcés wrote:

> I arrived at a rancheria which is on the Río Jabesúa [present day Cataract Creek], which I named (Río) de San Antonio; and in order to reach this place I traversed a strait (pasé por un estrecho) which I called the Nuebo Canfran. This extends about three quarters (of a league); on the side is a very lofty cliff, and on the other a horrible abyss (voladéro). This difficult road passed, there presented itself another and a worse one, which obliged us to leave, I my mule and they their horses, in order that we might climb down a ladder of wood. All the soil of these caxones is red; there is in them much mezcal; there are some cows and horses, most of which are branded, and some have several marks . . . I recognized none of them, but of a single one I doubted whether it were not of the mission of San Ignacio. I asked these Indians, as I had done before in other rancherias, whence did they procure these horses and cows; and they replied, from Moqui [Hopi], where there are many ill-gotten cattle and horses.[118]

In Cataract Canyon, Garcés encountered a ranchería of the Havasupai and spent five days with the inhabitants because they desired a missionary to be among them.

Departing from the Havasupai, Garcés traveled in a southeasterly direction, sometimes moving southward, then finally eastward until he halted before the Grand Canyon, which he described as "the most profound caxones which ever onward continue . . . and within flows the Río Colorado."[119] It was a warm day on 26 June 1776 when Garcés looked down into the Grand Canyon, which he named *Puerto de Bucaréli* after the viceroy of Mexico. He was the first European to have reached the Grand Canyon from the west.[120] Peering into the vast landscape, he saw "a very great sierra, which in the distance looks blue; and there runs from southeast to northwest a pass open to the very base, as if the sierra were cut artificially to give entrance to the Río Colorado into these lands."[121]

To the south of the Grand Canyon, Garcés could see the San Francisco Mountain peaks, which he called the *Sierra de Napac*. Crossing the

Little Colorado River which he named the Río de San Pedro, he kept the mountains to his right. Of the Little Colorado, Garcés wrote: "It was running water enough, but very dirty and red, that could not be drunk; but in the pools of the border of the river there was good water. This river runs to the westnorthwest, and unites with the Río Colorado a little before this passes through the Puerto de Bucaréli."[122] Near there, Garcés arrived at a ranchería of Yavapais where he met two Hopi traders dressed in "leather jackets almost as well as Españoles."[123] He talked with them, but they were reluctant to guide him and departed early the next day.

Garcés stayed at the ranchería from 28 June to 1 July; he then left in an east-southeast direction. That day, he was soon on the outskirts of the Hopi pueblos, traveling past ruins of a village and pastures and croplands. The next day, accompanied by Yavapai guides, he arrived at Oraibe. Although the inhabitants were friendly to him, it became fairly evident that the people at Oraibe did not want a missionary or any other Spanish frontiersmen living in their midst. Some young men from Zuñí Pueblo arrived and offered to take Garcés there; but, bowing to protocol, he desired to avoid crossing into the neighboring missionary field. Besides, he feared that his Yavapai guides would not be welcomed there, as had been the case in Oraibi. Garcés knew that the Yavapais also served as his bodyguards and felt he could not trust the Hopi on his return if the Yavapais were not with him.

On 3 July 1776 Garcés wrote a letter to the minister at Zuñí, Fray Silvestre Vélez de Escalante, describing his explorations and explaining his situation. His letter was forwarded to Santa Fe on 6 July 1776 where Escalante prepared his expedition to the Yuta country.[124] Thus, Garcés supplied Escalante with valuable information about a southern route from the land of the Cosninas and the Grand Canyon to Oraibe. Escalante already knew the route from Oraibe to Santa Fe via Zuñí. Together, Garcés and Escalante would gather new information and blaze the rudiments of a route that would eventually connect New Mexico with California along the later Route 66, the lesser-known part of the Old Spanish Trail. In any event, Garcés was the first Spanish explorer to traverse the Mojave Desert-northern Arizona segments of the Old Spanish Trail.[125] He was also the first to recognize the route as a direct pathway between Santa Fe and Los Angeles (Mission San Gabriel).

Garcés showed that one could cross from Mission San Gabriel near Los Angeles through the Mojave Desert to the Little Colorado and beyond to the Hopi villages, thence to the Río Grande in New Mexico. He also showed that the tribes along that route feared by New Mexicans,

such as the Cosninas, Yavapais, Apaches, and Navajos, did not constitute an insurmountable barrier, for he had literally met many of these
tribes who guided him through their lands. In the end, New Mexicans
would find Garcés generally correct in his assumptions about the various
tribes south of the Grand Canyon; however, they also knew that their
history with them ran contrary to Garcés's perceptions.

From Hopi, Garcés returned to the Colorado River, followed it
southward to Yuma, then eastward to San Xavier del Bac, arriving there
on 17 September 1776.[126] He had been on the trail for seven months.

A few years later, in 1780, Garcés and two fellow missionaries
founded two missions, Purísima Concepción and San Pedro y San Pablo
de Bicuñer, among the Yumas. A year later, the Yumas rebelled, killing
all of the missionaries, including Garcés, and many settlers who had established themselves at the Yuma crossing of the Colorado River. Pedro
Fages led the punitive expedition in 1781 to the Yuma crossing to investigate the rebellion and rescue Spanish survivors.[127] There he discovered
the remains of Father Garcés.[128] A year later, Fages, newly appointed
governor of California, crossed the Colorado River at Yuma and headed
northwest to his post in Monterey.

Nearly three decades after the death of Garcés, Spanish plans to
connect New Mexico and California persisted. During that time all of
the California missions had been founded, seven of them being established in the last decade of the eighteenth century. At the end of the
century, Governor Diego de Borica proposed a plan to populate California by bringing in settlers from New Mexico by way of the old Garcés
route.[129] Missionaries would be needed to pacify the tribes at the confluence of the Gila and the Colorado, but the Franciscans were loath to return to the desert after the Yuma uprising of 1781. Nonetheless, Garcés's
efforts proved to be a pioneering accomplishment that would eventually
contribute to the establishment of an immigration route to California
from New Mexico.

In the early nineteenth century, Californians continued to penetrate
the interior seeking new lands to settle and missionize within the Central Valley. In September 1806 Alférez Gabriel Moraga and Fray Pedro
Muñoz led an exploring party from San Juan Bautista Mission east of
Monterey Bay toward San Juan Junction, entering a plain near present
San Luis Creek. Their purpose was to determine sites for the establishment of missions and presidios in California's interior. Crossing the San
Joaquín River north of present Firebaugh in the Dos Palos area, they entered present Merced County and named the area *Mariposas* because of

the swarms of butterflies they saw there. Proceeding in two groups, the explorers marching northward discovered and named the Merced River, officially Nuestra Señora de la Merced. Beyond the Merced, they discovered another river they named the Dolores. Turning northeastward, the explorers marched twenty-five to thirty leagues toward the San Joaquín, naming the rivers encountered successively, the Nuestra Señora de los Dolores (probably the Tuolumne), Nuestra Señora de Guadalupe (probably the Stanislaus), the Dry San Francisco (probably French Camp Creek, or some other stream west of Farmington), and the Río de la Pasión (probably the Calaveras).[130]

Marching southward, the explorers reached an area near Millerton, the predecessor of present Fresno, where they camped. Near there, they learned of a chief named Sujoyucomu, who told them that soldiers from the other side of the sierras had been there and fought them twenty years earlier. That story was heard again by Moraga and Father Muñoz on the Río de los Reyes—present Kings River, which was named by an unrecorded expedition in 1805. Muñoz thought the soldiers mentioned must have been from New Mexico, which he reasoned must not be far away. Meandering, the party turned south and east. Crossing the Tulare River, they named it the San Pedro, and proceeded toward the Kern River. By November 1806 the party had reached Tejón Pass; it finally reached Mission San Fernando near Los Angeles before proceeding south to San Diego.[131] Muñoz made several recommendations, particularly, a proposal that Kings River be settled with a mission and a presidio.

The expedition of 1806 had run a course from San Diego to San Francisco, crossing through the Tulares region. Slowly, Spanish officials attended to the planning of the development of California's interior. In so doing, another step in the development of the California side of the Old Spanish Trail had been taken.

Between 1769 and 1806, much had been learned by Spanish explorers about the geographical features of the land from the California coast to Oraibe. The explorations of Captain Pedro Fages, Fray Francisco Hermenegildo Garcés, Alférez Gabriel Moraga, and Fray Pedro Muñoz created a familiarity with the interior of California beyond San Francisco Bay, Monterey, and San Gabriel in the Los Angeles area to the interior valleys. Beyond that, the California hinterland was comprised of high sierras to the northeast and the Mojave Desert to the southeast. Far to the east of the Colorado River lay New Mexico and the Hopi villages. To the southeast of the confluence of the Gila and Colorado rivers was Pimería Alta (southern Arizona and northern Sonora). Much information had been gathered and disseminated by word of mouth and through maps, diaries, and reports known to Spanish officials from Mexico City to Santa Fe, New Mexico, and San Francisco, California. This information was eagerly acquired by various governors of New Mexico who dreamed of a trade route to California. After Fages, Garcés, Moraga, and Muñoz, what lay between Santa Fe and Monterey through Arizona was no longer a mystery. The impetus for a route connecting the two points, however, came from New Mexico.

CHAPTER V

From Santa Fe to the Green River

The First Phase of the Dominguez-Escalante

Expedition, 1776

STANDING IN THE Plaza de Santa Fe on 29 July 1776, Fray Atanasio Domínguez and Fray Silvestre Vélez de Escalante distributed the Holy Eucharist among the members of their expedition to Monterey, California. Among those accompanying the two Franciscans were Juan Pedro Cisneros, chief magistrate from the Pueblo of Zuñí; Bernardo de Miera y Pacheco, a retired captain of the militia and citizen of Santa Fe; Lorenzo Olivares from the Villa of El Paso; Andrés Muñiz from Bernalillo; Antonio Lucrecio Muñiz, brother of Andrés, from Embudo south of Taos Pueblo; Juan de Aguilar from Santa Clara Pueblo; Joaquín Laín, a blacksmith from Santa Fe; and Simon Lucero, probably from Zuñí, who had served as Cisneros' servant. Of them, Andrés Muñiz, who had been with Juan María Rivera to the Gunnison River in 1765, spoke the Ute language. His brother Lucrecio had also been with the Rivera expedition and likely spoke, or at least understood, the language of the Yutas.[132]

Perhaps the most notable of the lay people on the expedition was Bernardo de Miera y Pacheco, who would later earn a place in the history of the cartography of New Mexico and the Southwest. In a letter dated 26 October 1777,[133] Miera y Pacheco, born in the mountain country of Burgos in Spain, recounted that in 1743 he came from Spain to El Paso del Norte. He participated in five campaigns against hostile Indians, and in 1754 he and his family moved to Santa Fe. In New Mexico,

Miera served as alcalde and captain of Pecos and Galisteo, where he campaigned against Comanches. In his letter, he wrote that he had journeyed to Hopi and drawn a map of the Navajo country. He also mentioned that, in 1760, he prepared a general map of the *Provincias Internas* of New Spain, which Nicolás Lafora, the cartographer of the marqués de Rubí expedition, had used. After his term as alcalde, Miera y Pacheco became the cartographer of the Domínguez-Escalante expedition.

As he stood in the Plaza de Santa Fe on that warm summer day, Friar Silvestre must have thought back to the day he first envisioned the possibility of such an expedition. Over a year had passed when he had returned from a reconnaissance to the Moqui (Hopi) villages in which he tested the possibility of a route from Santa Fe through present northeastern Arizona, south of the Grand Canyon and beyond the western bank of the Colorado River, which he would cross on his way to California. In a letter dated 28 October 1775 to Fray Fernando Antonio Gómez, Escalante recounted the purpose of his expedition to the Hopi pueblos. He knew that Governor Mendinueta had expressed interest in learning about the lands beyond the "Province of Moqui" (as noted in Spanish maps) and the tribes that bordered it.[134] His first visit to the "Province of Moqui" in the summer of 1775 resulted in meeting a Cosnina Indian who, through an interpreter, had drawn directions in the dirt leading from Oraibe to his land[135] and had given Escalante valuable information about the land beyond the "Province of Moqui."

His expedition to the Hopi had given him some insights in proposing a plan for a future expedition to Monterey. In June 1775 Escalante arrived at the Hopi pueblos with the intention of reaching the *Río Grande de los Cosninas*—the Colorado River. Finding the Cosninas unfriendly and fearing harm, Escalante did not accomplish his goal, although he spent eight days among them. He noted the Indians' location, defenses, herds, waters, and subsistence sources, as well as their population.[136] Given the hostility shown him, Escalante began to think that it would not be a good idea to pass through the Cosininas' land.

As part of his report, Escalante had Miera y Pacheco draw a map of the "Province of Moqui" (Map 11). The province, which later would be associated with the history of the Old Spanish Trail, was comprised of seven pueblos, almost in a direct line, wrote Escalante, from east to west on three mesas. On the western end of the first mesa at its narrowest point, were three pueblos. The first one, said Escalante, was inhabited by the Tanos, known as Teguas there. Their language was different from that of the Hopis. The other two pueblos, one a stone's throw from the first, and the second a musket shot distant, were Hopi speaking. Over 300 families lived in the three pueblos on the first mesa.

West of the first mesa, stood the second-mesa pueblos, called Gualpi. The first pueblo was called Mossasnabi, the second was Nipaolabi, already in ruins and abandoned; its people had moved to the newly built third pueblo called Nangopabi. The people of Second Mesa, observed Escalante, appeared more prosperous than those of First Mesa, for they possessed more horses and sheep.

On Third Mesa stood proud Oraibe, built stronger and larger than the others. It had 800 families, many horses and cattle, and a great number of sheep. It also had six large cisterns to supply its large population with water. The "Province of Moqui" with its three mesas, including the friendly tribes of Yochies and Fasabuests within it, was bordered by the Navajos on the east, by the Cosninas on the west and northwest, by the Yutas on the north, by the Gileño Apaches on the south, and by the Mescaleros on the southwest.[137]

Escalante, however, was not as much concerned about the tribes that surrounded the "Province of Moqui", as he was with the Hopi themselves. He felt that the prosperous Hopi were rebellious, despite their professed loyalty to the crown following the Pueblo Revolt of 1680. The Hopi people, furthermore, had obstinately refused to acknowledge obedience to Spanish authority as well as to the Christian religion. He proposed an expedition against them to compel them by force or by intimidation to accept their legitimate sovereign.[138] He also proposed that a fort be established to maintain peace between Spaniard and Hopi. He felt that the fort would also deter Apaches from raiding in the area. Once the Hopi were pacified and converted religiously, their land could be used to march against the Cosninas. Escalante suggested that the establishment of the fort among the Hopi would serve to subjugate the Cosninas.[139] Perhaps, Escalante hoped that his proposal to find a route to Monterey would receive a more receptive ear if he suggested an alternate route that was not fraught with complications such as the route which required crossing the land of the hostile Cosninas, or another which crossed through territory claimed by the warlike Apache leading to the Gila River, thence westward to its confluence with the Colorado River.

Escalante's proposal showed his belief that the expedition to Monterey would be easier through the land of the Yutas than through that of the Cosninas. Besides, by comparing "Vivas's maritime directory" printed in Manila in 1766 with the "newest" map of the area drawn by Nicolas de Lafora in 1771, Escalante determined that the Port of Monterey was at "37° and some minutes" and Santa Fe was at a "latitude of 36 degrees and 11 minutes." Between them, therefore, lay the land of the Yutas who were at peace with the Spaniards.[140] Besides, the expedition would have to march northward anyway to the latitude of Monterey.

Escalante alluded to the possibility of finding a "lost" tribe of Spaniards, whom he believed now lived as Indians. Rivera had earlier sought them in 1765. Two years after his expedition of 1776, Escalante, in a letter to Father Juan Agustín Morfi, confused the bearded Indians he met among the Yuta tribes with the story of the lost Spaniards. In his letter, 2 April 1778, he wrote that

> "from the misunderstood stories of the heathen Indians, many [Spaniards] were persuaded that on the other side of the Colorado River, which with the Gila enters the Gulf of California, live a nation similar to the Spanish, wearing long beards, armor, like our ancient kind, with breast plate, iron helmet and shoulder-piece; and these, no doubt, are the bearded Yutas of whom the Reverend Father Custodian [Domínguez] and I speak in the diary of the journey which we made through those lands in the year 1776; who live in rancherias and not in pueblos. They are very poor; they use no arms, other than their arrows and some lances of flint, nor have they any other breast-plate, helmet or shoulder-piece than what they brought out from the belly of their mothers."[141]

Escalante's visit to the Hopi pueblos had, indeed, stimulated his excitement about a possible route to Monterey.

It is important to note, however, that the actual leader and organizer of the expedition was Fray Francisco Atanasio Domínguez, who bore the burden of responsibility in planning, making critical decisions on the trail, disciplining members of the party, assuring the safety of the men, and was the final authority upon whom fell the judgment of his superiors whether the expedition was a success or failure.[142] In this regard, Escalante, as the subordinate to Domínguez, had the "task to act as amanuesis," that is, as the scribe of the expedition.[143] In reality, both men collaborated in the writing of the diary. Perhaps, because Escalante was better known and Domínguez virtually unknown to contemporary authorities in New Mexico, it was Escalante who received recognition for having written the diary and was subsequently credited by some later historians as having led the expedition.

Francisco Atanasio Domínguez was born in Mexico City around 1740. By age seventeen he had joined the Franciscan Order in the Convento Grande located in the Mexican capital. In 1772 he was serving at the convent of Veracruz as commissary of the third order there. His assignment to New Mexico began in 1775 as the *visitador* (inspector) of the Custody of the Conversion of St. Paul, as New Mexico was known to missionaries. The office of canonical visitor was given only to most qualified clergymen, a reputation well earned by the esteemed Father Domínguez.[144]

The instructions given to Domínguez ordered him to make a thorough and detailed report of the spiritual and economic status of the New Mexico missions, including geographical and ethnological information. On 4 September 1775 he arrived in El Paso, then the ecclesiastical headquarters of the Custody of the Conversion of St. Paul. After a six-month sojourn, he left El Paso and arrived on 1 March 1776 in Santa Fe. During the spring of that year, Domínguez made his inspection of the New Mexico missions from Santa Fe to Taos Pueblo. In late spring he visited the missions south of Santa Fe on the Río Abajo, the lower Río Grande. During those months, he made preparations to meet the objectives of his instructions, which included finding a route to Monterey. On 15 April, Friar Domínguez ordered Father Escalante, who had been assigned to Zuñí Pueblo and who had been working on a plan to find a route to Monterey, to join him in Santa Fe. Their friendship was immediate. After consulting each other on the best route to California, they enlisted the service of Miera y Pacheco and several other frontiersmen who had been to the Yuta country.[145]

Francisco Silvestre Vélez Escalante was born in 1749 in Treceño, Santander, Spain.[146] He died in 1780 in Parral, Chihuahua, Mexico. His parents were Clemente Nicolas Vélez Escalante and María Josefa Fernandez de los Ríos. Escalante was baptized on 9 June 1749. Little is known about his early life, but by age seventeen, having committed himself to the life of a missionary, he took the Franciscan habit at the Convento Grande in Mexico City. Fray Silvestre (he rarely used his first name) arrived in New Mexico sometime in the early 1770s; one of the earliest records of his New Mexican assignment is dated 21 December 1774.[147] In the next two years he earned recognition among New Mexican officials as an explorer in addition to his growing reputation as a missionary.

Having said their prayers, and bidding goodbye to their friends and families, the ten men of the Domínguez-Escalante expedition set out from the Villa de Santa Fe. Meandering along the camino de Taos, they stopped for the night, after an uneventful day, at Santa Clara Pueblo.

Their first day's journey, by their count, was barely nine leagues, or a little more than twenty-four miles. The next day's going was equally slow, making another nine leagues and spending the night and the next day, 30 and 31 July, at Santa Rosa de Abiquiú. Bearing northwest for the next few days and suffering from heavy rainfall, the expedition passed through rugged terrain in the direction of Arroyo del Canjilon, Río de la Cebolla, and Río de las Nutrias. They reached a small pine forest and descended to the Río Chama.[148] Wending their way over small pine-forested mesas, short valleys, and open grassy meadows, they continued northwest from sunrise to sunset.

By 4 August, the expedition, bearing north at times and northwest at others, swung within sight of Piedra Parada, today's Chimney Rock, "a sight known to our people who have traveled through here," wrote Escalante in his entry for that day.[149] That night they camped in a canyon named *Cañon del Engaño* on Amargo Creek. The next day they left the canyon, traveling toward the southwest to the Río de Navajó, which flows from the *Sierra de las Grullas,* a part of the Rocky Mountains, featured in Miera y Pacheco's map. The Río de Navajó, today's Navajo River, runs from the northeast to the southwest to a point near *Cañon del Engaño* where it turns north until it joins the Río San Juan. Crossing the Río Navajó, they continued southwesterly through canyons, over inclines, and through heavy brush country where they lost their trail. Not even their guides could determine where they were. Domínguez and Escalante held a council and decided that their best guess was to turn northwest. The next afternoon, they stopped and took a reading of the sun's meridian, somewhere near present Carracas, Colorado, in the vicinity of Pagosa Springs. They reckoned that the place they named *Nuestra Señora de las Nieves* was at 37° 51' latitude.[150] Fray Silvestre scouted ahead to the confluence of the San Juan and the Navajo rivers, which he said was three leagues in a straight line almost due east of Las Nieves. The two rivers formed a drainage previously unknown to the Spaniards, who called it the Río Grande de Navajó. Across it began the territory of the Yuta nation.[151] They described both banks of the river as "leafy and extremely dense thickets of white poplar, scrub oak, choke-cherry, *manzanita, lemita,* there is also some sarsparilla and a tree that looks to us like the walnut."[152]

For the next few days, they traveled westward along the river's edge, stopping now and then to allow Miera y Pacheco to rest and care for "the stomach trouble" he had been experiencing. Passing near present Ignacio, Colorado, and the flat land along the Pine River south of there, they turned west-northwest and arrived at the Río Florido (Florida River), which they crossed. Continuing down a rocky incline, they arrived at the Río de las Animas. They camped on its west side not too far south of later Durango, Colorado.[153] By 9 August they had reached the La Plata River and took note that the Rivera expedition had been there before them. They wrote:

> [The Río de la Plata] rises at the same western point of La Sierra de La Plata and descends through the same canyon in which there are said to be veins and outcroppings of metallic ore. However, although years ago certain individuals from New Mexico came to inspect them by order of the governor, who at the time was Don Tomás Vélez Cachupín, and carried back metal-bearing rocks, it was not ascertained for sure what kind of metal they consisted of. The opinion which some formed previously, from the accounts of various Indians and from some citizens of the kingdom, that they were silver ore, furnished the sierra with this name.[154]

Complaining of the "excessively" cold nights during the months of July and August, members of the expedition suffered headaches, colds, fevers, and exhaustion. A heavy downpour on 10 August increased their maladies and forced them to camp a couple of days at the East Mancos River near its confluence with the main Mancos River.[155] While there, Andrés Muñíz, who had been on the Rivera expedition, told the others that the Sierra de la Plata's metallic rocks were a short distance from their camp. However, they were too fatigued to verify his claim.

Having rested, they traveled west by west-northwest; a few leagues later, they went north and crossed the Dolores River, where they took another compass "bearing on the polar elevation of this site and meadow of El Río de los Dolores. . . . The bearing was taken by the sun, and we saw that we were at 38° 13½' latitude." There they noted an ancient ruin on the river's south side, writing "there was in ancient times a small settlement of the same type as those of the Indians of New Mexico, as the ruins which we purposely inspected show."[156] No description of the ruin was made, although they did note that pasturage, irrigable lands, timber, and firewood were characteristically abundant in the area and recommended it suitable for settlement.

By mid-August the expedition had moved away from and then back to the Dolores River, satisfying their need for water, which they could not find away from the river. In their meanderings they had been overtaken by a mestizo named Felipe, and an Indian of mixed Plains parentage from Abiquiú called Juan Domingo. Domínguez and Escalante were not pleased by their appearance because the two had left New Mexico without permission, and the friars feared if they sent them back they might run afoul of wandering Ute bands. So they felt obligated to keep Felipe and Juan Domingo with the expedition.

Again, moving along the Dolores River, they entered a canyon they named *El Laberinto de Miera* "because of the varied and pleasing scenery of rock cliffs it has on either side . . . and because Don Bernardo Miera was the first one to go through it."[157] That day, 17 August, they camped on the Dolores River in Summit Canyon near Disappointment Valley. Near there they found human tracks and followed them hoping they might be those of Tabehuachi Yutas who could guide them; but they failed to make my contact. In that sortie, they reached present Disappointment Creek.

The remainder of August they spent traveling in western Colorado, reaching the point the Rivera expedition called La Sierra de los Tabehuachis, present Uncompahgre Plateau. To get there they had followed the Dolores River past Steamboat Hill to the Little Gypsum Valley at the south end of Andy's Mesa, where they noted they were at 39° 6' latitude. Somewhere southeast of present Spectacle Reservoir they entered the west fork of Dry Creek Canyon and camped at a place they named San Bernabé. By the third week in August they had moved northwest of present Naturita, Colorado, as they crossed and followed the San Miguel River, which they called the Río San Pedro, in a northeasterly direction.

Having left the San Miguel, they encountered the Sierra de la Sal, present La Sal Mountains, named for the salt beds near them. Stopping in a narrow valley, they described its pasturage potential, for they had seen little such land since leaving the river. They also described an ancient ruin they saw on a ridge: "On top of this are ruins of a small and ancient pueblo, the houses of which seem to have been made of the stone with which the Tabehuachi Yutas have fashioned a weak and crude rampart."[159] Near the ruins they found pasturage for their mounts. Although the land appeared dry, intermittant rains pelted them along the route. Somewhere along this line of march, they met with a Tabehuachi Ute who exchanged information with them for some food. He agreed to guide them to the Sabuagana tribe Rivera had mentioned. As agreed, the Tabehuachi left them and returned two days later with his family members who desired to trade with the Spaniards. After their guide was paid with two large knives and sixteen strings of white glass beads, the family members returned to their camps, and the

Tabehuachi proceeded to guide the expedition to the land of the Sabuagana.

On 24 August they crossed present Red Canyon and camped near Horsefly Creek, which runs through the canyon. Meandering south, southeast, then northeast, they proceeded to a point near Johnson Spring, after which they reached the Uncompaghre River, noted on Miera y Pacheco's map as El Río de San Francisco, but which the Utes called the Ancapagari, meaning red lake, "because they say that near its source there is a spring of red-colored water, hot and ill-tasting."[160] Three days later, the expedition was back on course, moving northwest downstream on the Uncompahgre River. Along their march they met a Ute called the Left-handed with his family from whom they learned nothing of the land ahead.

The hot August sun beat down on the expedition as it moved northwestward toward the Gunnison River, shown on Miera y Pacheco's map as the Río San Xavier; the Utes called it the Tomichi.[161] Near there, Andrés Muñíz told them that Rivera in 1765 had carved a cross, his name, and the year 1765 on a poplar sapling. Muñíz reiterated that he had been there with the Rivera expedition and had returned in 1775 with Pedro Mora and Gregorio Sandoval. They had also been with Rivera and had crossed the Uncompaghre, having reached the Río del Tizón, present-day Colorado River.[162]

The last days of August were spent in contacting the Sabuaganas, who had been exchanging goods with Laguna traders, whom Spaniards knew as the Timpanogotziz from Timpanogos, or present-day Utah Lake and the Great Salt Lake. Actually, the Timpanogotzis were the present Uintah Utes. The Old Ute word Timpanogos appears to mean "the stone person," referring to the figure of a reclining human being formed by the ridges of Mount Timpanogos.[163] The Spaniards took a reading of the sun's meridian at 39° 13' 29".[164] At one point, they met a group of Utes who tried to discourage them from proceeding any farther west. They were told that the Yamparica Comanches would kill them if they found them. A day later, the expedition's scouts brought the Sabuaganas they sought and one Laguna Ute to the camp. They too told the Spaniards to turn back, for the Comanche would kill them, and, besides, none of them knew the way to Timpanogos. Finally, the Spaniards offered the Laguna Ute a woolen blanket, a large knife, and white glass beads to lead them to Timpanogos. He readily agreed. Seeing this, the Sabuaganas acknowledged that they too knew the way. Suddenly, all the potential difficulties with the Comanches disappeared. The next day, they all set out for the Sabuagana encampment two days' distance from their camp at a little river they called Santa Rosa, today known as Leroux Creek. Heading northeast, then north, they reached a water source they named San Ramón Nonato, where they stopped north of the confluence of present Willow Creek and Hubbard Creek in Hubbard Canyon.[165]

As August turned into September, the weather began to cool noticeably. Somewhere in the Colorado wilderness near present Electronic Mountain Hunting Lodge on Grand Mesa, they encountered eighty Yuta warriors "all on good horses and most of them from the encampment to which we were going. They told us that they were going out to hunt, but we figured that they came together like this, either to show off their strength in numbers or to find out if any other Spanish people were coming behind us or if we came alone; for, since they knew from the night before that we were going to their encampment, it was unnatural for almost all of its men to come out at the very time that they knew we were to arrive, unless motivated by what we have just said."[166] Once at the Ute encampment, the Spaniards set about to trade for fresh mounts, while the padres, using Andrés Muñiz as their interpreter, began to proselytize among the natives. Meanwhile, a separate camp was set up for the Spaniards.

Domínguez and Escalante were astute frontiersmen who perceived that they were involved in a sort of ruse being played out between the Utes and some of their own men who wanted to turn back. In the evening, the Sabuagana chieftains sat with the Spaniards and again attempted to convince them to turn around, for they were certain the Comanches would not let them pass westward. As it turned out, Andrés Muñiz, the lead interpreter, and his brother Lucrecio had ulterior motives for secretly prompting the Sabuaganas to oppose their plan to proceed westward. Wrote Escalante:

> Ever since La Villa de Santa Fe, we had reminded all of the companions that those who wished to be part of this expedition were not to take along any goods for trading and that those who did not agree to this condition were to stay behind. All agreed not to bring a thing, nor any purpose other than the one we had, which was God's glory and the good of souls. For this reason, everything that they requested for their equipment and to leave to their families was rationed out to them. But some of them failed in their promise by secretly carrying some goods we did not see until we were near to the Sabuaganas. And here we charged

and begged them all not to engage in commerce, so that the infidels might understand that another motive higher than this one brought us through these parts.[167]

The friars felt betrayed by the two brothers because they threatened the hope that the Christian God would grant them safe passage through the lands of the Comanche. By trading for weapons from the Utes as insurance against an anticipated lack of divine intervention in the event of an attack, the two men had presumably weakened the friars' message about their Christian God. Escalante felt sorrow for the two, for they not only lacked faith, their actions proved them "unfit for ventures of this kind."[168] A day later, the Ute chieftains agreed with the friars and granted them passage through their land, exhorting their tribesmen to stop presenting barriers to the Spaniards' desire to travel west.

Led by two Laguna Indians named Silvestre and Joaquín, the expedition, on 2 September, continued up Cow Creek, crossing over to Dyke Creek and then westward to Chimney Rock, reaching Mule Park on the upper West Muddy Creek.[169] They went westward through present Buzzard Park, passing along the south face of Bronco Knob, down Plateau Creek to the Meadows in a north-northwesterly direction until they reached Campbell Mountain, known to the Utes as Nabuncari.[170] Continuing northwesterly, and experiencing cold temperatures at night, the expedition passed present Jerry Gulch, reaching the Colorado River by way of Battlement Mesa, east of Castle Peak, then down Alkali Creek to the south bank of the Colorado River. They turned northward, seeking a ford near present Una bridge.[171] On 7 September the expedition approached the confluence of Brush Creek and Roan Creek.

The march was not without its intrigue. Escalante could not help but think that certain members of the expedition still hoped to turn back to Santa Fe, rather than proceed westward. His fears were confirmed when he was confronted by a new threat which he and Father Domínguez had to decide was real or imagined. The expedition's interpreters attempted to convince the padres that their Laguna guide Silvestre was leading them into a Sabuagana ambush. They told the priests that they had heard many Sabuaganas tell Silvestre to walk the expedition in a roundabout way for eight or ten days to make them turn back. Domínguez and Escalante realized that the northerly route they had embarked upon since leaving the Sabuaganas constituted a great detour, but they pondered the contradiction presented to them by their own men: why, if what they said was true, did they not reveal it before?

After a debate among the expeditionary members, the priests decided to trust their Laguna guide. Not long after this, they encountered
a lone Sabuagana Ute "of the most northerly ones," and they asked him
about the route. He recommended that they bear west to get to the great
lake because the trail they presently followed went further north. Later,
they encountered three camps of Sabuaganas who had been stealing
horses from the Comanches. They informed the Spaniards that the Comanches had gone eastward toward the Río de Napeste, present Arkansas River. With that report, the dissenting voices in the Spanish camp
about encountering Comanche warriors subsided.[172]

Leaving their campsite near the confluence of Brush Creek and
Roan Creek, they moved to the top of Brush Mountain, and thence to
the junction of East Douglas and Cathedral creeks. By 9 September
they were in Douglas Canyon south of Rangely, Colorado, where they
saw a lofty rock cliff with crudely painted shields, spearheads, and two
men depicted in combat. From there they went through the canyon
where they saw some iron pyrite, or fool's gold. Traveling north-north-
west, they arrived at the White River, which they named the Río San
Clemente, where they camped at the confluence of Douglas Creek and
the White River at present Rangely, Colorado.[173] The expedition pushed
forward, marching west-northwest, passing over arroyos and embank-
ments. Tracking a buffalo on 12 September, they crossed into present
Utah east of Snake John Reef and K-Ranch, after which they followed
Cliff Creek westward to the Green River Valley.[174]

The Green River was known to the Spaniards by the name Río San
Buenaventura and to the natives of the area as Seeds-Kee-dee. The
Spaniards camped on the east side of the Green River near the future
town of Jensen.[175] Water sources leading to there were few, and they had
collected water two days after leaving the painted canyon at Fuentes de
Santa Clara, about ten miles east of the Green River.[176] Escalante knew
a little about the Río San Buenaventura, for he had studied previous
Spanish reports of the area. He recounted how Fray Alonso de Posada,
the Custos of the Province of New Mexico in the previous century, had
written about the river in 1686. Posada had said that the river was the
boundary between the Comanche and the Utes.

Mid-September was spent exploring the region around the Río San
Buenaventura. Somewhere along the river, Joaquín Laín took an adze
and carved on a cottonwood tree the letters and numbers "Año de 1776."
Having crossed the river, they headed in a south-southwesterly direction. Near present Asphalt Ridge, the Spaniards found horse and hu-

man tracks. After studying the indications, they concluded that whoever had been there had been lying in wait at that place, probably to ambush them and take their horse herd. The priests suspected that it could have been some Sabuaganas who thought to attribute the deed to Comanches, since they were apparently in Comanche territory. Their suspicion turned on their Laguna guide, Silvestre. They had learned that, the night before, Silvestre had gone off to sleep alone some distance from the camp. They also noticed that throughout the march, he had never once wrapped himself with a blanket. Now, they observed that he wore a blanket, even in the daytime. They suspected that if he had negotiated with the Sabuaganas, he wore the blanket to be recognized during an attack on the Spaniards. Silvestre, nevertheless, was not confronted with the circumstantial evidence the priests had quietly gathered. Soon, the priests decided that their fears were unfounded and that time had proven Silvestre's innocence.[178]

The San Buenaventura River could represent what Spanish officials and explorers knew about the Yuta country. Since 1686 when Father Posada had written about it, albeit vicariously through the eyes of colonial informants, until 1776 when the men of the Domínguez-Escalante expedition saw it and described it, knowledge about the river was only from hearsay evidence. New Mexican frontiersmen who had been there kept what they knew about the area to themselves, for they had been there without license. Their illegal entry into the area would not have been without penalty. But now, the Domínguez-Escalante expedition stood on the threshold of a new land. Beyond the Río San Buenaventura lay *Teguayo,* a place few, if any, Spanish New Mexicans had seen.

Chapter VI

The New Eden

Beyond the Río San Buenaventura to Utah Lake

and the Grand Canyon

THE COOL SEPTEMBER air announced that fall was upon them. The expedition, now fifty days out of Santa Fe, had reached the farthest known point of any official expedition to the Yuta country. Their New Mexican guides, who had tried by trickery or persuasion to turn the expedition back, probably did so out of fear of the unknown. Now they were committed, they had crossed the San Buenaventura, the historic boundary line between the Comanche and the Ute tribes. It was 17 September when the expedition broke camp on the "Stirrup" bend of the Green River. They had named their campsite *Las Llagas de Nuestro Padre San Francisco,* "the wounds of our Father St. Francis," a leafy poplar grove and meadow, where they had found human tracks and concluded that they had been left by Comanches in pursuit of Ute hunters.[179] Certainly, the Comanche had made their presence felt, and the expedition hoped to avoid them. Looking westward into the distance, beyond the meadow, the expedition members traveled to a high ridge from which they could see the junction of the present White River and the Green River. Descending to a plain, they headed for the junction. Ironically, on 17 September 1776, as Domínguez and Escalante were about to embark into the new land, Friar Francisco Garcés had just returned to San Xavier del Bac, ending his exploratory travels from Mission San Gabriel to Oraibe.

Marching toward the west, they crossed a large meadow and arrived at the juncture of two medium-sized rivers which they named the Río de San Damián and the Río de San Cosme—present-day Uinta River and Duchesne River, respectively. Along the Duchesne, they came across the ruins of an ancient pueblo and noted the fragments of stone used for grinding maize as well as shards of jars and pots of clay. The pueblo, wrote Escalante, was circular "as indicated by the ruins now almost completely in mounds."[180] That day they camped at a place they called *La Rivera de San Cosme,* east of Myton, Utah.

The meandering Duchesne caused the expedition to cross it five times in one day. Once across the river, they headed directly west as they moved to higher ground. Stopping to camp along the Duchesne River, near its namesake town in present Utah, Domínguez and Escalante estimated that they had traveled 287 leagues, or over 750 miles, from Santa Fe. From their camp, they could see the Uinta Mountains, which they named the *Sierra Blanca de los Lagunas* because they were snow covered. Their destination, the Laguna settlements, was located at the far end of the Uinta Mountains, a high sierra running east to west. Formidable as the mountains appeared to the Spaniards, Domínguez and Escalante made plans to cross it the next day at its lowest point, "where it appears less lofty."[181] It appears, however, that they crossed over the Wasatch Plateau.

From their camp on 19 September, the Spaniards set out toward the southwest, camping in a meadow near a water source they named *San Eustaquio,* present Red Creek. Continuing southwest, they crossed the Río San Cosme as they proceeded through a narrow valley, stopping at a spring they named *Ojo de Santa Lucía,* present Deep Creek drainage.[182] Climbing hills and crossing small or medium-sized rivers, the Spaniards continued southwesterly. At a place they called *Valle de la Purísima,* in the vicinity of present Strawberry Reservoir, the Spaniards fished for trout, but their Laguna guide was more successful shooting fish with his bow and arrows. Finally, after crossing a small stream with very cold water, they came to a very dense forest of white poplar, scrub oak, chokecherry, and spruce.[183] In the forest, Father Domínguez, moving his mount faster to keep up with his guide, received a hard blow to one of his knees when it hit a poplar as he rode swiftly by. That night, the fatigued expedition camped at a site they named *San Mateo,* on present Sixth Water Creek. The cold air seemed somewhat frigid to them in comparison to that of previous nights.[184]

Each day they traveled, they came closer to the salt lake the natives had told them about. They knew from their guide that soon they would be making contact with the Lagunas. Traveling west-southwest from their camp at *San Mateo,* they climbed a high ridge. From there they could see smoke signals rising from a nearby mountain. Their guide Silvestre said they belonged to some of his people who had probably been hunting. Their anticipation mounted at the prospect of meeting the Lagunas, but so did their fears of being mistaken for enemies. They took precautions by asking Silvestre to be on the lookout and ready to intercede in their behalf.[185]

By 23 September 1776 the Spaniards believed that they were approaching the lake. Heading southwest, they climbed a hill, noting a large anthill on top of it. Crossing modern Diamond Creek, which they named *Río de San Lino,* they followed it downstream passing some hot springs similar to those near Jemez Pueblo in New Mexico.[186] Moving west, they entered the narrowest part of the river's canyon, present Spanish Fork Canyon. There they described three other springs and a river on the northern side they named *Río de Aguas Calientes,* present Spanish Fork River. Traveling northwest, they crossed the river, climbed a hill, and from its summit, first viewed present-day Utah Lake and Utah Valley, which they named *Nuestra Señora de la Merced de los Timpanagotzis.*[187] From the hill, they could see smoke signals, likely announcing their arrival. Entering the valley, they noticed that the Lagunas had tried to burn the pasturelands along their route. The Spaniards speculated that the Lagunas had thought them to be a hostile force and tried to deprive them of pasturage. Fires had been started in several places. Finally approaching a settled area, they were met by armed warriors ready for combat. Quickly, the interpreters calmed the Indians' fears and a peace was made.[188]

Once at the main village, they were given lodging. The friars told the natives about the Christian God, and about the safe travel He had granted them. Then they asked about continuing their travel through the land since, wrote Escalante, "we had to continue our traveling in order to learn about the other padre, our brother, we needed another one from among their own to guide us as far as another nation they knew, which might grant us another guide."[189] The friars were hoping to arrange for a guide to advance them westward to California. The "other padre" to whom they referred was likely Father Francisco Garcés, their contemporary who had communicated to them before they had left Santa Fe that he had explored a route from California to Oraibe. The rest of September, prior to their departure from the Utah Lake area, was spent exploring the vicinity, and learning about the Great Salt Lake, which was connected by a river approximately forty miles long, the modern Jordan River.[190]

The natives told them that the salt at the Great Salt Lake was very harmful. They told the priests, furthermore, that the Great Salt Lake was inhabited by the *Puaguampe,* or "bewitchers." The *Puaguampe,* Escalante believed, spoke a Comanche language, but they were not foes of the Lagunas; however, there had been some hostility between them.[191] The *Puaguampe* lived on wild plants, and they drank from springs surrounding the Great Salt Lake. Their homes had grass and sod roofs. The usual route from the Lagunas to the *Puaguampe* was through a gap in the mountains.

Toward the end of September 1776, the expedition began to meander away from the Laguna settlements. Exploring the vicinity of modern Provo, the Spaniards moved west, then south, reaching *Valle de las Salinas,* present Juab Valley, by 27 September. The salt flats of the valley were ones the Lagunas had said they used. Two days later, upon leaving the southern end of the valley, they turned southwest and came upon "a very old Indian of venerable countenance. He was alone in a tiny hut, and he had a beard so full and long that he looked like one of the ancient hermits of Europe."[192] Influenced by the generalization that Indians lacked facial and body hair, the explorers were astonished at seeing the bearded Indian. The bearded man told them that in the direction they traveled, they would come to another river. Upon reaching the river, which they did not see until they were at its very edge owing to the flatness of the land and the undergrowth, they named it the *Río Isabel,* present Sevier River.

The next day, very early on 30 September, twenty Indians came to trade at their camp. They were covered with robes of coney and jackrabbit furs. They talked until nine o'clock in the morning. Escalante noted that "these ones, more fully bearded than the Lagunas, have their nostril-cartilage pierced, and in the hole, by way of adornment, they wear a tiny polished bone of deer, fowl, or some other animal. In their features they more resemble the Spaniards than they do all the other Indians known in America up to now, from whom they differ in what has been said. They employ the same language as the Timpanogotzis. From the river and site of Santa Isabel onward begin these full-bearded Indians, who perhaps gave rise to the report about the Spaniards who were said to exist on the other side of El Río del Tizón."[193] For a long time, a story persisted in the eighteenth-century lore of New Mexico about bearded men living somewhere in the Yuta country north of the Colorado River who were said to be Spaniards who had been shipwrecked. Miera y Pacheco noted the place and sketched the bearded Indians with their fur robes on his 1778 map of the expedition.

The cold October nights, the dwindling supplies, and the scarcity of potable water for long stretches at a time began to concern the expedition's leaders. On 1 October, searching for water, Escalante wrote, "We thought we saw a marshland or lake water nearby, hurried our pace, and discovered that what we had judged to be water was salt in some places, saltpeter in others, and in others dried alkaline sediment."[194] That day they traveled fourteen leagues (thirty-six miles) without finding water or pasturage for their horses. They stopped at a site they called *Llano Salado,* Salt Plain, northwest of Pahvant Butte, because their horses "could go no farther."

Having camped for the night, the Spaniards decided to continue seeking water as soon as the rising moon offered some night light. The decision almost ended in disaster, for, during the night, those who had taken the herd fell asleep and the herd got away from them. The next morning at six o'clock one of the herdsmen came in to report what had happened. One of the men was still missing. As soon as he reported the bad news, Juan Pedro Cisneros rode off bareback to find the herd, which he found halfway back the trail toward the Sevier River. No sign of the missing man was found.

Meanwhile, at their camp on the salt plain, they were visited by more bearded Indians with pierced-noses who called themselves *Tirangpui.* Still in amazement about their beards, Escalante noted that "the five of them who came first with their chief were so fully bearded that they looked like Capuchin padres or Bethlehemites."[195] Upon hearing about the missing Spaniard, the chief ordered four warriors, each taking a different direction, to go look for him. Just as the warriors were about to set out, the missing man showed up. Still, the chief's gesture to help the expedition was overwhelming. At the camp, the friars spoke about the Holy Gospel to the chief, who appeared interested in what was said. Escalante wrote that the chief and his men wanted them to return with more padres.

Breaking camp, the expedition pursued a south-southeasterly course to avoid marshes and lakes. For the next few days, they continued looking for potable water and pasturage for their horses. Passing modern Beaver River which they named *El Arroyo del Tejedor,* they reached *San Atenógenes,* northeast of present Red Rock Knoll, Utah. There they camped, for there seemed to be plenty of water and pasturage. However, the cold increased as winds blew in snow clouds and the snowfall reached the lower elevations. On 6 October the snow fell all day. So unceasing was the snowfall that when night came and it continued, the priests implored the intercession of "Our Mother and Patroness . . . by praying aloud in common the three parts of her rosary and by chanting the Litany, the one of All-Saints. And, God was pleased that by nine at night it should cease to snow, hail, and rain."[196]

Digging out from the snow was difficult, and they also were in great distress without firewood. The snow and mud made the terrain unfit for travel and they were forced to spend another night at *San Antenógenes*. The next day, 8 October, they broke camp and made slow progress, marching only three and a half leagues (nine miles), to the south. The cold north wind blew all day, beating down on the small expedition. Suffering greatly, they stopped at a place they called *Santa Brigida*, eleven miles north of modern Milford, Utah. There, they took a bearing by the North Star and computed that they were at 39° 3' 30" latitude.[197] They then called a council to discuss their situation, including the likelihood that winter had set in upon them. They concluded that they still had many leagues left to travel toward the west and their destination. Fearful of being stranded for months in the bitter cold, Escalante wrote:

> . . . all the sierras we managed to see in all directions were covered with snow, the weather very unsettled, we therefore feared that long before we got there the passes would be closed to us, so that they would force us to stay two or three months in some sierra where there might not be any people or the wherewithal for our necessary sustenance. For the provisions we had were very low by now, and so we could expose ourselves to perishing from hunger if not from the cold. We also figured that, even granting that we arrive in Monterey this winter, we could not be in La Villa de Santa Fe until the month of June the following year.[198]

Slowly, in their discussions, another plan emerged.

The expedition realized that by following the well-known route from Santa Fe to Abiquiú to the *Río San Buenaventura* (Green River), and by blazing a new pathway from that river to the Laguna settlements near present Provo they had taken a very long and arduous route. Because they felt that they were still a long way from Monterey and the cold weather along with their diminishing supplies would cause them much suffering along an unknown route through mountainous country where they could perish, they decided to modify their objectives. They decided that their new plan would be to discover a shorter and better route along a lower latitude that would take them from Santa Fe to the Laguna settlements at Lake Timpanogos and to the "full-bearded Indians." Besides, wrote Escalante, there might be a tribe living on the Colorado River that could help them.[199] Thus, by backtracking from *Santa Brigida* to Santa Fe, they would be able to describe an easier route to the salt lakes, should anyone wish to go there, or to the western portion of the Colorado River.

Their "new itinerary," as they called it, began at *Santa Brigida* on 9 October 1776. For the next few days, they headed southward. Along their way, they reported passing three outlets of hot sulphurous water south of present Thermo Siding, patches of nitrous soil, and long, waterless expanses. They derived their drinking water from melted snow. They also determined that the southern boundary of the "full-bearded Yutas" was at a place they called *San Eleuterio*, near present Brown Knoll.

The question of the "new itinerary" came up again, as members of the expedition argued with the priests virtually the entire day, so much so that very little else was discussed. Finally, to put the matter to rest, the priests decided to gamble. By agreement, the members of the expedition would draw lots with two names on them: one signifying the route to Monterey, the other the route to the Cosninas. The Cosninas route would be one similar to that followed by Father Garcés to Oraibe in summer 1776. Also, as part of the agreement, if Monterey were chosen, Miera y Pacheco would be the new leader, for it was he who believed that they were closer to California, and "everything started from his ideas."[200] In his entry for 11 October 1776, Escalante wrote:

> They all submitted in a Christian spirit, and with fervent piety prayed the third part of the rosary and other petitions while we ourselves were reciting the Penitential Psalms with the Litany and other orations which follow it. This concluded, we cast lots, and the one of Cosnina came out. This we all heartily accepted now, thanks be to God, mollified and pleased.[201]

With new resolve, the expedition continued with the "new itinerary."

Marching southward for the next five days, they passed present Horse Hollow and Cedar Valley, and skirted the vicinity of present Cedar City, stopping at Indian settlements south of there to gather information about what lay ahead. Following present Ash Creek, they crossed *El Río Sulfero*, present Virgin River, and on 15 October pitched camp just south of the present Utah-Arizona border at a place they named *San Dónulo*, or *Arroyo del Taray*, near Hurricane Wash.[202]

On 16 October 1776, the expedition encountered some Indians from an undetermined tribe called the Parussi who told them that in two days they would reach the Colorado River. They described the river as deep and boxed in by canyon walls with very tall rocks. The Indians also told the Spaniards that the river could not be crossed at that point. Despite their feeling that these Indians were trying to lead them astray, the Spaniards were determined to continue south.

Weakened from lack of food and water, the nearly exhausted expedition pushed south looking for the Colorado River. Their Indian guides sought water for them, but found little. Their food supply gone, the padres decided to slaughter one of their mounts for food. Meanwhile, their guides who had gone out to find sustenance returned with other Indians, among them a Mescalero Apache, who brought them some wild-sheep meat, dried prickly pear cactus, and seeds from wild plants.

On 20 October, the expedition took an astronomical bearing at a place they called *Santa Gertrudis,* on modern Bull Rush Wash, placing them at 36° 30'.[203] Meandering over hills and crossing the *Arroyo de Santa Gertrudis* several times, the Spaniards finally came to a beaten path which their guides told them led directly to the river. But the path proved unreliable, and the Spaniards left it for their tried and true methods of using ravines and other topographical features to find their direction. Shortly, they came upon an Indian campsite where they spent the night. The Indians were afraid of them, despite the padres' attempt to assuage their fears. Trade proved to be the universal language, however. As soon as the friars brought out ribbons and other trade items, the Indians warmed up to them. Four hard days' march placed them near the Colorado River. Having crossed Coyote Wash, Soap Creek Canyon, and a place near present Marble Canyon Trading Post, they reached the Colorado River on 26 October; they called it *El Río Grande de los Cosninas.*[204]

At the confluence of the modern Paria River and the Colorado, the expedition halted at a place they called *San Benito de Salsipuedes* (meaning "get out if you can"), indicating the rough terrain they were in. They were surrounded on all sides by mesas and large hogbacks impossible to climb. The river ran high, yet two volunteers offered to swim across and explore the other side. Entering the water naked with their clothes over their heads, they were lucky to get across, but their clothes were swept away by the current. Nude and barefoot, the two men swam back, having failed in their mission. The next day the Spaniards and their Indian guides unsuccessfully looked for a way to get themselves and their animals across the river.

The padres sent scouts up the river, hoping to find a ford the Indians had told them about. The Spaniards even tried rafting the river to get across, but the current was too strong. Finally, after a week of probing the river, they found a possible spot. There, on 4 November, near the mouth of Navajo Creek Canyon (presently inundated by Lake Powell), the expedition attempted to cross the river; but they then thought better of it and continued walking upstream looking for a passable ford.

On 6 November, southeast of present Gunsight Butte, they suffered through bitter cold brought on by a tempest consisting of rain and thick hailstones accompanied by lightning and thunder. So terrified were the Spaniards that they huddled reciting prayers imploring God to bring the storm to an end. The next day they found a place where finally they could ford the river. Cutting steps with axes on a stone cliff "for a space of three yards or a bit less," they lowered their horses down the canyon and followed the river bank to a place where the water was low enough to wade across.[205] The crossing, later known as the "Crossing of the Fathers," was dramatic. Escalante described it:

> On the 7th [of November] we went out very early to inspect the canyon and ford taking along two mixed-breeds, Felipe and Juan Domingo, so that they might ford the river on foot since they were good swimmers. In order to have the mounts led down to the canyon mentioned, it became necessary to cut steps with axes on a stone cliff for the space of three yards or a bit less. Over the rest of it the horse herds were able to get across, although without pack or rider.
>
> We got down to the canyon, and after going a mile we reached the river and went along it downstream for about as far as two musket shots, now through the water, now along the edge, until we came to the widest part of its currents where the ford appeared to be. One man waded in and found it all right, not having to swim at any place. We followed him on horseback, entering a little farther down, and in its middle two mounts which went ahead missed bottom and swam through a short channel. We held back, although with some peril, until the first one who crossed on foot came back from the other side to lead us, and we successfully passed over without the horses on which we were crossing ever having to swim.[206]

Their equipment, saddles and other effects were eventually brought across. The entire day, from early morning to "about five in the afternoon," was spent getting across. The eastern side of the ford was named *La Purísima Concepción de la Virgen Santísima.* There, they took a reading of the north star showing them to be at 36° 55'.[207]

The entire week following 8 November 1776 was spent finding a way out of the maze of canyons or looking for trails that would take them across the mesas and forests of the area. Lacking food, the explorers were in constant search of sustenance and water. Their horse herd turned out to be their main source of food, although the explorers were loath to eat horsemeat unless they had no other choice. The Indian groups they saw were too fearful of the Spaniards and very little contact was made during this time. The cold weather worked a hardship on the expedition, as well. The expedition moved away from the Colorado River southward, camping five miles north of modern Tuba City.

By 14 November the expedition knew it was in the vicinity of the Hopi villages as it approached some farmlands of the Cosninas. The next day they saw cattle herds which they assumed belonged to the people of Oraibe. Even though they were near starvation, the explorers knew that they could not kill a cow for food because it would cause trouble between them and the Hopi people. On 16 November the Spaniards and their guides arrived at Oraibe. There they traded for food and lodged for the night. Their stay among the Hopi was not pleasant; but it was, nevertheless, a respite from the cold and hunger they had suffered for the past month.

On 20 November the expedition set out from the Hopi villages, following the trail to Zuñí, which town they reached on 24 November. Suffering from extreme cold brought on by a blizzard, the expedition arrived in Zuñí at night and remained at *Nuestra Señora de Guadalupe de Zuñí*, Escalante's assigned mission, until 13 December recuperating their strength. From there, they sent a message to Governor Mendinueta.

After a brief rest, they resumed their march to Santa Fe via Acoma, Laguna, Isleta, Los Padillas, Pajarito, Armijo, Atrisco, Albuquerque, Sandia, and Santo Domingo. On 2 January 1777 they reached Santa Fe. More than five months had passed, and the members of the expedition spent the next few days telling their friends what they had seen in the Yuta country.

The significance of the Domínguez-Escalante expedition of 1776 lies in its eyewitness descriptions of the immense tract of land that stretched from northern New Mexico past the southern end of the Rocky Mountains to the Great Salt Lake of Utah. Its members were the first to leave a documentary record of the land beyond the Green River, and they were the first to describe the Yuta country and add a historical note to mythical *Teguayo*. The early literary tradition of the Yuta country, begun in part with the Rivera expedition of 1765, is extended with the journal of Domínguez and Escalante. The written descriptions of the Grand Canyon ethnology, as well as its flora and fauna, begins with the journal of

Domínguez and Escalante. Also, the Domínguez-Escalante expedition established the north fork of the Old Spanish Trail and complemented the efforts of Rivera, Fages, Garcés, Moraga, and Muñoz. Indeed, together with the countless unknown Indian peoples who hunted, lived, and died in the Utah wilderness and who guided Spaniards across their lands, these early explorers are a part of the national story of the United States.

Spanish interest in the Yuta country soon was interrupted by the need to consolidate New Mexico's defenses against different enemy challenges that threatened to destroy New Mexico as a province. Tribes from the eastern plains of New Mexico continued their raids against the scattered Spanish villages between the Pecos River and the Río Grande. Particularly, from their *rancherias* along the western confines of New Mexico, Navajo and Apache raiders ravaged New Mexican villages and homesteads almost at will. From the north, New Mexicans were beset by hostile Comanche and Yuta tribes that continually hammered against every Spanish village, ranch, and farm. From all directions, New Mexico throughout the latter part of the eighteenth century faced possible destruction. In 1778 Juan Bautista de Anza was appointed governor of New Mexico with instructions from the commandant general of the *Provincias Internas* to resolve the dilemma caused by incessant Indian raids throughout the province. Anza turned his attention to the north, toward southern Colorado. In so doing, he pointed to the eventual Spanish occupation of southern and western Colorado.

CHAPTER VII

Juan Bautista De Anza's Expedition to the San Luis Valley in 1779

IN 1779 Teodoro de Croix, Commandant-General of the Provincias Internas, a large geographic area defining the northern frontier of New Spain, reviewed the deplorable situation in New Mexico in regard to increased raids by Comanche bands. Realizing that the Spanish military effort could not stop Comanche raiders, he reasoned that the best result would be a lessening of the raids through improved defenses and well-timed punitive expeditions against Comanches with Ute and Apache allies, their traditional enemies. That year, Juan Bautista de Anza was appointed governor of New Mexico. His primary objective at the time of his appointment was to establish communications between Santa Fe, Sonora, and California. Pacification of the Hopis was at the heart of Anza's mission, for the Hopis had long held Spanish progress in that area in abeyance. Anza's purpose in New Mexico, however, would take on a completely different direction as Comanche raids increased.

The choice of Anza as governor of New Mexico was excellent from the point of view of the colonial administration of the area—he was one of the ablest and most experienced frontier administrators of his time. Born in the summer of 1736 in Fronteras, Anza, of Basque origin, was reared on the frontier. He was not quite four years old when his father was killed in an Apache ambush. By the time he was a teenager, he had joined the garrison at Fronteras under the command of his brother-in-law Gabriel Antonio de Vildósola. In 1755, at age nineteen, he had been commissioned lieutenant. Four years later, Anza was promoted to captain of the presidio at Fronteras.[208] Charismatic and inspiring, he soon became a legendary figure in Sonora because of his military prowess, especially against Apache warriors, with whom he had engaged in hand-to-hand combat. By 1779 much had accumulated around Anza's name. His participation in numerous campaigns and explorations, especially the Sonora campaign (1767–71) and the founding expedition of San Francisco, California in 1776, attracted the attention of Spanish officials. Soldier, explorer, and administrator, Anza, who had served as captain of the presidios at Tubac in present Arizona and at Fronteras, Terrenate, and Horcasitas, was destined for greater services to the crown. His star had risen steadily, and, by 1782, he had been promoted to colonel. His appointment to the governorship in New Mexico was no accident, nor did it happen for lack of a better person to fill the needs of an embattled frontier defense in that area of the empire.

The route to California from New Mexico continued to stir considerable interest among Spanish officials who wished to consolidate the frontier. At first, Anza's instructions included establishing a route from New Mexico to the Colorado River. The dream inspired by the Domínguez-Escalante expedition of 1776 had persisted but had cooled somewhat when the two friars had proposed expanding the New Mexico mission frontier to the Ute country. Indeed, Governor Mendinueta was taken aback when Captain Bernardo de Miera y Pacheco rode south to Chihuahua to propose that three new settlements and three new presidios be established to consolidate Spanish control of the area between New Mexico, California, Nueva Vizcaya, and Sonora. One presidio and settlement, proposed Miera, would be established at the lake of the Utes, and another on the San Juan River near present Four Corners.[209] The plan would come to naught.

Meanwhile, the scholarly Father Juan Morfi, who served as secretary to Commandant Teodoro de Croix, advised his superior that Anza should, on his way to New Mexico, march from Sonora along the north bank of the Colorado River and rendezvous with Fray Escalante at a point in the territory of the Sabuagana Utes. Meanwhile, Escalante would explore the Colorado and the Río Grande on his way from New Mexico to meet Anza. Once united, the two would then proceed to Santa Fe by way of the Hopi and Navajo provinces, making careful observations about the land and people for future plans to conquer the area. Morfi suggested that a line of presidios should be established along the Colorado River to protect the route from Santa Fe to Monterey.[210] One major obstacle stood in the way of Morfi's plan: the Apache and Comanche proclivity to wage war against Spanish New Mexico. He hoped that Anza could form a peaceful alliance with the Comanches, but fate would intervene in yet another way. Anza's path lay along a different direction, for he would be drawn to war against the Comanches in southern Colorado.

When Anza finally did leave Sonora for New Mexico, he swung over to El Paso, where he reformed the militia, equipping them and creating two new units to guard the area against Apache raids. Proceeding northward, Anza marched along the Camino Real past Socorro, Belen, Tomé, and the Albuquerque area. Along the route, he could see the devastation caused by Comanche raiders. Tomé had been struck hard, having suffered twenty-one settlers killed in summer 1777 and another thirty dead at the hands of Comanche warriors in summer 1778. Albuquerque similarly presented special problems for Anza.[211]

New Mexico's defense problems were linked to a particular characteristic that marked its settlement pattern: most homesteads were dispersed throughout the province, making them easy prey to raiding tribes. Anza, armed with orders from Croix, methodically convinced the frontiersmen living in scattered and isolated circumstances to move to towns with defensive walls and towers. Albuquerque was one such collection of scattered frontiersmen living on farms and ranches who Anza virtually forced into the defensive plaza for their own good.[212]

The root of New Mexico's dilemma with the Comanches lay far to the north, in present southern Colorado, known to New Mexicans as *Comanchería*. It was clear to Spanish officials that the road from New Mexico to southern Colorado had been marked by war between Spanish colonial frontiersmen and their Indian counterparts, particularly the Comanche and the Utes. Both tribes, however, were just as frequently warring with one another as they were with the Spaniards and their Pueblo Indian allies. To Anza, the improved defenses in New Mexico were only a part of the solution against raiders. He needed to make a decisive strike against the Comanche in their own territory if the New Mexican defenses were to work. Holding councils with New Mexican frontiersmen and Indian allies including the Utes and Pueblos, Anza developed a plan for a punitive expedition into southern Colorado. Raising the expectations and morale of New Mexicans, Anza organized an army of a hundred veteran soldiers of the Santa Fe garrison, 203 militiamen, and 259 Indian auxiliaries. They were equipped for forty days of campaigning. The small army was divided into three divisions of approximately 200 men each. By mid-August the punitive expedition against the Comanches was ready.

On Sunday, about 3 o'clock in the afternoon, 15 August 1779, Anza and his troops began their march against the Comanches.[213] Marching north from Santa Fe, along the Camino Real, the Spanish troops reached the pueblo of Pojoaque, where they halted for the night. At daybreak the next day, Anza continued his march northward, reaching San Juan de los Caballeros. There, he assembled his Sonoran troops with soldiers from New Mexico. Disappointed at what he saw, he reviewed his command, for he suspected that the poorly equipped New Mexicans would have to receive new issue if they were to continue on the expedition.

In his review, Anza noted that the forty-day campaign upon which they were about to embark required that each soldier have three horses, arms, munitions, and food to last for the duration of the expedition. Seeing the poverty of his New Mexican troops, Anza felt obliged to share horses and weapons from among his Sonoran troops. He reorganized his command into three divisions, armed them, and loaned them horses from his remuda. The three divisions were organized as follows: the first served as the vanguard under Anza; the rear guard was under a first lieutenant; and the third was commanded by a second lieutenant.[214] At the end of the inspection, Anza sent out a scouting party to reconnoiter the road before them and to find out what they could about the Comanches. The scouts were instructed not to return until 20 August, four days later, unless they learned something about any movements made by the Comanches.

Meanwhile, Anza and the main body of troops moved northward, proceeding along the Camino Real for a short distance until they crossed the Río Grande bearing northwest. At the deserted pueblo of Ojo Caliente, they camped for the night, having reached, as Anza noted, "the end of the Camino Real." In August 1779 Ojo Caliente was comprised of nearly thirty families scattered in a line almost ten miles in length. They lived scared, almost all of the homes were fortified. Life, for them, was hard, and their crops which were their subsistence were constantly threatened by raiding bands of Comanches or Utes.[215] The next day, Anza moved his troops to the Río de las Nutrias and set up camp for the night.

For the next few days, the expedition members moved northward, passing the Río de San Antonio, the Río de los Conejos, Río de las Jaras, Río de San Francisco, Río de las Timbres, and Río de San Lorenzo until they again rejoined the Río Grande at a ford they named El Paso de San Barolomé. During their march on 20 August, the day they reached the Río de los Conejos, they rendezvoused with their scouts as they had previously arranged. The scouts reported that they had seen no sign of Comanches. At their camp on the Conejos, Anza was joined by 200 men from Ute and Apache tribes who wished to make war on the Comanches.[216] After a brief council, Anza agreed to let them join the Spaniards as allies against the Comanches. Given the complexity of frontier alliances and their reasons, Anza clarified that should the Comanches be defeated, he would decide how to divide the spoils, meaning that everything would be divided equally between all members of the force under his command. To that, they all agreed.

The next day, Saturday, 21 August, Anza's small army rose early. By dawn they were on the trail marching north-northeast through a series of ravines; they reached Las Jaras after crossing the Río del Pino. From the scouting reports that Anza had received, he learned that his army was getting closer to Comanches. Consequently, he decided to march only at night so that the troops would not be easily detected. He explained, "It was necessary to make the next march at night so that the enemy might not descry the dust of our troop and horse herd from the sierra, not very distant, which we are keeping on our right. For that reason the march of this day was reserved for the night."[217] At sunset, the Spaniards and their allies broke camp and continued their route northward, crossing the Río de los Timbres. By two in the morning, they reached the Río San Lorenzo, where they camped for the day. The next night, they continued their course northward, and then bending northwest they reached the Río del Norte at a ford they named San Bartolomé. Noting that the river emptied into the Gulf of Mexico, Anza figured that he was fifteen leagues from its source. His Ute guides and three Spanish New Mexicans who were part of the expedition and who had been on the Rivera expedition in 1765 told him that the river "proceeds from a great swamp, this having been formed, in addition to its springs, by the continuous melting of snow from some volcanos which are very close."[218] They also told him that beyond the sierra one could see seven rivers, which united formed the Río Colorado. Anza deduced that the Colorado was the same river which was fed, farther south, by the Río Gila before draining into the Gulf of California. Of the New Mexican guides in his force, Anza wrote:

> The same settlers mentioned, who explored the seven rivers referred to, by order of Governor Don Tomás Vélez, affirm that on all of them, which are very fertile, they observed that in ancient times they were well

populated with Indians, this being demonstrated by the large size of the formal pueblos of three stories and other remains. Among these was [evidence] that the settlers themselves had practiced the art of taking out silver, as their ore dumps and other remains of their use were found. They assured me moreover they delivered these fragments to the aforesaid governor, who, according to other reports, sent them to the city of Mexico."[219]

Who were the New Mexicans? Anza does not say.

Each night the expedition set out on its march toward the Comanche rancherias. Suffering from unexpected cold, the expedition did without fires so that the Comanches would not detect their presence in the area. In the next few nights they passed by an arroyo they named Santa Xines and El Aguage de los Yutas, a swamp in the San Luis Valley of the Río del Norte, which valley narrowed as they marched northwest between the two mountains that formed it. They then went to the Río San Agustín, beyond which they crossed the Río de Napestle, present Arkansas River, after which they stopped to rest their horses. Their march continued until eight o'clock in the morning of 29 August at a place they called Las Perdidas because of trouble they had from snow and fog, which dogged them all the previous night. Near there, the Spaniards and their allies killed fifty head of buffalo "in less than ten minutes."[220] At that place, Anza replaced the twelve scouts that had been out on the trail since 26 August with thirty others who were to report back on 31 August.

On the appointed day, two scouts returned with news that they had found signs of Comanches. Indeed, they said a considerable number of the enemy had raised a cloud of dust not far from their scouting encampment, which was located near a place the Spaniards called Río del Sacramento. Anza decided to move his men to that place. Meanwhile, the Comanches had discovered the scout's camp and fled. Anza, realizing that he might not have another chance, moved his army forward as quickly as possible to attack the Comanches in the area. The advancing Spanish army with their allies formed a long skirmish line which Anza hoped to use as a drag net, entrapping Comanches as they advanced in the woods.

Never having seen this type of formation before, the Comanches, who were all mounted, including women and children, attempted to flee. Anza's scouts told him that there were probably 120 wooden frames of tents in the area, indicating that the Comanches had left precipitously, if not nearly panic stricken. Within three leagues, the Spanish army caught up with the Indians and a running battle ensued in which eighteen warriors were killed and many wounded. Over thirty women and children were taken captive as well as 500 horses. All goods and baggage carried by the Comanche were lost in the flight. Anza returned to the Comanche campsite, proclaimed a victory, and divided the spoils.[221]

Anza learned from informants that the Comanches he had attacked were a band traveling to a rendezvous with the chief or captain-general of the Comanches named Cuerno Verde. It seems that Cuerno Verde had returned from a sixteen-day raiding sortie into New Mexico and had asked all Comanche groups in the area to join him in a celebration. Anza decided to try to find Cuerno Verde "to see if fortune would grant me an encounter with him."[222] The next day, 1 September, Anza, with the aid of scouts and informants, found Cuerno Verde's trail. His troops followed the trail from mid-morning until sunset.

At sunset on 2 September, Anza caught up with the Comanches. Attacking in a column, Anza punished his enemy, but night fell, and the Comanches, scattering in all directions, fled into the darkness. The Spanish army camped on the Arkansas River that night. On the morning of 3 September, at seven o'clock, Anza broke camp in search of Cuerno Verde. Anza's plan was to feign pursuit of the Comanches to make them fatigue their horses. Taking the main body of his troops, Anza then turned around as if in retreat, for he knew he was being watched by Comanches. By this maneuver, Anza hoped that the main body of Indians with Cuerno Verde would stop their flight and make a stand. Meanwhile, as their Spanish Indian allies pursued the rest of the scattered bands, Anza turned his attention to the group led by Cuerno Verde. In the woods nearby, Anza saw a group of Comanche warriors firing muskets at the Spaniards, who were out of range. The insignia and devices used by Cuerno Verde were identified. Mounted on a spirited horse, Cuerno Verde defiantly challenged the Spaniards to advance. Viewing this, Anza determined "to have his life and his pride and arrogance."[223]

In a gully near the Arkansas River, Anza trapped Cuerno Verde. Anza described what happened next.

> There without other recourse they sprang to the ground and entrenched behind their [fallen] horses made in this manner a defense as brave as it was glorious. Notwithstanding the aforesaid Cuerno Verde perished,

with this first-born son, the heir to his command, four of his most famous captains, a medicine man who preached that he was immortal,
and ten more, who were able to get in the place indicated.

A larger number might have been killed, but I preferred the death of
this chief even to more of those who escaped, because of his being constantly in this region the cruel scourge of this kingdom, and because he
had exterminated many pueblos, killing hundreds and making as many
prisoners whom he afterwards sacrificed in cold blood. His own nation
accuse him, ever since he took command, of forcing them to take up
arms and volunteer against the Spaniards, a hatred of whom dominated
him because his father who also held the same command and power
met death at our hands.[224]

Not far from the gully, Anza interviewed the defiant survivors of the
battle, who told him that they would lament their lost leader. Anza reflected only on Cuerno Verde's folly, for he had dared attack 600
Spaniards in formation with only fifty warriors. In the battle, Cuerno
Verde exposed himself needlessly, refusing to load his own musket while
someone else loaded it for him, such was the disdain he had for the
Spaniards. Tarrying near the battlesite, Anza named the place Los Dolores de María Santíssima, in the present Greenhorn Mountains, ultimately named after Cuerno Verde. Near sunset on 3 September, Anza
turned his army around—heading south to the Villa de Santa Fe. Passing by Taos Pueblo, where they picked up the old colonial road leading
southward, the army reached the capital on 10 September.

The success of the expedition was reinforced in July 1785 when 400
Comanches sought amnesty in Taos. Anza told them that lasting peace
could not be realized until the Comanches united. By fall, the Comanches met on the Arkansas River at a place called Casa de Palo and
elected as their leader Ecueracapa, called Cota de Malla (Coat of Mail)
by New Mexicans, uniting those tribes present. Rumors of the treaty
spread to the Yutas, who feared the Comanches and Spaniards would
unite against them. Hurriedly, they sent two chiefs, Moara and Pinto, to
protest the arrangement. They complained that Anza preferred to make
peace with unfaithful rebels rather than with obedient and loyal friends.
Angrily, they refused for hours to smoke or accept gifts from Anza. Finally, Anza convinced them to join him in the peace process with the
Comanches.

In February 1786 a peace was negotiated at Pecos Pueblo between the
two tribes. The astute Anza offered the Yutas and Comanches present

trade privileges and correctives against abuses by Spanish and Pueblo traders in exchange for their agreement to wage war against the Apaches, either as auxiliaries with Spanish forces or singularly whenever they met their common foe.[225] Anza meant to keep the peace, even if it meant punishing New Mexican frontiersmen to do it. Although Anza had used New Mexicans as guides to southern Colorado, he had made it clear as part of his defense plan that future trips to the Yuta country would be prohibited. Especially after his expedition against the Comanches, Anza doggedly enforced *bandos* providing that anyone going to the Yuta country without license be punished under the law.

In the long run, the expedition of 1779 to the San Luis Valley through Poncha Pass to the Arkansas River to present South Park resulted in an interest in the eventual settlement of northern New Mexico and southern Colorado. Still, Hispanic settlers would not confidently move northward until the first decades of the nineteenth century. The settlement of southern and western Colorado by Hispanic settlers from New Mexico would generally follow the lines of established routes such as those run by Domínguez and Escalante toward the Yuta country and that blazed by Anza in his campaign against the Comanche Indians. The pacification of southern Colorado had only begun, decades would pass before it was completed. Meanwhile, Hispanic traders from Santa Fe would continue to use known trails and routes into western and southern Colorado to trade with the Utes. Often, they would continue westward to Utah and the Great Basin.

Chapter VIII

New Mexican Traders and Slavers

Illegal Trade and the Yuta Country,

1778–1821

ESPECIALLY AFTER the expeditions of 1765 by Rivera and of 1776 by Domínguez and Escalante, New Mexicans turned their attention toward the Yuta country for trade. Interest in reaching California was joined by the desire for trade with the Yutas and other tribes in the region, and New Mexicans soon looked to the Great Basin as an outlet for trade. But their hopes for trade there were quickly dashed by Spanish authorities, who, hoping to stabilize relations with the Utes, prohibited New Mexicans from going to the Yuta country. Although the Domínguez-Escalante expedition sought to establish a route to California through the Yuta country, it resulted in creating a greater interest in the possibility of trade in the Great Basin, the farthest point reached by the expedition. In the thirty years following the Domínguez-Escalante expedition, numerous unofficial trading parties went northwestward from New Mexico to Utah for trade. Still, the danger of making enemies of the Utes that would result in increased Ute raids motivated Spanish officials to continue to outlaw any expeditions into the area without license. Each trading expedition added knowledge about the various valleys through which were forged variants of the Old Spanish Trail, however, until finally, after nearly five decades, interest in a direct route to California through southern Utah was revived.

In 1778, Teodoro de Croix, commandant general of the Provincias Internas, issued an order prohibiting trade with the Yutas. Aware of previous *bandos* prohibiting trade with the Yutas, especially the most recent one by Governor Pedro Fermín de Mendinueta publicized in 1775, Croix sought to enforce the law by reinforcing the penalties against the prohibited trade. Chastising Spanish officials in New Mexico for winking at violations of the laws, Croix stated that those officials were "seriously obligated to execute and observe the law and punish the transgressors accordingly under penalty of law." Croix understood one of the underlying causes of Yuta raids into New Mexico: the illicit trade carried on by New Mexicans in the Yuta country. By going among them, New Mexicans invariably would commit some form of insult against the Indians, creating conditions for revenge. He observed that the "Yutas resenting some bold act or an evil deed against them, commonly break the peace with little reflection." With his *bando*, Croix hoped to curb, if not stop, New Mexican trading in the Yuta country. Croix further accused New Mexicans in the illicit trade of impeding the expansion of *"Nuestra Santa Fee Catholica"* among the Yutas because missionaries were fearful of going to them.[226]

Croix's *bando* expressly prohibited any Spaniard, *genízaro*, or Indian from trading with the Yutas and provided that no one would be permitted to go or send someone in their stead to the Yuta country. The penalties for participating in the illicit trade commonly included incarceration; fines of one hundred pesos, which were considerably stiff in a society that depended on barter for trade; confiscation of all items traded; and servitude or public works in government installations for a period of time. Additionally, if a Spaniard was caught breaking the ban on trade with the Yutas, he would be prohibited from holding any public office; if a *genízaro* or Indian broke the law, he would be subject to a fine of one hundred pesos and suffer 100 lashes.[227] So that no one could plead ignorance, Croix ordered that the *bando* be read aloud by a crier and posted in a public area in various plazas in New Mexico. As instructed by the *bando*, the *alcalde mayor* of Taos Pueblo, Manuel Vigil, published it immediately, as did Antonio Baca, *alcalde mayor* of the Villa de Alburquerque, and Nerio Antonio Montoya at Picuries Pueblo. This *bando* and others similar to it were in effect throughout the rest of the Spanish colonial period in New Mexico.

It did not take long for New Mexicans to violate Croix's *bando*. Croix recognized that the New Mexican tradition of trading with the Yutas was a longstanding one. Traders from Abiquiú, Taos, Picuries, and Chama were especially tied to the Yuta trade; and, they knew routes to the Yuta country as far as the Great Basin.

The reasons New Mexicans risked their lives to go to the Yuta country varied. Some who were in debt to creditors in their own communities sought sources of income through bartering with native groups on the Great Plains or in the Yuta country. Mules and horses bought slaves held by stronger tribes, a bushel of corn or wheat flour bought a buckskin shirt, and knives and awls were traded for pelts, blankets, and saddle blankets. Some New Mexicans did not go to the Yuta country only for trade; they went to recover stolen animals or kidnapped kinsmen. Such unauthorized punitive expeditions by Spanish frontiersmen often resulted in open warfare between New Mexicans and Utes.

By the early 1780s, despite the *bandos,* illicit trade was flourishing. New Mexican officials also were caught in the same economic bind. Disregarding the prohibitions, some officials often sent relatives to the Yuta country to carry trade items for them. And when their relatives or close friends were caught, they, as officials, sought to diminish the crimes or reduce the penalties. The *bando* did not address the complexity of the problem, it merely offered short range penalties, which did not halt the proliferation of trade to the Yuta country.

On 3 February 1783, eleven Hispanic frontiersmen from Santa Rosa de Abiquiú stood before the magistrate Santiago Martín. They were charged with disobeying the prohibition imposed by Croix and reissued by Governor Anza. Actually, they were apprehended before they were out of the jurisdiction of Abiquiú. Just as they were preparing to leave, Friar Diego Muñoz reported to Martín that Antonio Cordoba, a settler from Abiquiú, had told him that eleven men including a servant of the alcalde mayor of Abiquiú were leaving for the Yuta country. Rounding up a posse of ten Spaniards and two Indians, Martín rode out to arrest the party. Having imprisoned the frontiersmen and confiscated their trade goods, Martín summoned them to explain why they dared go to the Yuta country to trade without a license.[228]

After the charges were read against them, each admitted to the trade items they were carrying. Encarnación Espinosa said that he carried eight *almudes*[229] of corn, twenty-five awls, ten trading knives, called *cuchillos de rescate,* three *almudes* of flour, a sack of *biscochos,* a type of biscuit, his own horse, and two mules, one belonging to Gaspar Ortiz, the other to Aban Cordoba, settlers from Abiquiú. Clemente Benavides listed fourteen *almudes* of corn and a mule belonging to Andrés Roybal, a neighbor. José Mariano Mondragon confessed to carrying ten *almudes* of corn, four *almudes* of flour, and a mule and a horse which he said belonged to the settler Tadeo Espinosa. Manuel Vigil said he was taking

forty *almudes* of corn, his own food, two mules belonging to other settlers, and a horse belonging to the settler Francisco Arellano. Pablo
Gonzales reported one *fanega* of corn, six awls, one knife, six rolls of
tobacco, and his own mule and horse. Juan Cayetano Gonzales and
Melchor Lopes listed fourteen *almudes* and two *fanegas* of corn, fourteen
awls, two trading knives, tobacco, flour, and four mules. Carlos Vigil,
brother to Manuel, said he carried nothing other than his own mare, the
rest of his trade goods were mixed with whatever his brother recorded.[230]
The inventory made, the men were returned to their cells to await res-
olution of their case, which had been sent to *Alcalde Mayor* Joseph
Campo Redondo at Santa Cruz de la Cañada, who consulted with
Governor Anza on the matter.

On 14 February 1783 three of the men, Encarnación Espinosa, Carlos
Vigil, and Pablo Gonzales, were called before Santiago Martín to explain again why they had attempted to leave Abiquiú for the Yuta country without license. Martín asked them to name the person who had
given them license to go trade with the Utes. They said that Salvador
Martín, the alcalde of Abiquiú, not only had given them the license to
trade but had sent one of his servants with them. Called to verify their
statement, Salvador Martín swore that everything they had said in that
regard was true. The testimony was sent to Redondo. Martín felt that
they had fulfilled the letter of the law by having been granted a license.
Nearly three weeks passed before a third hearing was held, this time at
Pojoaque, an intermediate place between Abiquiú and Santa Cruz de la
Cañada, where Redondo met with the prisoners, who had been trans-
ferred there for that purpose. Redondo said that the governor, who was
inclined to grant them their freedom since they had not actually gone to
the Yuta country, wished to know what kind of arrangement the prisoners had made with those who had given them items to trade in their behalf. The men were further advised that, meanwhile, their property
would remain confiscated.[231]

Regarding the vicarious trading arrangement, Encarnación Espinosa
declared that of the three animals which he had with him, one had been
loaned to him by Aban Cordoba out of friendship, other items he was to
trade in return for a commission in the form of goods. The other animal,
a mule, belonging to Gaspar Ortiz was consigned to Espinosa to be used
on the trading trip in return for three tanned buckskins or chamois
called *gamuzas*. The third animal was his own property. Second to speak,
Clemente Benavides stated that the mule which he had was consigned
to him by Andrés Roybal in return for three *gamuzas*.

Of the three animals he had with him, declared Manuel Vigil, one mule was consigned to him by Domingo Labadia for whatever *gamuzas* he could pay for the animal; another mule belonged to Juan Pacheco, who had consigned it to him for three *gamuzas;* and, the third animal, a horse, had been consigned to him by Francisco Arellano in exchange for three *gamuzas.* Each one understood that Vigil was going to the Yuta country for trade. Likewise, Juan Cayetano Gonzales declared that José Gonzales, a relative, had consigned a mule to him, but that the second mule he had when arrested belonged to him. The other men testified similarly about animals that had been consigned to them.[232] If anything, Redondo and Anza learned that the trading patterns in New Mexico could be very complex. They also learned that Encarnación Espinosa and his men were no strangers to the Yuta country. If the *bandos* were to have any effect in stopping the illicit trade, licensing would not be enough to control the trade, for New Mexicans would find ways of expanding the trade through licensed traders.

At mid-decade, New Mexican traders continued to go to the Yuta country despite the prohibition against trading there, but José Campo Redondo still held court against those who were apprehended. In one case presided over by Redondo at San Antonio de Chama, a Spanish official, José Garcia de la Mora, was arrested and convicted for having given permission to Salvador Salazar and two others to trade among the Yutas.[233] As usual, the traders carried knives, awls, corn, tobacco, and horses to trade for hides, pelts, blankets, and slaves.

When, on 22 April 1785, the case against Salazar and his companions began, they were charged with violations of the ban against trade with the Yutas. When asked whether they had received license to trade, they responded that they had received such from José Garcia de la Mora. Redondo was interested in whether Garcia de la Mora was authorized to grant such a license. The case deepened when Salazar, Lucero, and Valverde revealed that Garcia de la Mora had asked Salazar to carry various goods including a large box of knives for him. Mora, furthermore, outfitted the traders with twenty-five small knives *(navajas),* tobacco, awls, corn, and a horse among other effects. Salazar also stated that Garcia de la Mora had given him permission to take along Lucero and Valverde.

Redondo summoned José Garcia de la Mora before him. Garcia de la Mora testified that he had indeed given Salazar and his companions license to trade with the Yutas. He proposed, furthermore, that the situation was not a conflict of interest as it appeared. He explained that the license was not for Salazar and his men to go to the Yuta country; it was to be used when the Yutas came to trade in New Mexico. Despite Garcia de la Mora's testimony, Redondo had him placed under arrest. Redondo then conferred with Governor Anza, who found all parties guilty. They suffered the usual penalties, except that Garcia de la Mora's fine was doubled.[234] Because of his ability to read and write, he served out his penalty in the *casas reales* at Santa Cruz de la Cañada as an assistant notary in cases involving illegal traders to the Yuta country. Much later, Garcia de la Mora would be restored to his office of alcalde mayor and captain of war.

One interesting question had been asked of all the accused in the Salazar case: did they know of the circumstances involving the death of a trader named Juan Garcia from Andalucia in southern Spain. Each responded that they knew nothing, nor did they even know who Juan Garcia was.[235] It seems that word had circulated throughout northern New Mexico that Juan Garcia had gone northward with a party of traders who, hit by cold weather and heavy snows, had left him for dead in the Yuta country. Almost everyone arrested for trading with the Yutas during that period was asked the same question. No one knew anything.

The death of Juan Garcia continued to be a mystery until a case involving certain settlers from Abiquiú unraveled. On 31 March 1785 Vicente Serna and four others were brought before alcalde mayor of Abiquiú Joseph Martín and charged with carrying on illegal trade among the Yutas. The charges included an inquiry into the death of Juan Garcia, who had gone on the trading trip. Swearing to tell the truth, Serna placed his hand on a crucifix, as was customary in all legal proceedings, and promised to tell all he knew about the venture to the Yuta country. He explained that he had gone to trade without license and that he had taken only trade items belonging to him and no one else. Indeed, he swore he had only taken his horse and some corn, which he said he could not trade. He said the trading venture had failed because he could not locate any Yuta camps due to the great amount of snow that had fallen. When asked about the death of Juan Garcia, Serna responded that upon reaching the Río San Miguel, which had taken them nine days to reach from Abiquiú, Garcia complained about a pain in his stomach. He died from whatever ailed him, and the expedition, leaving his body, continued as far northwest as the Río Salado. The other accused were similarly brought before the bench to testify. Francisco Serna, a relative of Vicente, similarly testified about Garcia's death and the failure of the traders to locate Yuta camps because of the heavy snows in the area. He reported that he had taken large quantities of corn and tobacco and a horse, which died during the journey, for trade. Vicente Luján testified that when the party reached the Río San Miguel and Garcia was near death he departed the party in search of the Yutas; but the deep snow impeded his progress. He learned later that Garcia had died. The other members of the party were Juan Manuel Gómes and Nicolas Sisneros. They, too, had taken similar trade items as the others, quantities of corn and a horse, which they ate after they had run out of food.

Their testimony was sent on to José Campo Redondo at Santa Cruz de la Cañada, who passed the documentation on to Governor Anza for adjudication. The five men were imprisoned, fined, and suffered confiscation of the property they had when they were arrested. In addition to their fines of one hundred pesos each, they were sentenced to perform public work service in the *casas reales* in the Villa de Santa Cruz. On 29 April 1785 Redondo visited the men in their jail cells and read them their sentences, which they pledged to obey.[236] The case was closed and the men gained their freedom only after all the terms of their sentences were completed.

Another case illustrated the proliferation of frontiersmen moving north and northwest from places like Abiquiú, Taos, and Chama. On 10 April 1785 Marselino Mansanares, Vicente Garcia, Miguel Sandoval, and Cristóbal Salazar were arrested for trading with the Yutas. Initially—and typically—their memories failed them when it came to discussing precisely what they had taken with them. Predictably, they took the usual items: knives, awls, horses, corn, flour, and tobacco. Mansanares said he had a license to trade, but his companions denied any knowledge of a license. Given the contradictions about the license and Mansanares's inability to prove that he had one, Governor Anza condemned the men to incarceration, fines, confiscation of trade items, and servitude in the *casas reales* of Santa Fe.[237]

At the end of the decade, illicit trade still flourished. Numerous New Mexicans had gone to the Yuta country for trade, many of which were unrecorded as they were not caught. However, the long arm of the law eventually caught up with some frequent traders who were arrested and tried. Throughout the 1780s and 1790s numerous cases, revealing the complexity of monitoring trade with the Yutas, had been brought to trial.

By the end of the 1790s little had changed. In out-of-the-way Puesto del Río Arriba occurred a case representative of many others. Most of the proceedings, such as that against Cristóval Lovato in 1797, began in the same way. Garcia de la Mora announced the following:

> In this Puesto del Río Arriba on the second day of the month of August of 1797, I, the alcalde mayor of this jurisdiction of Santa Cruz de la Cañada, don Manuel Garcia de la Mora, received notice about various individuals who had gone to the land of the Yutas and about what they were taking. And not having learned of this from my lieutenants in the districts, nor towns which correspond to them, I made myself forceful in the corresponding investigation in order to proceed with the punishment pertaining to this crime so that I could determine with which license they had gone knowing that this journey [to the Yuta country] is prohibited. So as to proceed with the penalties according to their circumstances, I approved and ordered [their arrest] on said day, month and year in which I testify. Manuel Garcia de la Mora.[238]

In this case, Mora ordered the arrest of Cristóval Lovato, José Miguel Naranjo, and Juan Domingo Sandoval. They were all asked the same questions:

> Asked: If he had gone to the Yuta country? He answered yes.
>
> Asked: With what license did he leave on the journey to the Yuta country? He answered that without one, that he went of his own accord and obligation.
>
> Asked: Who accompanied him? He answered José Miguel Naranjo
>
> Asked: What trade items did he take? He answered one *fanega* of flour and four *almudes* of corn.
>
> Asked: What did he buy with the above said items? He answered three *gamuzas*, and he could not sell the flour.
>
> Asked: How far did he get in this journey? He answered that he got as far as the Río de los Pinos.[239]
>
> Asked: Whether he knows that the journey to the Yuta country is prohibited. He answered that he knows it, but that his debts made him trespass there.
>
> This he said is all he knows and that nothing else happened to him on this journey and whereas he declares and gives in his statement which was ratified by one, two, and three times and which was read back to him, and he did not sign it because he did not know how, and I signed it with my two assistants to which I give testimony. Manuel Garcia, Assistant José Antonio Martinez, Assistant José Manuel Sanches[240]

Although Lovato said he was accompanied by only one person, there were other trading parties in the area, which Garcia de la Mora had arrested when they returned. These parties consisted of José Martín, Andrés Martín, Juan Ballejos, Juan Domingo Sandoval, Asensio Lucero, Juan Esteban Velasques, Gabriel Vigil, Nerio Gómes, Francisco Salazar, Mateo Garcia, Nicolas Martín, Pedro Sisneros, Ramón Saiz, Antonio Maese, Francisco Archuleta, José Manuel Montoya, Silvestre Lopes, Juan de Dios Trujillo, Antonio Torres, Pedro Aguilar, Antonio José Espinosa and Juan Griego. They also testified that they had reached a place called *Hancapagari* or *Aricapuaguro*—the present Uncompaghre Plateau, which the Domínguez-Escalante expedition had called Ancapagri. One group got as far as the Sierra de la Sal.[241] Although all were punished accordingly for violating the *bandos* prohibiting trade with the Yutas, subsequent court records show that some of those punished in 1797 would continue to return to the Yuta country, sometimes probing in different directions, but certainly learning about the area that extended from Abiquiú to the Great Basin.

Although there was little missionary activity in that direction, Father José Vela Prada, the custodian at Abiquiú, said that he had gone among the Yutas when he heard that they were in the area trading. He had heard that among them was a young Navajo woman, María Concepción, who had been taken during a war with the Navajos and had been brutally mistreated by her captors. In 1805 Father Vela Prada said he rescued her for humane reasons:

> I, as a religious moved by charity, took her from the tyranny of the Yutas who had captured her in just war . . . But they gave [her] by their barbarity very bad treatment, she had wounds all over her body from the stabs from their arrows. . . . But had I not taken her from their power, without doubt she would be in eternity, and from that hell, that from that loss, I desired to separate her, bringing to bear the office of the Church, it cost me 1,001 *pesos fuertes*, as she had been bought for two horses. . . . The only thing I did was to take this very unhappy creature from the heavens to where she was on the verge of going, and the tears that she poured out upon being freed . . . it broke my heart.[242]

The Navajos wanted her back, but María Concepción chose to stay in Abiquiú.

A flurry of activity in September 1805 revealed a glimpse into the life of a certain Manuel Mestas, who spun an incredible story about his exploits in Utah. Mestas, a seventy-year-old *genízaro* and a Yuta interpreter, had spent many years traveling to the Great Basin for trade. At one point he claimed to have pacified the Yuta Timpanogos, saying that he was the one who had "reduced them to peace."[243] Governor Joaquín Real Alencaster reported that Mestas had led men against the Yutas because they had stolen a number of horses from him. In his first attempt, Mestas succeeded in recovering eight horses.

Not satisfied with the partial recovery of his livestock, in July 1805 Mestas returned to the Yuta country for a month, during which he attacked at least one Ute band and returned with the eleven animals he sought as well as twenty mules and eight horses stolen from other New Mexicans. Some of the animals, Alencaster reported, had been stolen by Comanche raiders who had been attacked by Yuta warriors who took their herds from them. Mestas, upon reaching the area of Utah Lake, identified the animals and retook them. However, it seems that hard luck followed Mestas, who it appears lost most of the animals on the way back to marauding bands, possibly Kiowas who were at war with the Yutas. Alencaster's report does reveal that New Mexicans like Mestas were familiar with the Yuta country and often traveled to it. The astute Mestas, however, also sought to be compensated for his services as translator, just like "the Frenchman Chalvet, the interpreter for the Pananas," had been. He applied to Governor Alencaster, who recommended he be paid accordingly.[244]

Throughout the early nineteenth century, various parties left New Mexico for the Yuta country. Although most went northwest for trade, Pedro Pino in his report on New Mexico to the *Cortes de Cadiz* in 1812 wrote of one New Mexican who went to the Yuta country out of curiosity: he sought the legendary lost Spanish settlement mentioned by the Domínguez-Escalante expedition of 1776. Of that expedition, Pino wrote:

Last year, 1811, Don José Rafael Sarraceno, postmaster of New Mexico, crossed that territory in an effort to locate a Spanish settlement which the Yutas have always asserted lay beyond their territory, supposedly completely surrounded by wild Indians. After having traveled for three months, he was finally stopped by a large river. Among the Indians living there he found many articles manufactured by Spaniards such as knives, razors, and awls; he obtained the same information there, that the manufacturers of those articles lived across the river (somewhere between the north and the west). Since they could not tell him exactly where he could cross the river, he decided to return home; he brought back with him a large shipment of beautiful pelts which he had purchased very cheaply; for example, he traded one awl for a perfectly tanned deer hide. At this price he could have afforded to bring as many pelts as he could load on his entire mule train if it had been possible to export them.[245]

Pino also pointed out the desire of New Mexicans to reach the Pacific coast. Although he did not specifically suggest a California route, he thought that a port along the Sonoran coast such as Guaymas "would be advantageous to Spanish commerce."[246]

On 12 July 1813, led by Mauricio Arze and Lagos García, Miguel Tenorio, Felipe Gómez, Josef Santiago Vigil, Gabriel Quintana, and Josef Velasques left Abiquiú bound for the "Salt Lake" (probably Utah Lake). The seven men traveled over what appears to have been a well-known route. When they returned, they appeared before the alcalde of Santa Cruz de la Cañada, Manuel Garcia, and filed affidavits about their trading venture to Timpanogos. Their testimony before Garcia was aimed at clearing the name of Miguel Tenorio, who had been on the expedition with them, but who had been accused of carrying on an illegal trade with the Yutas. They reported that they had visited the area of present Utah Lake for three days to carry on trade while they waited for two Ute bands to assemble in council. They stated that the *Timpanzanos* were only interested in trading Indian slaves to them as they had done in the past, but the New Mexicans said they had refused to trade for slaves and paid a heavy price when the *Timpanzanos* began killing their horses. Eight horses and one mule were slaughtered before the New Mexicans could stop the attackers. In fear of a deadlier reprisal for refusing to trade for slaves, Arze and his men set up a camp at some distance from their attackers and stood guard all night. The next day they set out for the Río Sebero, present Sevier River.

Somewhere in the wilderness of western Utah, they met a Sanpuchi (Sanpete) Ute who promised to guide them farther into the interior to trade with a tribe heretofore unknown to them. While Gómez and Quintana remained with the pack train, Arze, Garcia, and the three others set out to the west. Three days later they arrived at a settlement of Indians they had only heard about in New Mexican lore: the bearded Indians of the Domínguez-Escalante expedition. After a confrontation in which the Indians indignantly refused to trade with armed Spaniards, the New Mexicans were able to calm them and arrange to trade the next day. The New Mexicans testified that no trade took place, however, because they learned that the Sanpete had planned to attack them instead.

Arze decided to travel all night and the next day hoping to reach their pack train and head south toward the Colorado River. On the way they encountered a settlement of Guasache (Wasatch) Indians who desired to trade with them. The New Mexicans reported that their visit with the Guasache started out friendly, but, when they refused to trade for Indian slaves, the Guasache took offense. Seeing the danger they were in, Arze and Garcia decided it wise to trade for twelve slaves. In their affidavits, the New Mexicans indicated that they had also traded for pelts, indicating "only a few" pelts had been collected.[247]

The documentation does not reveal the results of the case against Tenorio, but it does permit speculation about what New Mexicans knew about the Yuta country in 1813. For example, it appears that Arze and his men were familiar with the country over which they had traveled. In the testimony, none of Arze's men describe the route they took to Timpanogos, possibly because it was so well-known by that time. Secondly, it appears that some of the members of the expedition understood enough of the language spoken by the *Timpanzanos* and the Sanpetes to "overhear" plans to attack them. Thirdly, it appears that Arze's men were acquainted with some of the Indian groups they encountered, such as the *Timpanzanos* and the Guasache, of whom they remarked that it was customary to trade with them.

Each illegal expedition invariably furnished knowledge of the Yuta country. As Spanish frontiersmen ventured beyond Abiquiú, they learned different ways to get to the Great Basin. Often, the more experienced served as guides to different places in the Yuta country. By the end of the Spanish period, much was known about the Yuta country, its peoples, and their languages. After Mexican independence in 1821, many of the old Spanish *bandos* were only weakly enforced, and New Mexicans continued to go to the Yuta country. While the old dream of connecting New Mexico and California seemed to have been abandoned during the late Spanish period, it was renewed at the beginning of the Mexican period. The heyday of the Old Spanish Trail was at hand.

CHAPTER IX

Antonio Armijo and José María Chaves

Two Men on the Old Spanish Trail,

1821–1850

FOLLOWING MEXICAN independence from Spain in 1821, official interest in the Yuta country was renewed. After years of talking about initiating trade with California, New Mexico governor José Antonio Chávez decided to take the matter before officials in Mexico City. In his letter of 14 May 1830 to the Minister of Interior Affairs, Governor Chávez, acknowledging that a licensed expedition to California had taken place, wrote:

> On the eighth of November of last year, a company of about sixty men left this territory for California with the purpose of trading for mules with the products of this country. They have been traveling through unknown deserts until now, and have succeeded in discovering a new way of communication which passes numerous savage tribes, who, from all appearances, fled in terror. The Indians proved no obstacle and this contributed not a little to the success of the expedition.
>
> From the itinerary which I am sending Your Excellency it can be assumed that the distance which separates California from this territory is not great. It should be taken into account that the discoverers often had to retrace their steps and make detours. In short, they had neither map nor compass, and no other guides than the enterprising natives of this country.

I believe that it would be greatly to the advantage of both territories for the Supreme Government to promote the commerce of this region, for which I entreat Your Excellency.[248]

It was clear that a direct trail from New Mexico to California had been blazed in 1829, not by way of the traditional Timpanogos route but farther to the south. Led by Antonio Armijo, the official journey sanctioned by Governor Chávez from Abiquiú to San Gabriel Mission near Los Angeles took eighty-six days. Carrying blankets and other trade goods, Armijo hoped to barter for mules in California.

Armijo's route quickly became the favored route to California for the next twenty years, as New Mexicans used it as a trade and immigration trail to the west coast. Other variations developed over time, but Armijo's route served as the basic line of march westward. Significantly, much of the route was already known, as other New Mexicans had crisscrossed that country for decades. Some of them had led Anglo-American trappers through the area; other trappers like Jedediah Smith had likewise become familiar with the terrain. For example, in 1828, Rafael Rivera, a member of the Armijo expedition of 1829, had been to the Colorado River as far as present Hoover Dam near Las Vegas Wash.[249] Indeed, some of the sixty men with Armijo probably had been in the region previously and their collective recollections permitted them to "retrace their steps and make detours" as Governor Chávez had reported.

According to Armijo's diary, the expedition left Abiquiú on 6 November 1829 with the intent of discovering a route to Alta California. Traveling northwest the group reached the Colorado River after nearly a month of travel. Having crossed the river, they discovered some smooth stones with inscriptions left by Domínguez and Escalante. Bearing northwesterly, the expedition reached the Puerco River on 7 November, then went to Cañon Largo by way of Capulin Peak. They traveled through Cañon Largo, reaching the San Juan River. Eight days out of Abiquiú, Armijo and his men arrived at the Animas River near Aztec, New Mexico.[250]

Passing within the vicinity of Mesa Verde on 19 November, Armijo's march took him to the La Plata River and then to the Mancos River, a route known to the Domínguez-Escalante expedition in 1776. Moving northwestward on 21 November, they again met the meandering San Juan, where they encountered Navajos without incident. Near present Mission Spring they met other Navajos with whom they traded and arranged for a Navajo guide to take them farther west. The guide's services cost them eleven mares, but the New Mexicans felt it worth the price for the guide would also protect them from possible hostility by other Navajos. A few days later they reached present Chinli Creek, that runs north from Canyon de Chelly National Monument. By 30 November the party had gone beyond the environs of Canyon de Chelly and reached present Piute Canyon near Upper Crossing Springs by way of Limita Spring, known to Armijo as *Las Lemitas,* east of present Kayenta.[251]

Literally backtracking the route followed by Domínguez and Escalante from 8 to 11 November 1776, Armijo and his scout, Salvador Maes, approached the same craggy canyon on 2 December, and the next day the entire party scaled up one side and down the other carrying most of their baggage in their arms. By 6 December they had reached the "Crossing of the Fathers" where the Domínguez-Escalante group had forded the river fifty-four years earlier. Near there they found the canyon where the friars had carved steps into the canyon wall to provide footing for their animals. In his entry for 8 December, Armijo wrote, "We stopped the train and repaired the upgrade of the canyon, the same one which had been worked by the padres."[252] Near present Wahweap Canyon, at a place Armijo called *Ceja Colorada* (Red Ridge), near Paria Creek, they encountered a settlement of Payuche Indians. From there they traveled three days to present Kanab Creek, which they crossed near Fredonia, Arizona. By 20 December Armijo and his men had reached the Virgin River which he confusedly called the Río Severo (Sevier River)[253] and which Escalante had called the *Río Sulfero* from the sulphur springs near Hurricane, Utah.

Moving westward from 21 December to 31 December, the party crossed the Virgin River several more times, as their straight-line march repeatedly met the meanderings of this long river which flows into the Colorado River. Christmas Day was like any other for Armijo and his men, who spent the day traveling and sending out reconnaissance parties to determine the nature of the terrain before them. On 27 December, the party visited a "settlement of Indians with rings in their noses." New Year's Day, 1830, was spent along the Colorado River. That day they noticed that Rafael Rivera was missing from the reconnaissance party that had been sent out on 31 December. Moving along the river near present Hoover Dam close to the mouth of present Las Vegas Wash, they spend the next five days looking for Rivera. Finally, on 7 January, Rivera turned up in their camp and explained that he had located a village of the *Cucha Payuches* (a Paiute tribe) and the *Hayatas* (probably the Mojave Indians).[254]

By 9 January the expedition had left the Colorado River and traveled due west toward Spring Mountains; they stopped on 11 January at Cottonwood Spring, seventeen miles from Las Vegas, later a familiar stopping place on the Old Spanish Trail. It appears that Armijo passed some eight miles south of present Las Vegas, known among New Mexican traders for its excellent water supply, otherwise it seems he would have noted it in his diary.[255] From Cottonwood Springs, the party traveled to present Stump Spring, then on to the Amargosa River, or Bitter Creek, which Armijo called the River of the Payuches, where they visited a Payuche village. Beyond the village, Armijo and his men crossed the Río Salitroso, present Salt Spring, and suffering the next day without water, they came to a lake Armijo called *El Milagro* (Miracle).

On this leg of the journey, the aridity of the land and the lack of water caused anxiety among the men. For the next few days lack of food caused the party to eat a horse and a mule. On 21 January they reached the Mojave River and recognized an Indian trail which Armijo noted was "traveled by the Moquis [Hopis] with the object of trading shells with the said Hayatas." (Father Francisco Garcés had been the first European to reach the Mojave River, which he called Río de los Mártires on 9 March 1776.) From 22 January to 28 January Armijo followed the Mojave River, basically a dry arroyo. Out of food on 26 January, the party ate a mule belonging to Miguel Valdés. The next day, wrote Armijo, "we met the reconnaissance party with supplies and men from the [mission] ranch of San Bernardino."[256] Three days later they reached Mission San Gabriel, after following the San Bernardino Valley possibly through Cajon Creek.

Armijo returned to New Mexico by backtracking along his outgoing route from California. He left California, probably from San Gabriel, on 1 March 1830 and arrived "in this jurisdiction of Jemez" in New Mexico on 25 April. Of his return he thought it virtually uneventful "with no more mishap than the loss of tired animals, until I entered the Navajo country, by which nation I was robbed of some of my animals."[257]

The eventual discovery of a practical route from New Mexico to California by Armijo was a culmination of decades of travel to the Yuta country by New Mexican traders and slavers. They had learned about the geography and shared their knowledge, they learned the language of the Utes and used it for trade, and they accumulated information about the people and the land and passed it into the oral tradition of their generations. The Old Spanish Trail and its variant routes owed its existence as much to illegal traders as it did to those adventurers who sallied forth with license in hand and the blessings of Spanish authorities. But Armijo's route was more than a trade route; after 1829, when Armijo first traveled the length of it, New Mexicans began to use the trail as a way to migrate to California. This use happened slowly and quietly, almost without notice among Mexican officials. Were it not for the rebellion against New Mexico's governor Albino Pérez, insight as to Armijo's route as an immigration trail might have escaped notice. In that rebellion, José María Chaves, a supporter of Pérez, fled over the route. When he arrived in California, he was greeted by relatives who had used the trail years earlier. Cháves, a soldier-trader who had ventured into the Yuta country since a young man, knew the region well.

Born at Santa Clara Pueblo in New Mexico on 25 September 1801, an aged General José María Chaves sat in one of his favorite chairs in his home at Abiquiú in 1901. Surrounded by his family, including grandchildren and great-grandchildren, Chaves sat quietly as well-wishers, some of them from the leading families of New Mexico, came from miles around to offer their congratulations and good wishes. The occasion was Chaves's one-hundredth birthday. That his life had been filled with great activity and hardship made the occasion all the more remarkable, for few who had led the kind of life of José María Chaves lived to become centenarians. José María came from a long line of New Mexican frontiersmen. He was descendant from Don Fernando Duran y Chaves, who came to New Mexico from Spain in the seventeenth century and had served under Diego de Vargas in the 1692 reconquest of New Mexico. The family was keenly aware of its military prowess. In one of the many sixteenth-century wars against the Moors, the Chaves family had been rewarded by the king of Spain for having captured a Moorish town and presented the king with its the keys. José María grew up with a family lore that had instilled in him a sense of his frontier heritage.

His father was Francisco Antonio Chaves, who was born in Atrisco, near Albuquerque. Sometime before José María's birth, Francisco Antonio moved to the Indian pueblo of Santa Clara. By the time José María was four years old, the family had moved to Abiquiú on the Río Chama. Abiquiú had been an important outpost for decades, being the northwesternmost settlement before the Anglo-American occupation of New Mexico. Situated along one of the Indian trails favored by Apaches, Utes, Navajos, and Comanches, Abiquiú suffered frequent attacks. Although sheep, cattle, and horses were the primary objects of those raids, women and children also were taken captives by raiders. Overlooking the Río Chama, the Chaveses built their home, the present

Georgia O'Keeffe house. From their vantage point on the bluff, the family saw much of New Mexico's history evolve.[258]

Like their indigenous counterparts, Hispanic youths were bred to arms. The people of Abiquiú, living always in dread of surprise attacks by raiders, tried to be ready to repel them, although frequently the Hispanics were on the losing end, suffering many casualties. Watchtowers in the vicinity of Abiquiú attested to the fear Hispanics had of the raiders who frequently attacked their village. The men of Abiquiú were sometimes in pursuit of raiders who had carried off women and children. The *cautivos* were sometimes rescued, but more often they were ransomed at *rescates* whenever one could be arranged.

In this changing and perilous frontier, José María grew to manhood. Bred in a military tradition, he eventually rose to lieutenant of the militia, after which he became a *capitán de escuadron*. By the time he was twenty-two years old, he had been promoted to adjutant in the colonial militia of New Mexico. After Mexican independence in 1821, Chaves continued to serve in the New Mexican militia. Family lore had it that he would "rather fight than eat or sleep." Similarly, legend had it that once after Indians had raided Abiquiú Chaves raised a company to pursue them. In his zeal, he outran his own men; when he came within sight of his enemy, he found himself alone. Striking their camp at full speed, Chaves routed the small band, which fled leaving their arms and provisions behind.[259] Whether true or false, the stories about Chaves exemplified the esteem in which he was held by his own people.

In the course of his life, Chaves took part in at least eleven campaigns against raiding bands of Comanche, Utes, and Apaches. Punitive expeditions frequently resulted in the capture of Indian children, who were distributed among the settlers of Abiquiú as servants. The two-way slave trade which had been historical between Hispanic and indigenous peoples continued. Expeditions to rescue Hispanic captives and take Indian prisoners motivated Chaves to lead New Mexican militiamen into northeastern Arizona, Colorado, and Utah. No distance was too far for him to venture, for the men of Abiquiú had always gone in those directions. As his reputation grew during the Mexican period, Chaves was promoted to colonel, then military inspector of the frontiers of Abiquiu, Ojo Caliente, and El Rito. Eventually he became a brigadier general.[260]

Unlike many New Mexicans who resented control by the Mexican government, Chaves was supportive of Mexican appointees to New Mexican positions. After independence from Spain had been won, Mexico developed a major political split in which Centralists, led by the conservative elite of Mexican society, opposed liberals who sought to define a democratic philosophy which would provide equality for the masses. Some Centralists favored oligarchic models of government and entertained the hope of restoring a monarchical form of government. Civil wars erupted in Mexico during the nineteenth century over the centralist-liberal philosophic rift; the trend generally pointed to dictatorship. By the mid-1830s Mexico was ruled by a dictator. On the Mexican frontier, especially in New Mexico, where liberalism and a rugged frontier isolationism were more established, the notion of a dictatorship did not set well. New Mexicans would express their feelings, as did others elsewhere, as rebellions tore the frontier areas apart. Yucatan rebelled in 1835; Texas did so in 1836, Sonora in 1837, and Californians rebelled several times between 1824 and 1848. New Mexico underwent political turbulence in 1837.[261]

Problems began with the appointment by General Antonio López de Santa Anna of an outsider from Veracruz, Albino Pérez, to the governorship of New Mexico. Arriving in New Mexico in April 1835, Pérez, with high hopes of improving the situation which confronted him, succeeded only in encouraging the resentment harbored against him by those who considered him an outsider appointed by a dictator without their consent.[262] Pérez's unquestioned loyalty to the central government, his noble qualities, and his military experience actually made him a fine choice for the New Mexican mission. His objective, to prepare the people of New Mexico for the change from an outlying frontier province to a department or state within the Mexican union, inspired opposition from New Mexican frontiersmen who interpreted the change to mean that they would surrender local power to a distant central government. Consequently, an explosive political issue of home rule undermined his mission.

Soon after his arrival at Santa Fe, Pérez began an inspection tour of northern New Mexico. He concluded that Indian depredations against Hispanic settlements were in part due to established trading patterns. On 16 October 1835, Pérez announced legislation regulating trade with Indians. Threatening a lucrative illegal Indian trade which he related to increased Comanche, Apache, Yuta, and Navajo attacks by well-supplied raiders, the October law provided that

> 1. *estranjeros del norte* [Anglo-Americans, in particular mountain men who were illegally living within Mexican territory] be prohibited from trading in New Mexico with all classes of Indians.

2. Both *estranjeros* and citizens of New Mexico not be permitted to trade arms and ammunition to *naciones barbaros* who surrounded the territory and raided into Chihuahua.

3. Trade with Indians be permitted only with a license issued by the departmental government.

4. No Mexican citizen, native or naturalized, be permitted to trap beaver without license from the departmental government.

5. No citizen be permitted to use his license to trap beaver for any *estranjero.*[263]

Pérez also reckoned that monies from the sale of licenses could be used to outfit troops for combat against raiders; but New Mexicans viewed the law as an example of Pérez's role as an agent of the central government bent on destroying home rule. Other laws levying taxes on trade items followed. If there existed any doubt concerning Pérez's authority to suggest or decree taxation provisions, it soon disappeared with the decree of 17 April 1837. Sent from Mexico City, the decree spelled out the role of *jefe politicos* in directing their departments toward improved fiscal efficiency. Granting investigatory, advisory, and appointive powers to department governors, the decree allowed Pérez to supervise treasury officials. As witness to the monthly and annual cash statements made by officials of the treasury, Pérez could observe omissions and abuses. Furthermore, he could report and suspend employees who did not perform their duties loyally. Control of custom houses also fell to *jefe politicos* throughout Mexico.

Pérez became the focal point of attention among New Mexicans. Chief among the issues was direct taxes. Demands on the people for aid against marauding Indians became another area of complaint, for the people felt that the central government should provide military protection. Such discontent led to a lack of cooperation by New Mexican frontiersmen. Still, Pérez enjoyed the loyalty of certain leading New Mexicans, some of whom served in his administration.[264] Pérez married into the Trujillo family of Santa Fe. New Mexicans Miguel Sena, Jesus María Alarid, Santiago Abréu, Ramón Abréu, and José María Chaves and his brothers were among Pérez's supporters. Under Pérez, Chaves served as *alcalde constitucional* of Abiquiú in 1837.[265] But his associations were not enough to salvage Pérez from the blow fate would soon deliver.

In the backlands of northern New Mexico, trouble brewed for the Pérez faction. A seemingly innocent court case in La Cañada de Santa Cruz began a chain of events that led to a political confrontation between Pérez and his opponents. Presiding over a trial involving his relatives, Juan José Esquivel acquitted them. The case was reviewed by Ramón Abréu, a supporter of Pérez, who not only reversed the decision but had Esquivel arrested when he refused to comply with the new decision. Public sympathy soon was with Esquivel, who sat in jail serving out his term. Moving swiftly, a mob formed outside his cell in Santa Fe, liberated him, and retreated to a mountain stronghold. Josiah Gregg noted that it was "an occurrence that seemed as a watchword for a general insurrection."[266] Although it began as an individual struggle against the *jefe político,* in reality it was the pretext for a rebellion.

On 3 August 1837 a revolutionary junta was formed at Santa Cruz. It was made up of twelve persons who called their district the *Canton de la Cañada.* They drew up their position as follows:

> Long live God and the Nation and the faith of Jesus Christ. The principal points which we defend are as follows:
>
> 1. To be with God and the Nation and the faith of Jesus Christ.
> 2. To defend our country to the last drop of blood in order to attain victory.
> 3. Not to admit the Departmental Plan.
> 4. Not to admit a single tax.
> 5. Not to admit the bad order of those who are trying to effect it. God and the Nation, Santa Cruz de la Cañada, 3 August 1837. Encampment.[267]

Meanwhile. as word reached Pérez of impending trouble, he hastened to gather a militia but could muster only 150 men including the warriors of the Pueblo of Santo Domingo. With his small force, Pérez left the capital on 7 August 1837 to suppress the rebels. Having spent the night at the Indian pueblo of Pojoaque, they continued the march to Santa Cruz. While en route they were attacked by the rebels, reported Francisco Sarracino, "in a disorderly manner . . . giving us a lively fire. . . . Colonel Pérez approached the cannon and said to me these words, 'Friend Sarracino do not abandon the cannon.' "[268] Sarracino abandoned the cannon. The battle lost and most of his men either captured or defected to the rebels, Pérez was chased back to the outskirts of Santa Fe, where on 9 August he was caught and brutally killed. It is unclear whether José María Chaves had been in the battle, but when he heard that the governor had been captured and killed he rushed to escape a similar fate. Others of Pérez's supporters were not so lucky. Josiah Gregg described the atrocity: "His body was then stripped and shockingly mangled: his head was carried as a trophy to the camp of the insurgents who made a football of it among themselves." Gregg's report on the death of the governor was secondhand, but he did claim to see the deaths of Jesus María Alarid and Santiago Abréu.[269]

The rebel forces gathered strength. Two thousand marched on Santa Fe. Preparing for the worst, the inhabitants fortified themselves in their homes. The rebels entered the city and elected a governor, José Gonzales, who Gregg described as a "good honest hunter, but a very ignorant man."[270] Two days later, they left. With Gonzales and the rebels at large, New Mexico was in a state of rebellion.

Meanwhile, Manuel Armijo, self-appointed governor, led an army against the rebels. By 1838 Armijo had captured and executed Gonzales, crushing the revolt. He reported to the central government that the situation was under control and there was no need to send troops northward. Instability in Mexico allowed New Mexico to revert to its customary geographical remoteness and political isolation. Eight years later, New Mexico fell to the United States Army under Stephen Watts Kearny in the Mexican War and was annexed under the American flag.

What of José María Chaves's participation in the insurrection of 1837? No word is found in the historical record until 1902 when his granddaughter Rosa Chaves wrote to Governor L.B. Prince detailing, in glowing terms, his life. Rosa recounted the story her grandfather had told to her. After Pérez had been beheaded, Pablo Montoya, José María's uncle, who was in the fight against the governor, advised his nephew to get out of New Mexico as fast as he could. As Montoya had been one of the leaders in the rebellion, he knew that Chaves had been marked for execution. José María had been commissioned by the revolutionaries to raise a force from Abiquiú against the governor, though he did not do so. Instead, he hurriedly returned to Abiquiú, packed his baggage, and bought *serapes* to take with him as trade items in his escape with other New Mexicans to California.[271] Rosa did not detail her grandfather's route to Los Angeles, but Chaves knew the route from Abiquiú to the San Juan River beyond the northern rim of the Grand Canyon and then past present Kanab, Utah, to the desolate stopping place known as Las Vegas. From there it was westward to Los Angeles. It is likely he took Armijo's 1829 route.

Arriving in California in November 1837, Chaves presented himself as a trader from New Mexico. According to Rosa's account, he went to Los Angeles, where he had two brothers, Julian and Mariano. Soon after, Chaves became involved in another rebellion, this one against Governor Mariano Chico. Although the California rebellion reflected the centralist versus liberal rift, personal and local prejudices were equally as potent, and, like the New Mexican insurrection, they were based on a local antipathy toward Mexican appointees. Situated in their camps near San Buenaventura in March 1838, the rebels recruited the Chaves brothers, who joined them there. Hubert Howe Bancroft states that "the New Mexicans had been promised all the mares at San Fernando for their services, and were therefore known as Yegueros."[272]

By 26 March 1838 José María and others who had fled New Mexico with him, were involved in a twenty-four-hour gun battle with Mexican forces under General José Castro, who had moved his army south from San Francisco to suppress the rebels. In the battle, Chaves claimed to have killed Castro's artilleryman, Juan Coronado.[273] Taking command of some New Mexicans and Californios, Chaves ordered them to take refuge in an adobe building, where they were heavily bombarded by government forces. The battle lost, Chaves and his men were forced to surrender, especially after the building where their gunpowder was stored was hit and exploded. Oddly, the story goes that the government forces were too low on munitions to force Chaves and his men to surrender their arms. So the government forces invited Chaves and other rebels to a makeshift banquet, asking them to leave their arms at "an arsenal" before taking their seats at the table. At that point their guns were collected. Chaves and his men were taken prisoner and forced to march from their encampment at San Buenaventura to Los Angeles. Good fortune, however, attended Chaves and his men, especially since Castro, raising a sword, had threatened to behead Chaves. On their march, rebels under Juan Castañeda blocked the road and prepared for battle against Castro. A standoff ensued, and subsequently both sides met and negotiated an armistice and an exchange of prisoners. The armistice lasted thirty days, during which time Chaves and his men took advantage of the lull and quickly left California.[274]

Although lacking specific details, Hubert Howe Bancroft's account is at variance with that of Rosa Chaves. Regarding the role of New Mexicans at the battle of San Buenaventura, Bancroft writes:

> There is a very general tendency to grossly exaggerate the forces engaged, really a little more than 100 men on each side, and to speak of assaults repelled, and other purely imaginary details. Castañeda's force had, as it would seem, no artillery, but included a party of New Mexicans

armed with rifles. Castro's approach was altogether unsuspected until at dawn he made his presence known, having by that time seized all the garrison's horses, cut off communications with Angeles, and also probably cut off the water supply, thus obliging the soldiers to quench their thirst mainly with the mission wine. Two guns were placed on the shoreline on the direction of the chapel, and one perhaps on the elevation back of the mission. Early in the fight a rifleman from the church tower killed one of Castro's men. The guns were then directed upon the church, which in 1874 still bore some slight marks of the cannonade, and from the walls of which in the course of certain repairs some time in the past decade a cannon-ball is said to have been taken. The 'continuous firing of two days' was perhaps continuous only with considerable intervals between the volleys, and it could not have continued into the second day for a longer time than was necessary to make known the flight of the garrison during the night. The fugitives or such of them as kept together, were easily overtaken by the horsemen near Saticoy on March 28th. Castañeda and a few of his officers were sent under arrest to Santa Bárbara, and perhaps to Santa Inés. Nearly all Californians state that after the occupation Castro found concealed in the mission church certain other men of some prominence, who were sent north with the other prisoners. . . . There is no contemporary records respecting any of the prominent prisoners nor the circumstances and length of their captivity.[275]

Bancroft does not identify the New Mexicans. The battle of San Buenaventura was neither bloody nor glorious. Significantly, however, the presence of New Mexicans living in California prior to the rebellion as well as those recently arrived who participated in the battle of San Buenaventura gives testimony to the fact that the Old Spanish Trail was being used for immigration purposes as well as for trade. In the case of José María Chaves and his New Mexican compatriots, the Old Spanish Trail was used for purposes of political asylum.

Meanwhile, the situation in New Mexico had calmed. Probably before 1840 Chaves returned to New Mexico. It appears that he quickly reestablished himself in Abiquiú, for he was soon in command of a militia unit which undertook sorties against Ute and Navajo raiders in northwestern New Mexico. The problems of frontier defense remained. The pacification of southern Colorado and northern New Mexico continued well into the nineteenth century as Utes, Apaches, Navajos, and Comanches refused to bow to the power of the Mexican nation and later to that of the United States.

Throughout the early 1840s, Ute raiders had consistently attacked New Mexicans, making off with an appreciable number of livestock and captives as well as leaving many dead settlers in their paths. In 1841 and in 1843 Chaves led campaigns against the Utes in northern New Mexico and Colorado and against the Navajos in northwestern New Mexico. In 1845, Ute raids against New Mexican settlements increased at an alarming rate. Aroused to war, Hispanics under Adjutant General Juan Andrés Archuleta organized an army against the raiders. In command of the militia was José María Chaves, who led over 1,000 militiamen and 100 regulars. The army mustered at Taos Pueblo on 19 July 1845. Marching into southern Colorado, the New Mexicans terrorized and routed the Utes before them. Their march from Taos ran north to *El Saguache,* a small range in the Sangre de Cristo Mountains, and thence to Ponche Pass.[276] Pressing hard against the Utes, Chaves forced them as far north as the Río Napestle, also known as the Arkansas. The river, however, formed the Mexico-United States boundary established by treaty in 1819. Once across, the Utes were safe from Chaves and his frontier army. Chaves immediately sent a messenger to Santa Fe asking permission to cross the river; but permission was denied as it would constitute an invasion of U.S. soil. Frustrated, Chaves turned his army loose on remaining Ute encampments, which were overrun and destroyed. All belongings left behind by fleeing Utes were divided as spoils or destroyed as a message to Utes who would invade New Mexico. For his campaign against the Utes, the Mexican government rewarded Chaves with a handsome sword, which he proudly displayed over the fireplace of his home in Abiquiú.[277]

After the American occupation of New Mexico by General Stephen Kearny, Chaves became a citizen of the United States as provided by the Treaty of Guadalupe Hidalgo, which granted citizenship to all Mexicans living in the ceded territories. Under the United States' territorial government of New Mexico, Chaves served as a brigadier general of the militia. He also served in the New Mexico territorial legislature for seven years. In 1851 Governor James S. Calhoun appointed him prefect of Río Arriba County, and later Governor David Merriwether commissioned him probate judge of the same county.

In 1859, Navajo raiders attacked villages in central New Mexico, killing several persons and carrying off cattle from the outskirts of Santa Fe. Citizens of Santa Fe, realizing that the incidents took place within ten miles of the capital, demanded retribution. The territorial legislature passed a law permitting private citizens to organize volunteer militia companies to punish marauders. Fearing the territorial army incapable and noting that "our people prefer to carry on Indian wars in their own way," Governor Abraham Rencher approved the formation of volunteer militia units.[278] In order to protect themselves, some New Mexicans held a council in August 1860 and decided to take matters into their own hands. They organized a punitive expedition against the Navajos. Money was raised, a call for a regiment of mounted volunteers followed, and officers were appointed. José María Chaves was asked to serve as lieutenant colonel under the command of his cousin Manuel Chaves; Miguel Pino agreed to serve as a colonel of the regiment but never joined the expedition. Units were formed from villages such as Peralta, Santa Cruz de la Cañada, San Miguel, Bernalillo, and Santa Fe. The troops numbered almost 450 men, who supplied their own horses, arms, rations and clothing. By 23 September 1860 all units met at San Isidro, where they underwent an inspection by General M.L. Cotton.

The expedition followed the old Jemez Trail southward past Laguna Pueblo, then westward to Bear Springs. The march was arduous. Once beyond the Tunicha Mountains, the expedition marched toward the Hopi pueblos in northeastern Arizona. The inhospitable land, vast and arid, became increasingly difficult to cross on horseback. The hostile environment cost the expedition greatly, for several companies lost over 50 percent of their horses, and the pack train lost thirty-three mules.[279]

In the campaign of 1860, however, Manuel Chaves marched his men into Arizona and inflicted a severe punishment against the Navajos. Having taken the war into Navajo territory, the expedition recovered a large number of stolen livestock, took captives—mostly women and children—and inflicted as many casualties as they could. Running low on supplies and with colder weather approaching, Manuel Chaves ordered his men back to Santa Fe in early December. Little is known of José María Chaves's activities other than his participation in the war as an officer. A native poet who accompanied him in the campaign, nevertheless, saw it fit to write a poem glorifying Chaves.[280]

At the outbreak of the Civil War, José María Chaves served on the Union side as a lieutenant-colonel of a volunteer mounted regiment. Finally, in 1875, seventy-four-year-old José María Chaves was appointed school commissioner of Río Arriba County.[281] Given his age, his experiences, his longevity as a settler of Abiquiú, and his knowledge of northern New Mexico, Chaves later served as an expert witness in land grant cases, due to his keen memory and because he had witnessed the establishment of many property boundaries.

Chaves had led a long and fruitful life on the Abiquiú frontier. Significantly, when Chaves led his small party to California in 1837, he demonstrated that Armijo's route likely had been used as an emigrant trail by other New Mexicans living in the Los Angeles area for nearly a decade. Chaves died in 1902. Today, there is at least one memorial of the Chavez family experience in California: at the western end of the Old Spanish Trail is Chavez Ravine, where Dodger Stadium stands.

CHAPTER X

Mountain Men and Hispanic Traders on the Old Spanish Trail,

1822–1853

FOR NEARLY TWO centuries French, English, and Anglo-American trappers had been slowly moving westward, first up the St. Lawrence River, then along the Appalachian Mountains, and finally west from there until they reached the Mississippi and Missouri rivers. West of there, the Great Plains, stretching virtually from the Mississippi River to New Mexico, posed a barrier for several decades. After crossing the plains, in 1739 French trappers reached Santa Fe and began trading in the area. By the early nineteenth century, Anglo-American trappers also had reached Santa Fe from their rendezvous camps north of New Mexico. The way to the Great Plains from the Mississippi and Missouri river drainages had been blazed by Spanish trappers from St. Louis, before the Lewis and Clark expedition (1802–03). By 1821 a route known as the Santa Fe Trail had been developed from Missouri to New Mexico. That route linked up at Santa Fe with the Old Spanish Trail. Very quickly, a renewed interest in exploiting the Old Spanish Trail as a way to get to California attracted New Mexicans and Anglo-Americans alike. The Santa Fe Trail also linked up with another ancient road known as the *camino real de tierra adentro,* the Royal Road of the Interior, leading to Mexico City from Santa Fe. The Santa Fe-Chihuahua Trail became a famous route named for that segment of the Camino Real from Albuquerque to Chihuahua.

Anglo-American trappers, known as mountain men, following the Missouri River drainages, pushed deeper into the North American wilderness until they reached the Yellowstone River. From there they moved southwestward toward the Yuta country where they learned about new pathways—variants of the Old Spanish Trail—to reach California. Hispanic frontiersmen who lived along the Mississippi and Missouri rivers have often been ignored in the telling of the exploits of mountain men. Two such frontiersmen from Louisiana Territory were Manuel Lisa, who subsequently formed the Missouri Fur Company, and Louis Vásquez, who later, with Jim Bridger, founded Fort Bridger near the Green River in southwestern Wyoming. Vásquez traveled west to the Yuta country and eventually to California.

Pierre Louis Vásquez was the son of Benito Vásquez and Julie Papin. Benito Vásquez, born in Galicia, Spain, in 1750, arrived in Spanish St. Louis, present Missouri, with Governor Pedro Piernas in 1770. Benito, a farmer and trader, served as captain of militia. He married Julie Papin, a French Canadian, in 1774. One of twelve children reared by the couple, Louis, was born in 1798. His brother Antoine Francois "Baronet" Vásquez also became a trapper, who at one point worked for Manuel Lisa and later, in 1806, joined the expedition led by Zebulon Pike, whom he served as an interpreter. Auguste Pike Vásquez, another mountain man, was their nephew.

By the time he was in his early twenties, Louis Vásquez had joined an expedition, probably the Ashley-Henry company, involved in the fur trade along the Missouri River. Sometime after 1822 Vásquez reached the region of the Great Salt Lake, which he claimed to have discovered, although his claim has not been accepted by historians. Nevertheless, an interview published in the 29 October 1858 *San Francisco Bulletin* supported his claim by calling him "the oldest mountaineer in this country and the discoverer of Great Salt Lake."[282] The paper's correspondent continued his explanation by writing that Vásquez

> . . . first entered this valley [Salt Lake City] 36 years ago. In the fall of 1822, he, with a company of trappers, arrived in Cache Valley, where they determined to spend the winter, and trap in the numerous streams with which it abounds. The winter, however, became so severe—the snow falling to the depth of 8 feet—that they found it necessary to hunt out a better valley, in order to save their animals. Accordingly, Major Vásquez, with one or two of his party, started out, and crossing the divide, entered this valley, and discovered Great Salt Lake. This, they at first took to be

an arm of the Pacific Ocean. They found the valley free from snow, and well filled with herds of buffalo. Returning to their party, they guided them over into this valley, when they divided—one party, under Weber, wintering on the river which now bears his name; the other wintering on Bear river, near its mouth. The following spring, Vásquez built a boat, and circumnavigated this sheet of brine, for the purpose of finding out definitely whether it was an arm of the sea or not, and thus discovered that it was in reality merely a large inland lake, without an outlet. Since that time, the lake has been gradually receding.[283]

In his writings, Leroy Hafen credits the discovery to other mountain men or possibly Mormons who later occupied the area.[284] It is quite possible that the discovery was made much earlier by one of the many illegal traders from New Mexico who traded with the *Timpanogos* Utes. That discovery, however, would have gone unrecorded.

Vásquez was well regarded among mountain men and was a partner of Jim Bridger and co-founder of Fort Bridger in southwestern Wyoming. His son Hiram Vásquez was best friends with Felix Bridger, son of Jim Bridger. "We were raised together," Hiram would later write of their familial association.[285] This was one of many associations of Hispanic trappers and traders with their Anglo-American counterparts.

The push by Anglo-Americans into New Mexico began soon after Mexican independence from Spain had been gained in 1821. Almost immediately, a lively commerce between Missouri and New Mexico was established. The trade was begun by William Becknell, who became known as the "Father of the Santa Fe Trail." He began a commerce that depended upon pack mules and freight wagons. The Santa Fe–Chihuahua Trail trade ran its historical course from 1821 to the 1890s, when it was displaced by the railroad whose route ran from Missouri to New Mexico then south to Chihuahua. Trappers and traders alike quickly used the route into Mexican territory; from there, they picked up the Old Spanish Trail to California.

Before long, a connection was made between the Santa Fe Trail and the old Spanish dreams to reach California. The Santa Fe Trail became a feeder route for one of the many trails west that were developing with the westward expansion of the United States. Santa Fe, Taos, Santa Cruz de la Cañada, Chama, and Abiquiú were centers for Spanish traders and Anglo-American mountain men. From there, Hispanic and Anglo trappers and traders often pushed westward to California. The desire for a regular route to California received new interest. A major impetus occurred soon after the fur traders' Bear River rendezvous of 1826. The meeting was held forty or fifty miles north of where the Bear River enters the Great Salt Lake. At that meeting William Ashley sold his interest in his fur company to his partner Jedidiah Smith and several others.

Upon conclusion of the deal, Smith and fourteen men decided to move southwest of Utah Lake. Smith traced a route along present U.S. Highway 91 from Ogden, Utah, to Barstow and Victorville, California, then over the mountains near Cajon Pass into the San Bernardino Valley, and finally to San Gabriel. Although they were not the first non-Indians to do so, they were the first known Anglo-Americans to cross from Utah to California. Following Smith, some twenty-five parties of Anglo-American mountain men eventually reached California during that period. Even though Smith presented his credentials and trade license, some Californians sensed that the coming of the Anglo-Americans presaged important changes.

Smith's party retraced their steps back to the San Bernardino Mountains, then northward through Antelope Valley over the Tehachapi Mountains, from where they entered the San Joaquin Valley; where they had been preceded by Fages, Garcés, and Moraga. The party trapped the region for three months, bringing in over 1,500 pounds of beaver pelts. Smith had also gathered valuable information about the geography of the region for English-speaking parties traveling in the area.

By May 1827 Smith attempted another expedition to California by way of the Sierra Nevada; but the snow was too deep and he lost some pack animals. Retreating southward to the Stanislaus River where it was warmer, his party regrouped and planned a more southerly route to California. At the end of May, the party crossed the Jordan River near where it flows from Utah Lake, then went northward along the east shore of the Great Salt Lake to Bear River and then upriver to Bear Lake, where they camped.[286] On 13 July 1827 Smith separated from the main party and with eighteen men set out for California. But disaster struck while he and his men were crossing the Colorado River. They were attacked by the formerly friendly Mojaves Smith had met in 1826. The Mojaves killed ten of his men, and all of their supplies and trade goods were lost. Smith and his remaining men returned to the Stanislaus River. There, they rendezvoused with the main party.

The star-crossed Smith persisted in returning to Spanish California. On his next trip, he reached Mission San José and was arrested. Removed to Monterey, Governor José Echeandía held him for six weeks while John Rogers Cooper, a local resident, negotiated a bond of assurance that Smith and his party would conduct themselves well in California. Echeandía then authorized that Smith and his party could trap in the San Francisco area near Carquinez Strait and Bodega. After trapping 1,568 pounds of beaver, which were sold to the captain of the ship *Franklin,* Smith and his men returned to San José.[287]

Having outfitted themselves at San José, Smith and his party of twenty men and 300 horses headed northeast to the San Joaquin River. By January 1828 the party was trapping the tributaries of the lower Sacramento River. Three months later the men had made their way to the north end of the Sacramento Valley before departing to the northwest. Pushing their way to present-day Requa near the coast, Smith and his men marched into Kelawatset Indian territory. Three weeks later, while Smith and a companion were exploring for a route from there, his camp was attacked by Indians, who annihilated his party. Smith and two companions who were not in the camp at the time were joined by one other who had escaped the massacre.[288]

Smith had maintained to British authorities in Oregon and Mexican officials in California that his purpose of the traveling to the Pacific coast was twofold: he wished to trap for beaver and he wanted to learn the truth regarding the legendary San Buenaventura River that supposedly ran from Utah to California, possibly to San Francisco Bay. To his Anglo-American counterparts, Smith spoke ill of the British and Mexicans. Writing to General William Clark on 24 December 1829, Smith accused Governor Echeandía of ordering the Mojave Indians to attack him and his men at the crossing at the Colorado River. Smith also thought that "British interlopers" should be "dismissed from our territory." Meanwhile, his old partner, William Ashley, a member of Congress from 1831 to 1837, received a map drawn by Smith. Ashley took the map to Senator Thomas Hart Benton, who promoted the expansion of the United States.

Smith's trapping expeditions to California inspired others to go there. There were at least five major trapping expeditions that left New Mexico over the Old Spanish Trail between 1827 and 1830, including those of R. Campbell, who led an expedition from Santa Fe to San Diego in 1827; Sylvester Pattie, who left with a party from Santa Fe to San Diego the following year; Ewing Young, who in 1829 led a party from Taos to San José; William Wolfskill, who marched from Taos to Los Angeles in 1830; and David E. Jackson, who in 1831 traveled from Santa Fe to San Francisco Bay.[289]

Meanwhile, New Mexican traders continued to go to California via the Old Spanish Trail blazed by Armijo in 1829. Little information about what they traded is revealed in extant documentation of the period. More revealing are records that deal with misdeeds with which New Mexicans were charged in California. A certain Fray Cabot at Mission San Miguel complained about the conduct of New Mexicans by reporting that:

> Since the New Mexicans have come into this province with the commerce of wool and the purchase of horses, the mission has suffered a great loss of horses and 108 mules. . . . At the close of 1832 several of them passed by the Rancho of Asunción and four colts and a mule were taken from a herd. After a few days others passed and took with them a mule with a forged brand.[290]

Father Cabot suspected that the animals had been taken to New Mexico.

Following the alleged disorderly conduct and robberies of New Mexican traders, California authorities in 1833 established a series of policies restricting and regulating trade. Especially aimed at New Mexicans, the laws passed by the California legislative assembly provided that New Mexicans should not buy mules, mares, or horses at other than established prices set by the local justice of the peace; that New Mexicans must have a license to trade from the local alcalde; that New Mexicans bear proof of their purchases by keeping a signed itemized document listing their purchases. In Los Angeles it became the practice to assemble the traders at a predetermined place for inspection of their cargoes before they departed for New Mexico.[291] The practice helped officials to recover stolen animals and punish the culprits.

Unable to control the situation, California authorities asked assistance from the governor of New Mexico: that he provide New Mexican traders with authorization to go to California for trade as a testimony to their good character. The governor complied with the request, requiring New Mexico traders to observe the legal formalities imposed upon them in California or suffer the consequences.

On 21 January 1834 José Avieta arrived in Los Angeles from New Mexico with 125 men. The trade they undertook was brisk, involving 1,645 serapes among other goods. When revenue officers attempted to collect a duty, the traders intimidated them and told them they were exempt, quoting a law of 1830. Not wanting trouble, the officials backed down. Soon Fray Ramón Abella at Mission Concepción complained that New Mexican traders had stopped at his mission for two weeks and sold liquor in drinking horns to Indians there. Father Abella requested the governor establish a policy limiting the stay of traders to three days except in cases of illness. His request was granted. Apparently, Avieta's visit to California was the subject of much discussion and alarm. California officials discovered that members of Avieta's party had gone to the Tulare Valley, where they incited Indians to steal horses for them. A military force was sent after them to drive them out of California.[292]

In the intervening years, some Anglo-American traders had joined New Mexicans and combined their resources, much to the chagrin of Mexican officials in California. In 1835–36, Dr. John Marsh visited California with a party from New Mexico; in 1837 a suspected horse thief, one Charlevoix, was identified with a New Mexican group; in 1838 thirty New Mexicans showed up in Los Angeles with John Wolfskill. The party, comprising of the New Mexicans, one Italian, and two Canadians, was permitted to trade only south of San Fernando where its members could be easily monitored. In 1839 José Antonio Salazar entered California with seventy-five men. Highly respected, Salazar was able to keep close command of his men in the initial stages of their visit; however, over the course of three months, their discipline degenerated and trouble ensued. Salazar finally asked support from local officials to keep his men in line. The party was escorted from Santa Barbara to Cajon Pass. There the members were inspected and, on 14 April 1839, allowed to leave for New Mexico. For some reason, some of the men deserted the party, returned to California, and were quickly arrested. Because of the lack of administrative funds at the jail, the prisoners were released, and apparently they remained in California under bond of a local.[293]

Sometime during that period, New Mexicans began trading Indian slaves from Utah in California. On their way from New Mexico, the traders traveled through Navajo and Ute territories, trading with a few goods and horses. The horses were traded for children. Arrived in California, the New Mexicans would trade their slaves for horses and mules, other goods, or cash. On their way back through Utah, the New Mexicans with large herds from California would trade their jaded mounts for Indian children to take back to New Mexico. There, boys were sold for an average of $100 and girls from $150 to $200 as domestic servants. The slave trade became particularly vicious when certain Anglo-American traders began raiding weak tribes and taking children prisoners and selling them in New Mexico. The practice caused wars not only between tribes in Utah but between tribes and settlers in both Utah and New Mexico.[294]

In the early 1850s, lawmakers in Utah, like Californians, were troubled by the presence of New Mexican traders who crossed through their newly incorporated territory, but for other reasons. The Indian slave trade was considered a practice dating to "time immemorial," when the purchase of "Indian women and children of the Utah tribe of Indians by Mexican traders" began.[295] The Utah legislature recognized that certain Utah settlers, traders, and trappers formed the third party engaged in the slave trade. Between strong Indian tribes selling enemy captives, weak Indian tribes selling their children for food, New Mexicans buying Indian children to sell in California and New Mexico and Anglo-American settlers and traders in Utah also engaged in the Indian slave trade, the situation was complex. Utah lawmakers proclaimed their abhorrence to the human bondage and the ugliness of the trade:

> Whereas, It is common practice among these Indians to gamble away their own children and women; and it is a well established fact that women and children thus obtained, or frequently carried from place to place packed upon horses or mules; larietted out to subsist upon grass, roots, or starve; and are frequently bound with thongs made of rawhide, until their hands and feet become swollen, mutilated, inflamed with pain and wounded, and when with suffering, cold, hunger and abuse they fall sick so as to become troublesome, are frequently slain by their masters to get rid of them; and
>
> Whereas, They do frequently kill their women and children taken prisoners, either for revenge, or for amusement, or through the influence of tradition, unless they are tempted to exchange them for trade, which they usually do if they have an opportunity; and
>
> Whereas, One family frequently steals the children and women of another family, and such robberies and murders are continually committed, in times of their greatest peace and amity, thus dragging free Indian women and children into Mexican servitude and slavery, or death, to the almost entire extirpation of the whole Indian race; and
>
> Whereas, These inhuman practices are being daily enacted before our eyes. . . . It becomes the duty of all humane and christian people to extend unto this degraded and downtrodden race such relief as can be awarded to them, according to their situation and circumstances. . . .[296]

Part of the solution, as seen by Utah lawmakers, was to drive out New Mexicans engaged in the slave trade, prohibit Anglo-Americans from participating in it, and attempt to educate Indians about this wrong.

The manner in which Utah lawmakers, despite their good intentions, resolved the "New Mexican" problem, however, did not immediately stop the slave trade, it merely shifted its emphasis. In 1852 the Legislative Assembly provided that

> whenever any white person . . . shall have an Indian prisoner, child, or woman in his possession, whether by purchase or otherwise, such person shall immediately go, together with such Indian prisoner, child or woman, before the Selectman or Probate Judge of the country. If in the opinion of the Selectman or Probate Judge the person having such Indian prisoner, child or woman, is a suitable person, and properly qualified to raise, or retain and educate said prisoner, child or woman, it shall be his or their duty to bind out the same by indenture for the term of not exceeding twenty years at the discretion of the Judge or Selectman. . . . The master to whom the indenture is made is hereby required to send said apprentice to school . . . the master shall clothe his apprentice in a comfortable and becoming manner, according to his, said master's condition in life."[297]

The result of this law, as New Mexicans pointed out, merely replaced New Mexicans with Mormons in the slave trade.

Although slave trading and horse stealing by traders in California continued to be a major problem, Californians also faced a growing dilemma. After 1841 the Old Spanish Trail became increasingly used as an emigration route from New Mexico. Officials in California now had to contend with new immigration policies and the acceptance of New Mexican residents in their midst. A new era was dawning on the Old Spanish Trail, for in 1848 California became part of the United States by dint of the Mexican War. In the closing years of Mexican California, immigrating parties from New Mexico established themselves in California. One of the first was the Workman-Rowland party.

In 1841 Thomas Rowland and William Workman, resident traders in New Mexico, organized an emigrating party to California. Both men were familiar with the country, for they had trapped north of Santa Fe along the Green and Colorado rivers as early as the 1820s. They found support in Manuel Alvarez, the American consul in Santa Fe, who similarly was interested in trade with California, especially if there was a profitable business venture in transporting sheep there. Alvarez worked to get Rowland and Workman the proper licenses to go to California. Apparently, by the 1840s an annual trade caravan had been established between Santa Fe and Los Angeles via the Old Spanish Trail. Indeed, Governor Manuel Armijo had granted permission for a regular New Mexican pack horse caravan on 6 August 1841.[298] He authorized Francisco Estevan Vigil to travel to California. Meanwhile, Guadalupe Miranda, the Mexican secretary of state, had issued a prohibition against anyone leaving New Mexico because of impending trouble from Texans who had conspired to invade New Mexico. Mirabeau B. Lamar, president of the Texas Lone Star Republic, had claimed that the Texas boundary ran through the heart of New Mexico along the Río Grande. The Texas expedition, a bedraggled army by the time it reached New Mexico, was quickly defeated, much to the embarrassment of Texans.

In the midst of the trouble, the Workman-Rowland party slipped out of Abiquiú on its way to California. The party of twenty-five men included Anglo-Americans as well as native New Mexicans. Lorenzo Trujillo, J. Manuel Baca, Ignacio Salazar, and their families immigrated to California with the party. The party trekked over the familiar Old Spanish Trail, finally reaching Los Angeles after weeks of travel. Rowland wrote that the purpose of the expedition was to settle in California and establish trade: "They each had a firearm which they needed on this trip. The men with families come with the intention of establishing residence in this territory, and those having a trade to pursue same, and some of the others to examine and look over this territory for the purpose of settling here now or returning later to their country."[299]

As the Workman-Rowland expedition demonstrated, there were Hispanic traders who willingly led or participated in expeditions with Anglo-American mountain men through the Yuta country or over the Old Spanish Trail to California. The expedition further demonstrated that the Old Spanish Trail had, since the late 1820s when Antonio María Armijo blazed a route to California, become an emigrant trail to the west coast from New Mexico.

Although some Hispanics like Manuel Lisa and Louis Vásquez became mountain men, few from New Mexico did so. One who did was Mariano Medina. Because Medina was a part of the New Mexican trading and trapping tradition in the general region of the Yuta country, he deserves mention. Born in Taos sometime between 1808 and 1818, little is known about his early life other than that he had run away from home and joined a party of Anglo-American trappers who took him to the Snake River.[300] Small of build, Medina was a spry and active individual. His black hair showed no trace of greying even as he grew older. He generally dressed in the "Mexican fashion, with a scarf around his waist." By the 1840s, Medina had lived as far away from New Mexico as Walla Walla before settling at Fort Bridger. There he prospered by trading with emigrant wagon trains. After Bridger and Vásquez sold Fort Bridger, Medina, who owned a trading post on the Sweetwater River where the Oregon Trail left it to go over South Pass, operated a ferry on the Green River. He moved eastward on the Oregon Trail to trade cattle with emigrants. Later, he served as a scout for Captain Randolph B. Marcy. It is probable that Medina was the Mexican trapper who escorted Marcy across the Colorado River by finding Cochetopa Pass during the winter of 1857–58.[301] In 1859, Medina lived by Big Thompson Creek near the stage road between Fort Collins and Denver. He claimed to be the first white man on the creek. His establishment, a trading post, was west of present Loveland, Colorado. The adobe structure with its two-foot-thick walls served as a fort. The building also had a watchtower, and the walls had loop holes for firing from the interior. He built a bridge and charged a toll of one dollar for crossing it. In the 1860s he had trouble with Utes and Arapahoes who he claimed stole horses from his corral. On one occasion he led three men into present North Park after a party of eleven Utes. He killed four Utes and recovered his horses; the Indians swore revenge and threatened to kill him.[302]

Medina spent his last days in the Denver-Fort Collins area. He was married twice and apparently had fathered four children. In 1868 he was visited by Kit Carson, who had taken the stage from Cheyenne to Medina's house, where he spent the night. Medina, who had known Carson in Taos in their younger years, was pleased about the visit. Of his life as a mountain man, Harvey L. Carter, his biographer, wrote: Medina " is interesting because he is one of the few examples of a Mexican who became a successful free trapper and trader, and because he seems to have lived on terms with equality with Americans, whether they were trappers or settlers."[303] He died on 25 June 1878.

Another New Mexican who joined Anglo-American trappers at an early age was Marcelino Baca, who was born in Taos in 1808. Although he was a contemporary of Medina, it is not known whether they ever met. Easily over six feet tall, Baca was romantically described by George F. Ruxton in his novel *Live in the Far West* (1849) as having the "form of a Hercules, he had the symmetry of an Apollo; with strikingly handsome features, and masses of long black hair hanging from his slouching beaver over the shoulders of his buckskin hunting shirt."[304] Baca was a member of Jim Bridger's American Fur Company on the Yellowstone River and generally ranged in his trapping activities between the South

Platte River near present Denver and Fort Laramie. His westernmost activity may have been as far west as the Humboldt River. As a trapper and settler of northern Colorado, Baca had his share of trouble with Utes, who killed his brother Benito near Pueblo in 1854. Soon after, Baca moved back to New Mexico. When the Civil War broke out, he joined the New Mexico Volunteers. He was killed at the Battle of Valverde, New Mexico, on 21 February 1862.[305]

The general anti-Mexican sentiment among Anglo-American settlers in Utah tended to drive New Mexican traders from the area. Throughout the late 1840s and 1850s, New Mexicans found themselves unwelcome in Utah. Two events hastened the end to the New Mexican dominance of the Yuta trade: the settlement of Utah by the Mormons and the Mexican War of 1846. The latter resulted in the creation of territorial boundaries between Utah and New Mexico. Within a decade of the Mexican War, Mormon officials in Utah made it clear that New Mexicans were not welcome in the area.

One of the last major New Mexican trading parties in the area was led by Pedro León, whose party of twenty-eight men was arrested in 1851 at Manti in the Sanpete Valley. León and his men had been there trading horses for Indian children, and he had a license for trade dated 14 August 1851, signed by Governor James S. Calhoun in Santa Fe. During the winter of 1851–52, León and seven men were tried before the justice of the peace at Manti. Later, the case came before Judge Zerubbabel Snow of the First District court. Snow summarized the situation as follows:

> In September last, twenty eight Spaniards left New Mexico on a trading expedition with the Utah Indians, in their various localities in New Mexico and Utah. Twenty-one of the twenty-eight were severally interested in the expedition. The residue were servants. Among this company were the Spaniards against whom these suits were brought. Before they left, Pedro León obtained a license from the governor of New Mexico to trade on his own account with the Utah Indians, in all their various localities. Another member of the company also had a license given to blank persons by the Governor of New Mexico. The residue were without license. They proceeded on their route until they arrived near the Río Grande, where they exchanged with the Indians some goods for horses and mules. With these horses and mules, being something more than one hundred, they proceeded to Green River, in this territory, where they sent some five or six of their leading men to see

Governor Young, and exhibit to him their license; and as the Spanish witness said that if it was not good here, then to get from him another license. Governor Young not being at home, but gone south, they proceeded after and found him November 3rd at Sanpete Valley. Here they exhibited to the Governor their license, and informed him they wished to sell their horses and mules to the Utah Indians, and buy Indian children to be taken to New Mexico. Governor Young then informed them that their license did not authorize them to trade with the Indians in Utah. They then sought one from him, but he refused it, for the reason that they wanted to buy Indian children for slaves. The Spaniards then promised him they would not trade with the Indians but go immediately home. Twenty of the number, with about three-fourths of the horses and mules, left pursuant to this promise and have not been heard from since. The eight who were left behind are the men who are parties to these proceedings.[306]

León and his men lost their case and were sent back to New Mexico. The Indian slaves they had purchased were liberated. The next year, when José María Chaves attempted to trade in Utah with a license from then Superintendent of Indian Affairs James S. Calhoun, he too was rebuffed.[307] In turn, Chaves accused the Mormons of driving out New Mexicans so that they could dominate the trade of young Indian slaves traded by the more powerful Yuta tribes in the area.

In fact, Mormons had bought slaves to rescue them, one of whom was raised by church president Brigham Young. Charles Decker wrote that "During the winter of 1847–8, some Indian children were brought to the fort [the old Salt Lake Fort] to be sold. At first two were offered but the settlers peremptorily [*sic*] refused to buy them. The Indian in charge said that the children were captured in war and would be killed at sunset if the white men did not buy them. Thereupon they purchased one of them, and the one not sold was shot. Later, several Indians came in with two more, using the same threat; they were bought and brought up at the expense of the settlers."[308]

Despite hostile attitudes in Utah, New Mexican traders continued to go to the Yuta country for trade; but time was against them, and the Yuta trade with New Mexico steadily diminished. Conflicts between New Mexican traders and Mormons resulted in Brigham Young proclaiming that New Mexicans were no longer welcome in the area. In a proclamation of 23 April 1853, Young, as governor of Utah, proclaimed:

Whereas it is made known to me by reliable information, from affidavits, and various other sources, that there is in this Territory a horde of
Mexicans, or outlandish men, who are infesting the settlements, stirring
up the Indians to make aggressions upon the inhabitants, and who are
also furnishing the Indians with guns, ammunition, etc., contrary to the
laws of this Territory and the laws of the United States:

And whereas it is evident that it is the intention of these Mexicans
or foreigners to break the laws of the Territory and the United States,
utterly regardless of every restriction, furnishing Indians with guns and
powder, whenever and wherever it suits their designs, convenience, or
purposes:

Therefore, I Brigham Young, Governor and Superintendent of Indian affairs for the Territory of Utah, in order to preserve peace, quell
the Indians and secure the lives and property of the citizens of the Territory, hereby order and direct as follows:

1st. That a small detachment consisting of thirty men, under the
charge of Captain Wall, proceed south through the entire extent of the
settlements reconnoitering the country and directing the inhabitants to
be on their guard against any sudden surprise. . . .

3rd. The office and party hereby sent upon this service are hereby
authorized and directed to arrest and keep in close custody every stroll-
ing Mexican party, and those associating with them—and leave them
safely guarded at the different points of settlement to await further orders. . . .

5th. All Mexican now in the Territory are required to remain quiet
in the settlements and not attempt to leave under any consideration,
until further advised; and the officers of the Territory are hereby directed to keep them in safe custody, treating them with kindness and
supplying their necessary wants. . . . [309]

Young's proclamation was a sign that the New Mexican dominance of
the Yuta trade was at an end. In order to further control the slave trade
and force its elimination, the Utah Legislature passed a series of laws between 1852 and 1855 outlawing the Indian slave trade.

The pathways to California from New Mexico had been blazed in
part by New Mexican traders between the early eighteenth century,
when illegal traders ventured to the land of the Yutas, and 1829 when
Armijo blazed a route to Los Angeles. Other parts of the routes were
well known to various Native Americans who guided Spanish trader
and Anglo-American trapper alike across their lands. By the 1820s an ef-

fective route over a variant of the Old Spanish Trail had been established; and by the 1840s the route originally used for trade had become
an emigrant trail from New Mexico used by both Hispanics and Anglo-
Americans who wished to go to California. The importance of the Old
Spanish Trail as an emigrant trail took on added significance when it
was joined to the Santa Fe Trail. The New Mexican tradition of going to
the Yuta country had blossomed into a significant trail which aided in
the development of the West. Indeed, the Hispanic development of the
Old Spanish Trail had historical implications in the settlement of
southern and western Colorado, northern Arizona, Utah, Nevada, and
parts of California. It is a part of our national story. With the Camino
Real de Tierra Adentro and the Santa Fe-Chihuahua Trail, the Old
Spanish Trail has a special place in making New Mexico the heartland
of the Southwest, for once upon a time all roads led to Santa Fe.

CHAPTER XI

Epilogue

THE OLD SPANISH TRAIL lives in the lore of Native Americans, Hispanics, and Anglo-Americans of New Mexico, Colorado, Arizona, Utah, Nevada, and California. Similarly, its past and present are commemorated in literature and geography—in place-names, historical markers, and publications. Historiographically, the main event in the preservation of the Old Spanish Trail and its variants occurred in 1954 when *Old Spanish Trail: Santa Fé to Los Angeles* by Leroy R. Hafen and Ann W. Hafen was published. Historical markers are abundant in Utah, but not until 1976 when the United States celebrated its 200th anniversary did a regional interest arise seeking ways to preserve known portions of the trail. During the Bicentennial of the United States in 1976, many proposals were entertained by entities in Utah and New Mexico to "do something" about commemorating the trail and its variants. One significant action, taken by the Domínguez-Escalante State-Federal Bicentennial Committee (organized in 1973), was the publication of the *Domínguez-Escalante Journal,* translated by Fray Angelico Chávez and edited by Ted J. Warner. Nearly simultaneously, a book by Walter Briggs, *Without Noise of Arms: The 1776 Domínguez-Escalante Search for a Route from Santa Fe to Monterey,* was published. Although accounts had been published previously by Herbert S. Auerbach (1941) and Herbert E. Bolton (1951), the reissuance of the journal was a valuable contribution. The journal continues to be the premier document relating to the the Old Spanish Trail.

Perhaps the most significant outcome of the bicentennial in relation to the Old Spanish Trail was the beginning of a grassroots constituency to preserve the trail. During the Bicentennial, tourism seemed to be the driving force, as proposals for bike trails, hiking trails, turn-outs for viewing certain vistas along the route or its variants, and other related ideas were proposed, including re-exploring the route. Most ultimately came to naught. Today, a small but active constituency continues to pursue congressional action to help protect the remnants of the Old Spanish Trail. The Old Spanish Trail is a national treasure representing part of the tri-cultural prehistorical and historical development of the United States. The present volume speaks to the significance of it and its variants.

Translation of Incomplete and Untitled Copy of Juan María Antonio Rivera's Original Diary of the First Expedition, 23 July 1765

Translated by Joseph P. Sánchez

. . . [which is] a mountainous canyon covered with small *chamisos* and other trees of different species, although only a few. We ascended two small hills without any gravel. From there, we continued along another canyon in the same direction until we reached a very small river[1] which is named from the *Pueblo Colorado*. Our route is covered with much pasturage and good and copious waters. As we learned, the waters are permanent all year long. We passed the night there.

[June] 26th . . . We left that place following the same direction. Not long afterwards, we entered a canyon which was somewhat craggy and mountainous, which is about two and a half leagues long of bad road. It ends at the foot of a hill which is in the *Sierra de Abiquiú*. It is the one that has an incline of about one league, [and is] not too rugged. But as observed from the hill, the route, which appears to be little traveled, is palisaded by many oak trees and white poplar. From its descent to the

---

1. Rivera here corrects his diary from his original statement: " . . . *de ay seguimos por otra cañada al mismo rumbo, hasta llegar aun Río mui (profundo) digo pequeño.* . . . " The words *profundo* and *digo* are crossed out.

river called *Cangilones* are two leagues of flat land without any rock, although [it is surrounded by] very mountainous terrain. The water of the said river is very good, although there is little of it. Travelers through here say that the river became barren a few years ago. Although it lacks water during the dry season, it runs most of the year. Our campsite abounded with good pasturage. We passed the night along the said river.

27th . . . We camped there until a little after three o'clock in the afternoon. We left the place through good, open land which did not have any rock. Having traveled about three quarters of a league, we encountered two very small hills which were barren of any rock, not at all inconvenient [to cross]. [They are] low lying and somewhat covered with pine at intervals, not too thick [however]. We followed along this direction through flat, rockless land until we reached a small river called *Las Cebollas* which has good meadowlands, much pasturage, and little water. Having been told [by natives], the river was not permanent every year. During dry years the river dries up but it opens up near another river two leagues hence. Not having any information about whether there was any water ahead, we stayed there for the night.

28th . . . We left the said place following the same direction bearing a little to the northwest. We traveled about five and a half to six leagues until we reached the *Río Chama,* leaving behind us another river called *Las Nutrias* which we are told is permanent. The said route is along gentle land without any rock. [It has] many depressions with some sagebrush but well provided with much pasturage as well as sufficient and good water. We rested after lunch along this river in a large meadow adjoining it. About three o'clock in the afternoon, we departed in the same direction. Traveling through level land without any rock, we came to a small river which holds water all year long in pools. It is about a league and a half, [maybe] a little more, from the *Río Chama,* and it is covered with many varieties of flowers. We named it the *Río Señor San Joseph.* We stopped there for the night.

29 . . . We left the said place traveling in the same direction through flat, rockless land, until we came to a copious lake which had no exit. The water appeared murky and dense. It must be about half a league long surrounded by bald hills; it had no treeline, [and must be] about three *estados* deep. We named this place the *Laguna de San Pedro,* because it was his feast day. Along this way, are seen many meadows the principle one is called *El Coyote* by the Yutas; it has forty pools filled with water. We rested after lunch near the *Laguna.* From the previous campsite to this one is about six leagues. About two thirty o'clock in the

afternoon, we left in the same direction. We crossed over a small hill, with very little rock and no inconvenience, which is about the length of a musket shot. It has few rocks, and inconvenienced us little. Leaving the lake to our right, we traveled about three and a half leagues until we reached a small canyon which is about a league long, very narrow as the hills close in on it and not at all straight. It can be observed that this route leads to a spring which is very brackish and murky. The Yutas call it *la agua de el Berrendo*. Not far from there is another spring which is called *Tierra Amarilla*. In the said little canyon is a small river. We are told it has water year around. There is much pasturage here as well as sufficient firewood. More importantly for travelers to know is that upon descending into this little canyon there is a large outcropping of rock which is only a stone's throw long. Upon coming out of it, we camped for the night. We called it *Embudo* because it was so narrow.

30—On the 30th of the said month, we traveled in the same direction about five leagues until we reached the *Río de Navajo*. From the exit of the little canyon on this road can be seen a hill [that] is inconvenient because it is so long and somewhat steep in parts. Having ascended it, a trail through good land can then be taken. It has many natural depressions and a few hilly wrinkles in the area that are not inconvenient to go through. None of it is steep, but low lying, covered with much pine, small and scanty oak, and some good meadows with good pasturage; we rested there along the said river, and we collectively named it with much sentimentality *San Antonio de* [illegible]. From there we left along the same direction. And we traveled another five leagues until we stopped for the night along a much larger river than the previous one. [It was] of such large size and pleasant [ambiance], we named it *San Juan*. It has many meadows and is well provided with pasturage. The road runs to the brow of a hill which is somewhat steep. Up to the river, the road is along flat land without rock, although there is some broken rock along the way. [There is] one small hill that hardly measures a stone's throw. Similarly, one can see along the said road, two dry arroyos.

The 1st . . . July 1, we left the said river in the same direction as said previously, a little west by northwest. We traveled through a spring-filled canyon, following it along three others until we descended a very small hill which had little rock in it and from which flows a spring formed from many creeks. The Yutas call it *Lobo Amarillo*. There we stopped to rest for the afternoon. There must be from the said river to the spring five leagues. Afterwards we continued in the same direction, traveling about four leagues through good land until arriving at the river the Yutas call *Piedra Parada* where we camped for the night. There is much pasturage, good meadows, and sufficient water.

The 2nd . . . We left the said place meandering between west and west by northwest. We traveled more than six leagues through good land without rocks, although there were some broken rock [which of-fered] little inconvenience. We ascended and descended three small hills which had very little rock until we reached a small rincon. It is a place where the Yutas hunt. It has a very small stream with permanent water. We named it *San Xavier.* Before reaching the rincon, along this route can be seen three rivers; one very large and copious. It runs so high that it reached the withers or the breasts of our horses. And because of its at-tractiveness, its many flowers and the many groves of trees that grace it, we named it *Nuestra Señora de Guadalupe.* The second river which is be-tween the other two runs full. It runs from the *Río Chama.* The third one runs with so much water that it can fill an *acequia madre.* We camped for the night in the said rincon because our interpreter said that the next hill was too large with huge boulders. Given the heat of the day, our mules would quickly fatigue. Thus, it was better for them to travel the next day while they were fresh and they could climb it better; we, too, would find it advantageous.

On the 3rd . . . We began to climb the said ridge from a westerly di-rection without straying until we had finished descending it. The as-cents and descents were very severe and very narrow and steep. It is three leagues long, and so steep that it is nearly impossible to pass over with-out there being any more passage than a small trail so narrow that a single horse barely fits through. The hill is so enclosed with all kinds of trees that in some parts the trail is lost for the many small oak trees that abound. Reaching the bottom of the hill, we entered a canyon with soft soil and no rock. It is about three leagues long and exits into a large river which the Yutas call *Los Pinos.* It has many meadows, good pasturage and its waters reached the withers of our horses. We stopped for the night along the said river because our horses and mules arrived so fa-tigued from having climbed the steep and rocky ridge. . . . Near its banks we found the ancients ruins . . . which at one time must have been a pueblo. In it are many burnt adobes as if smelted. Having made the reconnaissance of it with great care, we found within the ruins of that pueblo a foundry in which they smelted metal ores. They appeared to be gold ores. We picked up some burnt adobes to show them to his lordship, the governor.

On the 4th . . . We left the said river in a westerly direction although bearing more to the northwest, and we traveled about four leagues through flat land without rock or undulations until we reached a large river. It was quite pleasant. The Yutas call it *Río Florida*. As we got to it, a very small hill came into view. The hill was somewhat inconvenient as it was very steep and covered with rocks. We stopped to rest that afternoon along the river. There, we saw similar signs of burnt adobes and metals, etc. that we had seen at the pueblo ruins at *Los Pinos*. Having surveyed it all, we left the said place in the same direction taken earlier. We went a little more than four leagues, arriving at a river so copious and big . . . that we called it the *Río de las Animas*. Along it, on the other side, we found the settlement of *Capitán Grande*, whom [his people] call *Coraque*. With him were three petty captains. They were *Joso, El Cabezón,* and *El Picado,* as they are called by them. Not having found a ford all day long, we did not cross until the next day.

On the 5th . . . We passed the entire day in crossing the said river as it had so much water which ran high and fast. So high was the water that it reached the cantle of our saddles. We set up camp between it and Coraque's settlement. After we had presented them with food, tobacco, corn, and pinole, Gregorio Sandoval began to talk about our reason for being there. They were well aware that the Yuta we sought, *Cuero de Lobo,* was not at that settlement. He was the one who had showed us the piece of silver or metal [he had found]. We were told that he had gone to a settlement of the Payuchis to visit his mother-in-law. They added that about five leagues down river was the settlement of the captain whose name meant *Caballo Rosillo*. Among them was an old Yuta woman who knew about other silver outcroppings. They suggested we should go see her instead of the Yuta *Cuero de Lobo*.

On the 6th . . . After we had discussed the new information among ourselves, all in agreement resolved that Gregorio de Sandoval, Antonio Martín, the interpreter, and I should go [to the Payuchi settlement]. Having finished our business, we went to see whether the said Yuta woman would give us new information about the Yuta we sought. When we got there, we presented her with gifts as we did with other Yutas. We communicated much more with her [than the others] and began the order of our business. Suddenly, she put on such a mean face that she had nothing over the devil. Seeing that we were getting nowhere with her, we returned to [the ranchería] of *Capitán Asigare* who demonstrated through signs his great friendship toward us Spaniards. His great certainty and swift action which he demonstrated was a favor, for he made sure that the other Yutas would not try to trick us into anything. In that way [he continued] until he pressured and made [the old Yuta woman] confess why she was in such a bad mood as shown by her grimace. She said because she had just come down from the *Sierra del Datil* bringing down red clay with others. She became abusive as she felt put upon. Given that, she could not go where they asked, [but] she would give them directions where it [the metal] was located. To which she responded with as good a facial expression that she could summon that we should go straight toward the *Moquinos de Albaro* through the upper part of a dry arroyo going north. Before the turn of the arroyo, we would see a house of a Navajo. At a short distance of two or three stone throws . . . [we would see] where the silver was covered [in the ground], and after little excavation, we would pull out ore like the ones the father of the said woman had taken to Abiquiú and sold to Joseph Manuel Trujillo Herrera whom it was said made two rosaries and a cross from it. Asked the whereabouts of the father of the said Yuta woman, she said that he had died as he was already too old.

On the 7th . . . With the information from the Yuta woman we decided to leave, but not before acknowledging the said capitán who had shown us kindness. We gave him a horse. We went to the said place, spending the entire day in getting there. As it was late, having covered about eighteen leagues, and having run our horses at a quick trot and gallop, we stopped with our jaded horses for the night along a stream two leagues back which was between two low lying hills, somewhat covered with pine trees. The river has water year around although slow moving around its bends. We named it *Agua Escondida.*

On the 8th . . . We continued the route, and after traveling a little way we came upon the Navajo hogan and the dry arroyo which were the signs that the Yuta woman had told us about. Leaving the route on the right side we entered up the arroyo to the part where the small turn begins which faces north. We climbed and moved from one to another part for about six leagues through forest and flat land. We surveyed different places trying to find the land the Yuta woman had told us about and as the Yuta *capitán* had shown us. So angry were we at the Yuta woman, that we returned where she was as thoughts to kill her for lying to us and costing us so much hardship crossed our minds. By the time we got to the settlement we had calmed down. At a fast trot and gallop, we encountered the [new] camp where our men were taking their siesta along one of the rivers which we had crossed before. We called it *Río de el Luzero.* It has ample water and many good meadowlands with abundant woods. There we rejoined our men after three days of absence without hardly anything to eat. We informed our men that our efforts had been without effect, and that it was more important to go find *Cuero de Lobo*. We resolved to ingratiate ourselves with the said *Capitán* [*Asigare*], giving him gifts once again so that he would guide us to the land of the Payuchi where we were told was the said Yuta [*Cuero de Lobo*]. The captain accepted and we undertook the trip. I took note of how long we had camped near *Coraque's* settlement which was along the *Río de las Animas* and the travel time from there to the *Río de el Luzero*. To that Andrés Sandoval responded that the men had been camped three days with knowledge that, as we had said, we were going to look for the silver [described by] the Yuta woman. As they were going to show us where it is, he tried to follow us and traveled two days to where we met. [He said that on] the first day they had departed from the *Río de los Pinos* heading directly west and traveled nine leagues reaching the foot of a hill that was not too big. Near it is a small river with year around water as the Yutas tell us where they camped for the night. On the said hill, we had left them a special sign of a large cross. At the foot of it we placed a rock which at a distance appeared to represent the figure of *Nuestra Señora de Guadalupe*. Thus, we named it the *Cuesta de la Divina Señora*. They did this part of their travel on the 9th [of July].

On the 10th . . . Which was the day we encountered our men at siesta, was the second day of the trip they had taken in following us. They had gone seven leagues and stopped to sleep along the *Río de la Agua Escondida*. Together they backtracked the two leagues from the *Río de el Luzero* to this one, following the said direction. The route with only two low-lying hills is along easy ground for our horses without any rock. It is so far that upon leaving the camp where we had been, even though we traveled fast, we did not meet until the next day. Hard as it was to believe, we would see as we began to fear that we could lose our horses and mules of the [main] camp. We sent Gregorio Sandoval, Antonio Martín, and Joseph Martín, trustworthy men, to go with the interpreter and Yuta guide ahead to the camp. . . .

On the 13th . . . The said men picked up the road at a fast trot and gallop. They traveled all day without reaching the spring until the next day in the morning. They had traveled part of the night before. The road appeared to them to run from the west. Although the said road runs through gentle country without rock, it does not have any pasturage and is very sandy, which tended to tire out the horses and mules. A short time after they left our said camp, they encountered a small canyon which had a spring with much water. It is about a league and a half. Near there, they surveyed a large pueblo that appears to be twice as large as the Villa de Santa Fe as its ancient structures show. It is in a large plain which stretches as far as the eye can see. They did not scout around to see if there were other ruins as they did not want to delay any longer and as the Yuta guide was rushing them.

On the 14th. . . . They came upon the spring in the canyon, after which they watered, foraged, and rested their horses. The spring is very small as the Yutas Payuchis had told them. They traveled along the same direction as the day before and they reached the river at sunset. On the other side of the river they could see about ten small settlements of unruly Payuchis. Upon seeing our men, one of them dove into the river to see who they were. Similarly, one of our men entered the river. He was received in the middle of the river and communicating through signs he persuaded the Payuchi to cross to our side and talk. Having met and talked with our Yuta guide and the interpreter, he returned to his people and told them that they were Spaniards. So interested were they to meet them, that they crossed where our men were and once peaceful overtures had been made, they announced it to the other side whereupon *Capitán Chino,* as he is called among the said Payuchis, crossed the river with others. Having formalized the peace in which they had confidence, *Capitán Chino* said that his people would gather with them that night and talk to them. He wanted them to trade and talk some more. This said, he took what gifts had been given him and returned to his people and told them what he had promised the Spaniards.

On the 15th. . . . In the morning the Yuta Payuchis appeared before the Spaniards and said they would go with them to meet and trade with the rest of us Spaniards. This our men did without hesitation, and they arrived where we were about the same time as there was no other better way there than the referenced one.

On the 16th . . . Our men, whom we quickly recognized, arrived accompanied by the Payuchis. They came to where we were, and shortly we met with them. Andrés Sandoval and I received *Capitán Chino* and his Payuchis in our camp and we gave them gifts of tobacco, pinole, flour, and corn; that is, whatever we had brought to win them over. That done, *Capitán Chino* ordered that we communicate. He began by asking about what we Spaniards were doing through such rough country. What was it we sought? To which we responded that we hoped to find a Yuta called *Cuero de Lobo* who was said to be living among the Payuchis. We also said that we wanted to know where was the largest river in the area called *Río del Tizón.* They responded by saying that it was true that

Cuero de Lobo had been among them; but he had returned to his land. He told us Spaniards not to be foolish, for the said river was too far and the way there was through rough waterless country with little pasturage. There, [he said] were many obstacles, and our horses would quickly fatigue, and we would get dizzy from the sun's heat which, on this route, is severe and insufferable. As we do not know the way, we will suffer many hardships or we would die from hunger if one of the many tribes which there are before we arrive at the said river did not kill us. We should return to our own land. If we still wanted to go, the best time would be when the leaves of the trees start to fall, this would be around October. Then, there would be pasturage and some water, and they would take us to the other tribes, of which there are seven or eight, could not harm us. Then, we could go along the entire river where we were presently which flows into the *Río del Tizón*. It would be possible to go through the said route in seven days among the tribes that are there. Before getting to the said river, there is the tribe of the *Orejas Agujeradas* who tell many lies about the *Coninas*, who are a very friendly people who spend all of their lives dressed in hides.

In the same way, the Payuchis, as did *Capitán Asigare*, say that there are among these tribes one that kills people solely with the smoke that they make without one being aware that they have done so. Once the smoke reaches the olfactory senses, the person dies quickly. More than that, on that route. . . . There is a great variety of animals. One in particular tears apart anyone who comes or goes through there who does not give him a pelt when they pass by. It is also said that on the other side of the river there is a large trench which is so broad that trade is made without crossing it. The people throw what they want to trade: bridles and knives which the Spaniards trade with the Yutas. These are passed from tribe to tribe to the *Río del Tizón*, and from that side to this the chamois [is exchanged].

The variety of languages is so great that there are some tribes that do not understand each other. The manner of crossing the river is on a vessel called a *jícara* which carries only two people. They sit back to back, with one facing where they have left, and the other where they are going. The river is so large that it cannot all be seen, only as far as the eye can see. On the other side are some bearded white men dressed in armor with metal hats. Even their women adorn both their arms with iron armlets called *brazaletes*. Their hair is styled with braids as do Spanish women. Among them is one they call *Castira*, which means *Castilla*. That is what is known about the said river.

On the 17th . . . Having acquired the foregoing information and considering for now, entering the *Río del Tizón* is difficult because of what the Payuchi have said and because some of our men had tried it, we decided to return to the search for *Cuero de Lobo*. We traded with the Payuchi as we seemed to be on quite friendly terms. Finishing our trade we took what little was left for our own use. We returned by the same route without discovering new lands as we were very low on supplies. We had brought only the precise amount to sustain us. We went to the said river, *Río de el Luzero,* to camp for the night, but we ended up walking all night to it.

We left the said river and went to the foot of the *Sierra de la Plata* called *La Grulla* where there is a river with abundant water. It originates there. We called it *Río de San Joaquín.* There we found about twenty Yuta camps. Among them was *Cuero de Lobo.* We gave gifts to everyone in a way that it would be possible to have enough. [Afterwards] we began to communicate. [*Cuero de Lobo*] said that if we gave him a horse for the next day, we would go to see the silver. We spent the rest of the day in conversation which we had with the Yutas about the referenced information without learning anything new.

19 . . . We got the horses ready. One of the Yutas named *Capitán Largo,* seeing that we prepared to leave, asked us for a horse so that he could accompany us. One was given to him. Then *Cuero de Lobo* said that not all of us should go, only Gregorio Sandoval, Joseph Martín, Miguel Abeita, Andrés Chama, the interpreter, and myself. That done, we traveled along the upper river through the water instead of the land route as both banks were formed by an escarpment which appeared eminent. We went about eight leagues until we arrived at a bend which the mountain makes. There is where the said river originates. On the mountain we found snow and a short piece of flat terrain. . . . There, we left the horses and we climbed to its summit where we saw a great variety of veins of various colors which are countless. It can be said without exaggeration that the entire mountain is made of pure metal. All around could be seen *pamino* which is red and yellow; in other parts there is caliche, small white pebbles, and large stone manifesting throughout great richness of metals. We particularly found some veins of black lead [*atescatetado*] and others of red lead. *Punta de ahuja* [needle point?] and other dark or whitish metals which look like quicksilver. In order to see better if various types of silver could be found as the Yutas had told us, we camped on that mountain for two days. We could not learn more because what the Yutas thought was silver was actually lead. Having re-

corded what could be learned about the said mountain, we found a hill which we named *Tumichi*. On it, we saw a ruined pueblo so large that it appeared to exceed the population of *Santa Cruz de la Cañada*. There, we saw many burnt metals with the same signs in the rocks of the pueblos we saw earlier on the route which we passed. We saw evidence of ancient towers, some of which still had parts of their walls.

On the 22 . . . Realizing we could not accomplish our objective, we descended the mountain carrying some loose metal ore as we did not have the proper equipment to dig for more other than a chisel for cutting silver.

On the 23 . . . We left the river where our main camp had been. We took seven days to return to the Villa de Santa Fe at the pace set by the burden-bearing mules as the road and its watering places, etc., are well known. We do not improperly claim everything to be true, for what we say can be reported anew by others. I signed it today, July 23, 1765 = Juan María Antonio Rivera =

Translation of Juan María Antonio Rivera's Second Diary, October 1765

Translated by Joseph P. Sánchez

[This is] the second diary which Juan María Antonio Rivera made on being sent again to find the *Río del Tizón* with Gregorio Sandoval, Antonio Martín, and the Interpreter Joaquín, *indio genízaro*, of the pueblo of Abiquiú. [*The Río del Tizón*] is reached from the *Río Nuestra Señora de los Dolores* which they followed on their first expedition.

The day we arrived at the river named *San Joaquín* which originates in the mountain where there is much metallic outcropping [which is] marvelous to the eye, we met two captains of the adjoining settlements who were *Asigare*, who guided us on our first expedition, and the other named *Cabezón* of the Mauchis nation. We gave them gifts in the best possible way so as to make it possible to converse with them about our desire for them to show us as friends to the other people and nations ahead so that we could trade with them without revealing our real purpose. After which they remained in agreement, and they offered us guides under the condition that we pay them. After this they went back [to their settlement] to sleep. Convening his people, *Capitán Cabezón* told them about our conversation. A [certain] Payuchi from *Asigare's* settlement attended that meeting, for a Payuchi had been proposed to accompany us. The Mauchis determined not to let us pass, saying that we were going to reconnoiter their lands and could ruin their trade. To which the Payuchi made a response, as they had not seen him when they considered whether to let us pass. Offering himself as a guide, he said he had no fear of what the Spaniards had twice said through interpreters. He quickly ran crosswise with a Mauchi as he defended the Spaniards despite being hit by him. *Asigare* arrived and announced that he would give the Spaniards guides although he was too ill to go; he did not support the immediate disturbance. The next day he sent the grandson of *Capitán Chino Payuchi* so that we could pay him. We did so gladly, ending the trouble between the two litigants, leaving them in peace and, likewise, others who could have been offended on either side. Shortly, we left following [the guide] to the *Río Nuestra Señora de los Dolores* where we slept.

The 6th . . . On October 6, 1765, we left the said river in a northwest direction, veering somewhat to the northeast and traveling a little more than 12 leagues. We did not find any good stopping places with water for our horses and mules until we reached some pools where *Capitán Chino Payuchi*, grandfather of our guide, awaited us. With him were five campsites, as many of his people were out hunting elk [venados alazanes] in the mountains. Having later given out our gifts, he thanked us, saying that we were good friends. As we had returned as promised, he bade us pass with his grandson whereever we wanted to go. Once there, we should ask for another guide as we were not far from the end of his land. Having said this, he departed. We called this place *Soledad* as the grey sky seemed so gloomy. [Nonetheless] we did admire in it the pools of good drinking water and other waters that were brackish. The route we followed went over the ridge of the mountain. It was not inconvenient nor rocky, but on descending into a canyon it has three steep, rocky inclines which are very small. It was not hard on the animals, for it was well provided with pasturage, firewood, and good shelter.

On the 7th . . . we traveled in the same direction about five leagues through good land, which in parts had beautiful valleys, with many basins and a small hill that were easily traveled with no delays. It is a stone's throw to the stream we reached. We named this permanent stream *San Francisco*. Near it were five Payuchi settlements which, when their people saw us, they sounded alarms and fled our intrusion. Others approaching the village also fled. Gregorio Sandoval, the interpreter, and our guide went out to bring back those who had responded to the alarms. We, that is, our guide and companions, attempted to talk to their guards and others who had fled to the mountain in fear and calm them by explaining in their language. After much persuasion, we were able to show we came in peace to trade with them. We accepted the suggestion to send messengers of their people [ahead] to announce that we were

Spaniards of Peace who came to trade with them. That way there would be less irritation among them. What was most useful at this place was that a Payuchi assured us that he would send his brother to guide us to the land where we wanted to go as he understood what we wanted. Here, our former guide resolved to return to his land, saying that he was thankful and that the Payuchi would guide us, suggesting that we adjust to him as he [our former guide] truly was leaving. Immediately, we brought him over and paid him what he wished. Having given him a horse, we bade him take care of it like no other.

On the 8th . . . the new guide took us toward the east about two leagues, ascending a very steep hill where we turned northward about three leagues. From there, we followed it northwest about a league and a half, reaching a stream which comes from on top a mountain with much water that can run along two lines. There, we stopped and took in the amenities of the beautiful valley and the various springs of water which run due west. There, I reflected on the short distance we had traveled that day and realized that from the crossing at the *Puerto de San Francisco* to this ridge the land is open with many valleys surrounded by mountainous terrain. From the ridge which runs from the mountain to this place, which we named *San Cristóbal,* there are four branching streams with much water which originate nearby. It is a land with much pasturage, streams, firewood, and shelter for our animals.

On the 9th . . . Our guide took us northwest about three leagues and leaving the road on the right side he guided us westward through a very pleasant canyon about a league and three quarters until reaching a very wide path that descended into other canyons, all very beautiful. From there, we followed the same direction through good land, without any rock like the previous area we had traveled for about four and a half leagues until we reached some small settlements of the Mauchi. There were three settlements. We asked them if there was water ahead. They said there was not much more than a small spring which was around the hill from where they stood. From there, it would take one day to reach the Tabehuachi nation. On the way, there is a very full river in which one cannot stand, for its canyon-like banks are too steep and narrow. There is no meadow there for one to walk on or to make camp until one ascends the hill away from the said canyon. Thanking them, we decided to stay there and camp rather than suffer ahead. Our camp was in a wide valley blessed with pasturage, firewood, and some water. We named it *San Estéban.*

On the 10th . . . We went west about three leagues through level terrain without any rock. It had some small oak along the route to a small, but very rugged, canyon which we entered. It had much rock in it. Getting on a trail which was so narrow that a horse barely fit on it, as from its trailhead to the end was three musket shots long. It cost us much work to get through it, having to lift much of our cargo which was made more difficult by the cold and furious winds from the north that blew through there. It was so strong that the horses and mules balked at it; we had to turn their heads away from the wind. The wind blew for more than a half hour. Had it been longer, we might have frozen to death. Descending the ridge, we looked for a place to get out through another canyon which was between two mountains, but it turned out impossible, for the only way out was the canyon or channel through which ran the river. This was so difficult that the only way out was to stay in the river which reached the breasts of the horses. It was that way until we ascended the next ridge of the mountain on the other side which was also steep and narrow like the previous one. In one, we had to remove the cargo off the animals to get through; on the other, we had to wend our way by pulling the animals through (some by the ears), and in another by their tails. Having ascended the ridge, we could see a very pleasant valley as far as the eye could see. In one of the mountainous parts, we met a Tabehuachi hunter who told us we were close to his people who were celebrating, as they had recently taken horses from the Comanche in battle a few days ago. Traveling three leagues, we descended a canyon which is three to four leagues long. At the end of it we came upon the settlement of *Capitán Tonampechi*, which in their language means *Flor de Capulín*. The place is called *Passochi*, as it is said three little boys of their tribe burned to death there. Some of the Tabehuachis came out happily to receive us. They showed us a good camping spot near their settlement. They gladly gave us rations of elk meat. Such elk are hunted frequently in that mountain. We responded in kind, sharing our provisions. The captain and his people decided not to hold their dances that night so that they could gather where we, the Spanish, were to talk about where we were going. Although they already knew it, having been told by the Tabehuachi who had been with us all day, and who, apparently, had been at the Pueblo of Abiquiú with our governor. He was glad to see us and spent the entire day in our company.

At night fall, the gentiles gathered with their captain and formed a circle to converse with us. They handed us much tobacco to smoke as well as food as a sign of true peace among us. They told us that Spaniards had never passed through the country where we were going, and the people would be agitated. They asked us not to cross where we planned, for the people on the other side would cause us harm. The captain told us to beware those who called themselves friends. They already knew that we were going to the big river to see where there might be other Spaniards. There was such great risk that one of his warriors who had been with our captain had not told us directly that they did not know the way to the part we wanted to go. But up from there toward the north, on this side [of the river] there was much risk from the Comanches from whom they had recently gotten their horses which they were celebrating with their dances. Thus, it was better for us to go back [whence we came]. To which we responded that we understood that these were nothing more than pretenses not to let us go there. We understood that the captain had so dictated. The young warrior knew full well, and although we might be killed, we still wanted to go forward. The warrior, who knew the land and the way, should tell us. They responded by saying that the warrior was there, but it was true he was confused exactly through where he had said [it was]. If we were friends, and they were very contented, we would pay the said warrior, and he would guide us to the *Río Grande del Tizón* toward the north where many go to trade with the people of the other side. [Otherwise] for them, it was difficult to obey our captain, their friend. As a test of friendship, they implored us to stay with them three days during which time they wanted to celebrate and trade with us. As we were good friends, they were pleased. Considering the safety in which we found ourselves in this land, and the secure disposition which we found for our horse and mule herds, which were safe there in their land and, as we did not wish to make them unhappy, we accepted their invitation. [But to the point], we did not like wasting two days in the same place participating in their style of trade, which we thought badly done, for our maintenance on food and tobacco was not useful. On the third day they gave us a celebration with a dance which began at sunrise, wasting in it much food. Likewise, we reciprocated with a good meal that left them very pleased. That night they drew us a plan of the *Río del Tizón* showing us the many watering places everywhere on the west side. All the while they kept saying about the impossibility of going with us to that part as there was no one in their entire nation who knew the way.

Upon ending his contract to guide us, our Payuchi guide, the brother of *Asigare,* left, and we had to contract a young Tabehuachi warrior. To assure he would do it, we entertained him and others that night so that his people could not dissuade him even though they insisted that we not pass foreward.

On the 14 . . . we quickly presented the said Tabehuachi with a horse and left on a northwest direction traveling a little more than two leagues. Our guide stopped and told us to get off the path because it would cost us more time and fatigue our horses and mules as there was too much rock, little pasturage, and almost no water along it. By crossing the mountain it was closer and there was little rock through there. He said we would travel along a stream just as they did whenever they went to the river. We trusted his judgement, and we traveled on the ridge of the mountain about fourteen leagues showing us that what he had said was certain. We continued going to the said stream which is in the most conspicuous place, but it had such little water that it lasted for only half of our herd; it also had little pasturage, poor shelter, but much firewood. That night occurred such a furious storm of wind and rain that given what had gone on before, we named this place *Purgatorio*.

On the 15th . . . we left this camp in a northward direction and we traveled about five leagues off the trail until we slowly climbed a very high hill. A little after climbing it, we followed a trail that took us to an area filled with small cactus plants that stretched for three leagues with such great abundance that the horses and mules could not go through it except over a trail until we descended to a very unappealing valley with no pasturage, and no shelter where we could take a siesta. But for that which happened that day, I agreed with the guide in determining to go to the stream that was in a canyon which turned out to be a small river that ran from a mountain. We traveled to it, a little more than 10 leagues. After the horses and mules had been watered, our guide told us that we would climb to the top of a hill which was on the other side of the small river and we would see the *Río Grande del Tizón* which we sought. There, we would have much pasturage and firewood, and we should go there because it was close by, a little more than league and a half and there on its bank in a beautiful meadow, we slept.

On the 16th . . . our guide resolved to send two boys who had accompanied him to call the people down from the other side so that they could trade with the Spaniards who were waiting in peace, which was done. Gregorio Sandoval and I went with them to scout out the river. We crossed the only ford it has, the high water reached the cantles of saddles on the horses. Upon getting out of the river, the water washed over their shoulders. The width of the ford is 60 to 70 varas, the rest of the river is very boxed with steep banks. Where it is very enclosed, the water is two to three estados deep. To the east, nine small rivers flow into it up river. When it floods, it fills the entire meadow which is more than a league. It reaches the bottom of a hill where it leaves debris. Upon our return, we communicated with our guide, telling him that this was not the *Río del Tizón* which we sought and that he had misled us. To that, he responded sadly that there was no other major river in the area than that one. He would never had brought us here had he not heard the people down [at the ranchería] say that the high river was not crossable for it was so wide and now reached the meadow and [where] all the large rivers we had crossed join it. We met some people who were coming to trade. We asked them [about the river], and we now felt certain [that it was the river]: here was the crossing to go to the Spaniards on the other side who were five or six *jornadas* or days march. It could be done at great risk owing to raiding tribes in the area. A short distance away after crossing the river, about one days' march, was a certain kind of people of whom it was said that because of the poor hunting there, they ate their children. Another day beyond, we would meet other people, very white with hair the color of straw. They are considered to be enemies of all the tribes in the area. It would take two days to cross their land, but we should do so only at night. After that, we should reach the foot of a small mountain where there is a bountiful lake which is inhabited by people who are like rocks. From there, a route toward the skirt of a mountain takes one to the Spaniards. They live on the banks of a small river with plenty of water. These are the first people one reaches who have houses like ours. They are Spaniards, we are told, because they speak just like us, they are very fair, with heavy beards, and they dress in buckskin, for they do not have clothes like us in our land.

We told him that if he should take us there, we would give him more than we had paid and given him. To that, he and another older Tabehuachi, who claimed to be his father, responded that we were too few in number to go there. Upon reaching a ruddy-colored people, they would take each of us by the hand in peace, and we would never again be seen or ever return to our land. They would kill our guides for having taken us there. As captain, I should go back and bring more people, only that way would it be possible to enter that land.

On the 17th . . . five young Indian messengers came saying that they were Sabuaganas and that there were no other people through that area because all of them were scattered throughout the mountains hunting. It was not possible to gather them or even send them messages as they did not know where they were. With that, we attempted to thank them and communicate with them as our guide and his father were asleep near the river. We asked them about what had occurred with our guide in relation to the river as expressed above. They confirmed the same, and we were then persuaded that it was the river we sought, although we did not feel we were at the right part of it. They added that their leader was *Capitán Cuchara* and reported that the Spaniards had been killed in a battle. Out of fear they had stayed back because they thought we were angry because they too had killed Spaniards. With that, the talking stopped. The next day, we stayed long enough to trade with them.

On the 18th . . . We traded with the said Yutas. While there, three Sabuaganas arrived saying that their captain had called us over to talk. He wanted to know why we had not gone to his land as there was a path in that direction. He said that the captain of the Spaniards was his great friend, and he sought our friendship. We asked them to our camp and gave them presents. We stayed until the 20th of the month giving our horses and mules time to rest and recover as they were very jaded and their hooves were in need of being pared. That being the case, we were not able to decide whether to go on, even if we could, given our condition and provisions.

On the 20th . . . We turned around along with our Sabuagana guides. Ascending to the east [at first], we descended toward the south through a pleasant land with large valleys which had neither pasturage nor firewood except some cactus plants and what appeared to be traces of *panino mineral*. The rest of the land was similar to those surrounding it. We traveled twelve leagues until we reached a very beautiful large spring. We slept there.

On the 21st . . . we left the spring for the banks of *Río de los Sabuaganas*. Continuing in the same said direction toward the upper [river], we arrived at their settlement about noon. Talking to their captain, he told us that he was too ill to take us to see the *cuchillo*, as they call silver. He assured us that as soon as he felt better, he would do so. When they went to trade, they would guide us there. But if we wanted to go, we would do so at great risk as the Comanches had presently caused them much harm. [He asked] Why did we want to go to the large river through that lower portion where it is said were Spaniards? That was the one they called the *Río del Tizón* where there was much deer. And, there was every risk on the way to see the Spaniards that the other people had told us about. Having said that, he ordered his people to come and trade with us Spaniards, their friends, as the next day they would return to their homes. That done and concluded, we decided to return [to New Mexico].

In the meadow of the Great *Río del Tizón*, on a white poplar, I carved a large cross with the words 'Long Live Jesus' at the top and my name.

At the foot of the tree, I carved the year so that it could be verified at a future time that we had gotten that far. The same certainty is contained in the above account which I signed on November 20, 1765. Juan María Antonio Rivera.

The return trip took fourteen and a half days by the most direct route with regular marches. It is estimated that the distance from the Villa de Santa Fe to the *Río del Tizón* is one hundred fifty leagues. I judge that it is the Colorado River that empties into the Gulf of California.

Notes

1. For an explanation of the possible location of the Coronado campsite see Stanley M. Hordes, "A Sixteenth-century Spanish Campsite in the Tiguex Province: A Historian's Perspective," 155–64; and Bradley J. Vierra, "A Sixteenth-century Spanish Campsite in the Tiguex Province: An Archaeologist's Perspective," 165–74, in Bradley J. Vierra, general editor, *Current Research on the Late Prehistory and Early History of New Mexico* (Albuquerque: New Mexico Archaeological Council, 1992).

2. Fascination with Teguayo continued beyond the Spanish colonial period. In the late nineteenth century scholars such as Cesáro Fernandez Duro, John Gilmary Shea, Adolph F. Bandelier, and Oscar W. Collet renewed the search for mythical Teguayo by sifting through historical documents, maps, and archaeological reports. See Ernest J. Burrus, S.J., "Quivira and Teguayo in the Correspondence of Bandelier and Shea with Collet 1882–1889," *Manuscripta*, vol. XI, no. 2 (July 1967): 67–83. Regarding the relationship of Teguayo to the Great Salt Lake, Burrus writes, "Teguayo, just as unstable cartographically as Quivira, had been variously identified with Salt Lake, Utah, and the regions from which the Pueblo Indians originally came," 69.

3. [Alonso de] Posada, Dictamen del Padre Posade, Año de 1686, Colección Muñoz, Real Academia de la Historia, (hereinafter cited as RAH), Madrid. Also see Alfred Barnaby Thomas, *After Coronado: Spanish Exploration Northeast of New Mexico, 1696–1727* (Norman: University of Oklahoma Press, 1935), 9.

4. Posada, Dictamen.

5. Alicia Ronstadt Milich, trans., *Relaciones by Zarate Salmeron* (Albuquerque: Horn & Wallace Publishers, Inc., 1966), 62.

6. Ibid., 91.

7. Posada, Dictamen.

8. Alfred Barnaby Thomas, *Alonso de Posada Report, 1686: A Description of the Area of the Present Southern United States in the Seventeenth Century* (Pensacola: Perdido Bay Press, 1982), 43. Also see footnote 147, p. 43, in which Thomas explains that the word "astrologist" is derived from "astronomis," which appears in other copyists' versions of Posada's report.

9. Ibid., 42.

10. Ibid.

11. Ibid., 45, item 44.

12. Alfred Barnaby Thomas, trans. and ed., *After Coronado: Spanish Explo-*

ration Northeast of New Mexico, 1696–1727 (Norman: University of Oklahoma Press, 1935), 1.

13. Posada, Dictamen, 6-3-1. See also Thomas, *Posada Report,* 44.

14. Diario del descubrimiento que hicieron los R.R. Padres Eusebio Francisco Kino, Marcos Antonio Kappus, Jesuitas, y el Alférez Juan Mateo Mange Teniente de Alcalde Mayor y Capitán a Guerra de la Nación Pima, azia el Poniente y Nación Soba y brazo del Mar de California desde 7 hasta 23 de Febrero de este año de 1694, Capitulo 11, del Principio de la Cristianidad de esta Pimería, Progresos y Contradicciones que ha tenido, y estado que al presente tiene, Colección Muñoz, RAH, 9/4873.

15. Ernest J. Burrus, S.J. *Kino and Manje, Explorers of Sonora and Arizona, Their Vision of the Future: A Study of their Expeditions and Plans* (Rome: Jesuit Historical Institute, 1971), 706.

16. Pedro de Rivera, *Diario y derrotero de lo caminando visto, y observando en el discurso de la visita general de presidios situados en las Provincias Internas de Nueva España que de orden de su Magestad executó D. Pedro de Rivera, Brigadier de los Reales Ejércitos, 1736,* Archivo General de la Nación (hereinafter AGN), Sección Historia, tomo 395, pt. 6, folio 1, no 161. Rivera pointed out that the Utes were among the enemy tribes that threatened New Mexico. His reference to Moctezuma and Teguayo is found in numero 241 of the *Diario.*

17. Malcolm Ebright, *Land Grants and Lawsuits in Northern New Mexico* (Albuquerque: University of New Mexico, 1994), 26.

18. Carta del Padre Fr. Carlos Delgado al Reverendo Padre Comisario General, Fr. Pedro Navarrete, Misión de la Isleta, 18 de junio de 1744, Colección Muñoz, RAH, Madrid.

19. See S. Lyman Tyler, "The Myth of the Lake of Copala and Land of Teguayo," *Utah Historical Quarterly* 20 (October 1952): 326–27. The original document is in Archivo General de la Nación, Historia, Mexico City, T. 25.

20. Ibid., 329. Original letter in AGN. Historia, T. 4.

21. *The Domínguez-Escalante Journal: Their Expedition through Colorado, Utah, Arizona, and New Mexico in 1776,* Fray Angelico Chávez, trans., and Ted J. Warner, ed. (Provo: Brigham Young University Press, 1977), 60. Escalante wrote: "The Timpanogotzis are so named after the lake where they reside, which they call Timpanogo, and this name is the proper one for this lake since the name or word by which they designate any lake is *pagariri,*" 61. The journal has been reprinted with a Foreword by Robert Himmerich y Valencia by the University of Utah Press in 1995.

22. *Domínguez-Escalante Journal,* 58–59.

23. The Spaniards were at present Provo, Utah, where they saw the Spanish Fork River, Hobble Creek or Dry Creek, the Provo River, and the American Fork River. They learned about the Jordan River which connects Utah Lake with the Great Salt Lake, which they referred to as "the other lake," forty miles away.

24. Dominguez-Escalante Journal, 59–60.

25. Ibid.

26. Ibid., 61.

27. Ibid., 60.

28. See Cyclone Covey, trans., *Cabeza de Vaca's Adventures in the Unknown Interior of America* (Albuquerque: University of New Mexico Press, 1961); Cleve Hallenbeck, *Alvar Nuñez Cabeza de Vaca: The Journey of the First European to Cross the Continent of North America, 1534–1536* (Glendale: Arthur H. Clark, 1940); George P. Hammond and Agapito Rey, *The Rediscovery of New Mexico, 1580–1594* (Albuquerque: University of New Mexico Press, 1966).

29. See George P. Hammond and Agapito Rey, *Narratives of the Coronado Expedition, 1540–42* (Albuquerque, University of New Mexico Press, 1940); Peter P. Forrestal, trans., and Cyprian J. Lynch, ed., *Benavides' Memorial of 1630 by Alonso de Benavides* (Washington, D.C.: Academy of American Franciscan History, 1954). See also Frederick Webb Hodge, George P. Hammond, and Agapito Rey, *Fray Alonso de Benavides' Revised Memorial of 1634* (Albuquerque: University of New Mexico Press, 1945).

30. Joseph P. Sánchez, "Twelve Days in August: The Pueblo Revolt in Santa Fe," in David Grant Noble, ed., *Santa Fe: History of an Ancient City* (Santa Fe: School of American Research Press, 1989), 40–44.

31. See Joseph P. Sánchez, *The Río Abajo Frontier, 1540–1692: A History of Early New Mexico.* (Albuquerque: Albuquerque Museum History Monograph Series, 1987; revised second edition, 1996).

32. Patente de Custos Zavaleta, Santa Fe, 2 July 1700, Archives of the Archdiocese of Santa Fe (hereinafter cited as AASF), Santa Fe, New Mexico, General List of Patentes, Patentes 1.

33. Marc Simmons, *Spanish Government in New Mexico* (Albuquerque: University of New Mexico Press, 1968), 185.

34. Francisco Cuervo y Valdés, *Bando,* Santa Fe, 5 August 1705, Spanish Archives of New Mexico, Santa Fe Archives (hereinafter cited as SANM), no. 118.

35. Juan Ignacio Flores Mogollon, *Bando,* Santa Fe, 16 December 1712, SANM no. 185. For similar *bandos* issued by other Spanish officials, see Alcalde Mayor of Taos, *Bando,* 9 September 1725, SANM no. 339; and Juan Domingo Bustamante, *Bando,* Santa Fe, 17 September 1725, SANM no. 340.

36. Patente de Custos Zavaleta, Santa Fe, 2 July 1799, AASF, General List of Patentes, Patentes 1.

37. For a detailed treatment of the period 1751–1778 see Alfred B. Thomas, *The Plains Indians and New Mexico 1751–1778* (Albuquerque: University of New Mexico Press, 1940).

38. Governor Tomás Vélez Cachupín to Viceroy conde de Revillagigedo, Santa Fe, 29 September 1752, in Thomas, *The Plains Indians,* 123.

39. Thomas, *The Plains Indians,* 32.

40. Elizabeth A.H. John, *Storms Brewed in Other Men's Worlds* (College Station: Texas A & M Press, 1975), 327.

41. See Francisco Marín del Valle, *Bando*, 26 November 1754, SANM, no. 530; Hubert H. Bancroft, *Arizona and New Mexico, 1530–1888* (San Francisco: The History Company Publishers 1889); Eleanor B. Adams, ed., *Bishop Tamaron's Visitation to New Mexico, 1760* (Albuquerque: Historical Society of New Mexico, 1954), 103; Thomas, *The Plains Indians, 33–34;* and Oakah L. Jones, Jr., *Pueblo Warriors & Spanish Conquest* (Norman: University of Oklahoma Press, 1966), 136.

42. Proceso contra Juan Baldes, *genízaro*, May 1762, SANM no. 548.

43. Jones, *Pueblo Warriors*, 139, 144.

44. Incomplete and untitled copy of Juan María Antonio Rivera's original diary of his first expedition, 23 July 1765, in Diarios de reconocimientos de una parte de la América septentrional española, 176, Archivo del Servicio Histórico Militar, Madrid, (hereinafter cited as ASHM). The diary was signed by Rivera on 23 July 1765. The diary is considered incomplete because the first page, at least, is missing. An English translation of the text of Rivera's first diary is found in Appendix A of this volume.

45. Donald C. Cutter, "Prelude to a Pageant in the Wilderness," *Western Historical Quarterly* (hereinafter cited as *WHQ*) 8 (January 1977): 14. An interpretation of the above-cited Rivera journals found in the Servicio Histórico Militar in Madrid (see footnote 44) is offered by Cutter in his article. Cutter believed at the time of the publication of his essay that identification of these journals was hampered by the fact that the cover page is missing. However, the incomplete and untitled copy of the first diary was signed by Juan María Antonio Rivera on 23 July 1765, as was the complete second diary dated 20 November 1765.

46. Incomplete and untitled diary by Rivera, 23 July 1765, ASHM. Also see Cutter, "Prelude," 7.

47. Ibid., 27 June 1765.

48. Ibid., 28 June 1765.

49. Ibid., 29 June 1765.

50. Ibid., 30 June 1765.

51. Ibid., 1 July 1765. In 1776 Domínguez and Escalante, using some of Rivera's men as guides, passed through this same territory. See *Domínguez-Escalante Journal*, 10.

52. Cutter, "Prelude," 8.

53. Rivera, Diary, 4 July 1765.

54. *Domínguez-Escalante Journal*, 11.

55. Rivera, Diary, 5 July 1765. Also see Cutter, "Prelude," 8.

56. Ibid., 6 July 1765.

57. Ibid., 8 July 1765.

58. Ibid., 16 July 1765.

59. Ibid.

60. Ibid., 16 July 1765.

61. Ibid.

62. Ibid., 17–18 July 1765.

63. Ibid., 19–22 July 1765.

64. *Domínguez-Escalante Journal*, 10.

65. Cutter, "Prelude," 9.

66. Ynstrucción que deverán observar, Juan María Rivera, Antonio Martín, y Gregorio Sandoval, con el Ynterprete Joachín, indio genízaro de el Pueblo de Abiquiú con la comissión que por su práctica se les carga in Diarios de reconocimientos de una parte de la América septentrional española, 1766, ASHM.

67. Ibid.

68. Rivera, Second Diary, 20 November 1765, ASHM.

69. Ibid.

70. Ibid.

71. Ibid., 6 October 1765.

72. Ibid., 7 October 1765. ASHM.

73. Ibid., 9 October 1765.

74. Ibid., 10 October 1765.

75. Ibid.

76. Ibid.

77. Ibid.

78. Ibid., 14 October 1765.

79. Ibid., 15 October 1765.

80. A standard vara is approximately 32.5 inches long.

81. Rivera, Second Diary, 16 October 1765.

82. Ibid.

83. Oddly, the Ute word "Timpanogos" has been defined as "the stone person," in reference to the figure of a reclining human being formed by the ridges of Mount Timpanogos. See *Domínguez-Escalante Journal*, 27, fn. 133.

84. Rivera, Second Diary, 16 October 1765.

85. Ibid.

86. Ibid., 17 October 1765.

87. Ibid., 21 October 1765.

88. Ibid., 20 November 1765.

89. Elliott Coues, translator and editor, *On the Trail of a Spanish Pioneer: The Diary and Itinerary of Francisco Garcés (Missionary Priest) in His Travels through Sonora, Arizona, and California, 1775–1776*, 2 vols. (New York: Francis P. Harper, 1900), 1:474. Coues comments about Garcés's apt remark that the Chidumas were a Yuman tribe "variously called Alchedomas, Halchedomas, Jalchedomas, Jalchedums, etc." 1:474, note 23.

90. *The Domínguez-Escalante Journal*, 26.

91. Cutter, "Prelude," 14.

92. Joseph P. Sánchez, *Spanish Bluecoats: The Catalonian Volunteers in Northwestern New Spain, 1767–1810* (Albuquerque: University of New Mexico Press, 1990), 8–9.

93. Ibid., 9.

94. Ibid., 53.

95. Ibid., 56.

96. Herbert E. Bolton, "In the South San Joaquín Ahead of Garcés," *California Historical Society Quarterly* 10 (September 1931): 214.

97. See Herbert I. Priestly, ed., *A Historical, Political and Natural Description of California by Pedro Fages, Soldier of Spain* (Berkeley: University of California Press, 1937).

98. Maynard Geiger, O.F.M., *Franciscan Missionaries in Hispanic California, 1769–1848* (San Marino: The Huntington Library, 1969), 93.

99. Ibid., 93.

100. Ibid., 94.

101. Herbert E. Bolton, *Outpost of Empire: The Story of the Founding of San Francisco* (New York: Alfred A. Knopf, 1931), 103.

102. Coues, *On the Trail of a Spanish Pioneer,* 1:44.

103. Bolton, *Outpost of Empire,* 103.

104. Ibid., 106.

105. Ibid., 107.

106. Coues, *On the Trail of a Spanish Pioneer* 2:469.

107. Ibid., 475–76.

108. Ibid., 1:268. Coues explains Garcés's roundabout route by writing: "This is a long lap, chiefly northward, with but little to guide us on the trail. But it appears probable, as well as I can gather from the scant indications, that the Santa Clara river was crossed at or near Castac, a place at the mouth of the creek of the same name; up which creek Garcés went as far as its first fork, there taking the right-hand branch, to be found on modern maps by the name of Cañada de la Laguna, and following this up over the Libra mts. There is no question that this range is the 'great sierra' he makes to-day; the course here noted is quite right for Garcés's 'north,' with due allowance for magnetic variation E.; and the laguna he finds to-morrow, half a league from to-night's camp, may not impossibly be the very one which gives name to the Cañada de la Laguna." Ibid., note 8.

109. Ibid., 278.

110. Ibid., 284.

111. Ibid., 1:288, note 25.

112. Ibid., 1:288.

113. Ibid., 1:291. Coues states that the Sierra de San Marcos extended to include the Sierra Nevada "as far as he [Garcés] knew it, on the east side of the whole Tulare and San Joaquin valleys," 1:291, note 31.

114. Ibid., 1:299.

115. Ibid., 1:307.

116. Ibid., 2:313.

117. Ibid., 2:313–335 *passim*.

118. Ibid., 2:336–339. Coues states that "the Cataract cañon system is of great extent; its ramifications, fissuring the great Colorado plateau in every direction and as it were dissecting the surface of the earth, may be traced to the vicinity of Bill Williams' mountain and Mt. Sitgreaves. The general trend of the system is northwest, but the collateral fissures run in every direction. This is an effectual barrier to travel east and west, almost to the head of the system. . . . The bed of the main cañon sometimes runs water from near its head downward; but it is ordinarily dry almost down to the Havasupai settlement," 2:340–41, note 21.

119. Ibid., 2:347.

120. Ibid., 2:348, note 29. In 1540, members of the expedition of Francisco Vázquez de Coronado were the first Europeans to see the Grand Canyon after marching from their base camp at Zuni Pueblo.

121. Ibid., 2:347.

122. Ibid., 2:354. Coues believes that Garcés "struck the Little Colorado in the vicinity of Moencopie Wash," 2:356, note 37.

123. Ibid., 2:356–57.

124. Eleanor B. Adams and Fray Angelico Chavez, trans. and eds., *The Missions of New Mexico, 1776: A Description by Fray Francisco Atanasio Domínguez with Other Contemporary Documents* (Albuquerque: University of New Mexico Press, 1956), 281–86. Also, Escalante refers to the report in his journal entry of 24 August 1776; see *Dominguez-Escalante Journal*, 22.

125. LeRoy R. Hafen and Ann W. Hafen, *Old Spanish Trail, Santa Fé to Los Angeles: With extracts from contemporary records and including diaries of Antonio Armijo and Orville Pratt* (Glendale: Arthur H. Clark Company, 1954), 79.

126. Geiger, *Franciscan Missionaries*, 94.

127. Sánchez, *Spanish Bluecoats*, 58–59.

128. Ibid., 110.

129. Herbert I. Priestley, *Franciscan Explorations in California.* Edited by Lillian Estelle Fisher. (Glendale: Arthur H. Clark Company, 1946), 77.

130. Ibid., 89–90.

131. Ibid., 91–92.

132. For a complete listing of all participants in the expedition, some of whom joined Domínguez and Escalante while the exploration of the Yuta country was in progress, see Ted J. Warner, ed., and Fray Angelico Chávez, trans., with a Foreword by Robert Himmerich y Valencia, *The Domínguez-Escalante Journal: Their Expedition through Colorado, Utah, Arizona, and New Mexico in 1776* (Salt Lake City: University of Utah Press, 1995), vii–viii.

133. The letter, dated at San Phelipe El Real de Chiguagua, 26 October

1777, is reprinted in Herbert E. Bolton, *Pageant in the Wilderness* (Salt Lake City: Utah State Historical Society, 1950), 243–50.

134. Herbert S. Auerbach, "Escalante's Letters to Fray Fernando Antonio Gómez, Custodian of the College of Queretaro, and to the Governor of the Province," *Utah Historical Quarterly* (hereinafter cited as *UHQ*) 2 (January, April, July, October 1943): 15.

135. "Brief of a letter from Fray Silvestre Velez de Escalante, written at the Mission of Nuestra Señora de Guadalupe de Zuni on April 30, 1776, addressed to Fray Isidro Murillo, Provincial Minister," in Auerbach, "Escalante's First Visit to the Moquis," *UHQ*, 2:12.

136. Auerbach, "Escalante's Letters," 15–16.

137. Ibid., 16–17.

138. Ibid., 17.

139. Ibid., 19.

140. Ibid., 22.

141. Ibid., 23, fn. 11.

142. *Domínguez-Escalante Journal*, xv.

143. Eleanor B. Adams, "Fray Francisco Atanasio Domínguez and Fray Silvestre Vélez de Escalante," *UHQ* 44 (Winter 1976): 53.

144. Adams and Chavez, *Missions of New Mexico*, xiv–xv.

145. Ibid., xv.

146. Libro de Bautizados, Parroquia Santa María de Treceño, Año 1736 al 1781, Archivo Diocesano, Santander, Spain.

147. Adams and Chavez, *The Missions of New Mexico*, xiv.

148. *Domínguez-Escalante Journal*, 4–6. For a synthesis of certain place-names associated with the Domínguez-Escalante expedition see Joseph J. Hill, "Spanish and Mexican Exploration and Trade Northwest from New Mexico into the Great Basin," *UHQ* 3 (January 1930): 3–26.

149. *Dominguez-Escalante Journal*, 8.

150. Bolton, *Pageant in the Wilderness*, following p. 128, lists all of the astronomical observations made by the expedition as follows:

5 August	Nuestra Señora de las Nieves	37° 51'
13 August	Dolores	38° 13 ½'
19 August	Cajón del Yeso	39° 6'
28 August	Santa Monica	39° 13' 22"
5 September	San Rafael	41° 4'
6 September	Roan Creek	41° 6' 53"
14 September	La Vega de Santa Cruz	41° 19'
14 September	La Vega de Santa Cruz	41° 59' 24"
14 September	La Vega de Santa Cruz	41° 19'
29 September	Santa Ysabel	39° 4'
2 October	Llano Salado	39° 34' 35"
8 October	Santa Brígida	38° 3' 30"

11 October	Valle de Señor San José	37° 33'
15 October	San Dónulo	36° 52' 30"
20 October	Santa Gertrudis	36° 30'
7 November	La Purísima Concepción	35° 55'

It should be noted that the bearings taken by the expedition are not accurate and where noted in this study, the correct readings are given in the appropriate footnotes herein as calculated by Fray Angelico Chávez and Ted Warner in their edition of *The Domínguez-Escalante Journal*.

151. *Domínguez-Escalante Journal*, 9.

152. Ibid., 10.

153. Ibid., 11. Also see footnote 53 in which Warner speculates that the expedition was "probably somewhat south of Colorado State Highway 172 toward Farmington Hill, which they descended to the Animas River and crossed it."

154. Ibid., 12.

155. Ibid., 13.

156. Ibid., 14. In footnote 69, Warner comments that their calculations were too high, correcting them to 37°. In footnote 70, he notes that the Anasazi site known as "The Escalante Ruin" may or may not be the one mentioned in the journal.

157. Ibid., 16.

158. Ibid., 18–19. See footnote 93 in which Warner notes that they were perhaps closer to 37° 30'.

159. Ibid., 21.

160. Ibid., 24.

161. Ibid., 26, fn. 127.

162. Ibid., 26.

163. Ibid., 27, fn. 133.

164. Ibid., 27, fn. 135, Warner notes that it was closer to 38° 45'.

165. Ibid., 29, fn. 141.

166. Ibid., 29.

167. Ibid., 32–33.

168. Ibid., 33

169. Ibid., 34, fn. 154.

170. Ibid., 35, fns. 157, 159.

171. Ibid., 37, fns. 164, 165.

172. Ibid., 38–39.

173. Ibid., 40–41.

174. Ibid., 42, fn. 187.

175. Ibid., 43, fn. 190.

176. Ibid., 43.

177. Thomas, *Posada Report*, 42.

178. *Domínguez-Escalante Journal*, 46.

179. Ibid., 46, fn. 202.

180. Ibid., 47.
181. Ibid., 48.
182. Ibid., 49.
183. Ibid., 50.
184. Ibid., 51.
185. Ibid., 52.
186. Ibid., 53.
187. Ibid., 53.
188. Ibid., 54–55.
189. Ibid., 55.
190. The Domínguez-Escalante expedition's descriptions of Timpanogos are cited in Chapter 1.
191. *Domínguez-Escalante Journal,* 61.
192. Ibid., 63.
193. Ibid., 64.
194. Ibid., 65.
195. Ibid., 66. Could this have been the pierced ears tribe Rivera heard about?
196. Ibid., 70.
197. Ibid., 70; fn. 290 indicates that the latitude reading was actually much higher—at 38° 15'.
198. Ibid., 70–71.
199. Ibid., 71.
200. Ibid., 74.
201. Ibid.
202. Ibid., 79–80.
203. Ibid., 88; fn. 342 places the latitude at 36° 59'.
204. Ibid., 93.
205. Ibid., 99; see also fn. 384. Near Padre Creek was a steep sandstone slope where the shallow footholds were hacked for about ten feet. The site is now covered with 550 feet of water from Lake Powell.
206. Ibid., 100–01.
207. Ibid., 101. Footnote 392 suggests that they were slightly above 37°. They were about three miles north of the modern Arizona-Utah boundary.
208. Hoja de Servicios, 1767, Sección Provincias Internas, tomo 47, f. 263, Archivo General de la Nación (hereinafter AGN), Mexico City.
209. Bolton, *Pageant in the Wilderness,* 343–46.
210. See Charles Edward Chapman, *Founding of Spanish California: The Northwestward Expansion of New Spain* (New York: Macmillan, 1916), 398–402.
211. Adams and Chávez, *The Missions of New Mexico,* 154.
212. Alfred Barnaby Thomas, *Forgotten Frontiers: A Study of Spanish Indian Policy of Don Juan Bautista de Anza, Governor of New Mexico, 1777–1787* (Nor-

man: University of Oklahoma Press, 1932), 101. Of Albuquerque, Morfi wrote: "The Villa of Albuquerque was founded in 1706 is distant twenty leagues from the Villa of Santa Fe in a large plain which will be a league from south to north and two and a half from east to west on the banks of the Río Grande. It possesses seven and one half leagues of land for crops and pastures which they irrigate with the waters of the river diverted by means of ditches. The climate is fair with respect to its elevation and very healthy because of the purity of its atmosphere. The land is fertile although it does not produce what it could because of insufficient cultivation for lack of oxen and leisure, the [threat of] enemies not permitting them to absent themselves from the villages for various tasks. Thus the land lies fallow. Scarcity of fuel obliges the settlers to utilize the manure of the horses. The settlement is scattered throughout the entire breadth of the valley. In 1779 the governor, Don Juan Bautista de Anza, reduced it to the regular form. At that time three hundred and eighty-one Spanish settlers lived there."

213. See Thomas, *Forgotten Frontiers*, 123.

214. Ibid., 123.

215. Ibid., 124.

216. Ibid., 125.

217. Ibid.

218. Ibid., 126.

219. Ibid., 127.

220. Ibid., 128.

221. Ibid., 130–31.

222. Ibid., 132.

223. Ibid., 134.

224. Ibid., 135–36.

225. Eleanor Richie, "General Mano Mocha of the Utes," *Colorado Magazine* 9 (January 1932): 153.

226. *Bando*, Don Francisco Trebol Nabarro, gobernador ynterino y comandante general de este reyno de Nuevo Mexico por el Señor Comandante General Caballero de Croix, 13 September, 1778, Spanish Archives of New Mexico (hereinafter cited as SANM), II, microfilm roll 10, frame 1055.

227. Ibid.

228. Proceedings in a suit against [settlers of Abiquiú] for having traded with the Utes without permission, 3 February 1783, SANM, II, microfilm roll 11, frame 520.

229. An *almud* is a dry or liquid measure with a capacity of 4.66 (Spain) or 6.87 (Mexico) dry quarts, or 5.133 liters (Spain) or 7.568 liters (Mexico). A *fanega* is a Spanish dry measure, about a bushel and a half.

230. Proceedings, 3 February 1783.

231. Ibid.

232. Ibid.

233. Proceedings against Salvador Salazar, Santiago Lucero and Francisco Valverde, 22 April to 9 May 1785, SANM, II, microfilm roll 11, frame 853.

234. Ibid.

235. Ibid.

236. Proceso contra Vicente Serna y los demas que expreza por infraciones del comercio del pais de los Yutas gente relados en la conformidad que refire 920, 31 March to 29 April 1785, SANM, II, microfilm roll 11, frame 837.

237. Proceso contra Marcelino Mansanares y demas que expresa por infraciones del comercio en el pais de los Yutas, y sentenciados come se refiere, 10 April 1785, SANM, II, microfilm roll 11, frame 845.

238. Proceedings against Cristóbal Lovato, et al., Río Arriba, 2 August to 2 September 1797, SANM, II, microfilm roll 14, frame 112.

239. This was the Río de los Pinos crossed by Rivera in 1765 and by Domínguez and Escalante in 1776.

240. Proceedings against Cristóbal Lovato.

241. Ibid.

242. Father José Vela Prada, Custos, to Governor Real Alencaster, Abiquiú, 18 August 1805, SANM, II, microfilm roll 15, frame 780.

243. Alencaster to Commandant-General Salcedo, 1 September 1805, SANM, II, microfilm roll 15, frame 810.

244. Ibid.

245. H. Carroll and Villasana Haggard, eds., *Three New Mexico Chronicles* (Albuquerque: The Quivira Society, 1942), 134. Also see footnote 353 in which the editors state that "Don José Rafael Sarracino was a member of the first and third territorial assemblies of New Mexico. At the fourth territorial assembly he was chosen as a delegate to the national government in Mexico City. He played a prominent part in New Mexican affairs during the two decades immediately following Mexican independence."

246. Ibid.

247. Proceedings against Miguel Tenorio, et al., Río Arriba, 6 September 1813, SANM, II, microfilm roll 12, frame 783.

248. Quoted in Eleanor Lawrence, "Mexican Trade Between Santa Fe and Los Angeles, 1830–1848," *California Historical Society Quarterly* 10 (1931): 27.

249. See Leroy Hafen, "Armijo's Journal," *Huntington Library Quarterly* 11: 99. Armijo noted in his diary that "[Rivera] recognized the ford where he had crossed the Río Grande [Colorado] the previous year in going to Sonora." All place-name identifications in the referenced publication of Armijo's diary cited hereinafter are Hafen's approximations of locations to modern sites and places.

250. Ibid., 92–93.

251. Ibid., 94.

252. Ibid., 95. Hafen, in note 43, quotes Escalante: "To lead the animals down by their bridles to the canyon it was necessary to hew steps with an ax in

a rock for a distance of about three yards or a little less. The animals could go down the rest of the way but without a pack or a rider."

253. Ibid., 96. In note 48 Hafen explains the confusion: "A closer study, however, convinces one that this identification is incorrect. The Sevier River runs north, instead of south, and does not flow into the Colorado as does Armijo's Río Severo. The Virgin River is the only stream that can be the Colorado affluent which the Spanish party follows; it meets all requirements."

254. Ibid., 97–99.

255. Ibid., 99, fn. 59.

256. Ibid., 101.

257. Ibid.

258. "A Famous Centenarian, General José María Chaves of New Mexico. An official under three flags," Anonymous. The Prince Papers: Contemporary New Mexicans. J.M. Chaves #4, New Mexico State Records Center & Archives, Santa Fe, New Mexico.

259. Ibid.

260. Ibid.

261. For a discussion of the New Mexican rebellion of 1837 against the administration of Governor Albino Pérez see Joseph P. Sánchez, "Año Desgraciado, 1837: The Overthrow of New Mexico's Jefe Político, Albino Pérez," *Atisbos: Journal of Chicano Research* (Summer–Fall 1978): 180–91.

262. Lansing B. Bloom, "New Mexico Under Mexican Administration," *Old Santa Fe* 2 (July 1914–April 1915): 4.

263. Albino Pérez, Order, 16 October 1835, Ritch Papers, microfilm reel 2, frame 153, University of New Mexico Library.

264. Sánchez, "Año Desgraciado, 1837," 187–88.

265. Rosa Chaves to Governor Prince, Abiquiú, New Mexico, 5 December 1902, Prince Papers. New Mexico State Record Center and Archives, Santa Fe, New Mexico.

266. Josiah Gregg, *Commerce of the Prairies,* (Dallas: Southwest Press, 1933), 81.

267. Benjamin Read Papers, Mexican Archives of New Mexico (MANM), microfilm roll 24, frame 807, University of New Mexico Library.

268. Depositions and certificates testifying to the loyalty of Donaciano Vigil in the fight with the insurrectionists in August 1837, Ritch Papers, reel 24, frame 169, University of New Mexico Library .

269. Gregg, *Commerce of the Prairies,* 82. Pérez was beheaded by Antonio Garcia, according to Rosa Chaves to Governor Prince.

270. Gregg, *Commerce of the Prairies,* 82.

271. Rosa Chaves to Governor Prince.

272. Hubert Howe Bancroft, *History of California* (San Francisco: Bancroft & Company, 1885) 3:555, fn. 23.

273. Bancroft, *History of California,* Volume 3:554. See footnote 22 in which

Bancroft states "The man is called by most Californians Cordero or Coronado. Alvarado says he was Aquilino Ramirez; and Jesus Pico calls him Olivas."

274. Rosa Chaves to Governor Prince.

275. Bancroft, *History of California*, 3:554–55.

276. Rosa Chaves to Governor Prince.

277. "A Famous Centenarian."

278. Marc Simmons, *The Little Lion of the Southwest: A Life of Manuel Antonio Chaves* (Chicago: Swallow Press, 1973), 158–59.

279. Ibid., 159–60.

280. The poem reads: "El teniente coronel,/Del condado del Río Arriba,/Es distinguido hombre fiel,/Gritemos todos que viva./Decir la verdad no estriva,/Que ese si es hombre valiente,/Gritemos que vive y viva,/Merece ser presidente./En el campo es elocuente,/Avoz de las companias,/Por el norte y el poniente,/Relucen sus maravillas." In "On the Road," Prince Papers, J.M. Chaves #14, New Mexico State Record Center and Archives, Santa Fe, New Mexico.

281. "A Famous Centenarian."

282. In LeRoy R. Hafen, "Louis Vasquez," in Hafen, *Mountain Men and the Fur Trade of the Far West* (Glendale: Arthur H. Clark Company, 1971), 2:32–22.

283. Ibid., 336.

284. Ibid., 322. Hafen writes, "Positive data on the activities of Vasquez in the middle and late twenties are lacking." In footnote 9, p. 322, Hafen cites Dale L. Morgan, who "presents the various conflicting claims to discovery of this inland sea but without resolving the problem." Regarding the interview by the correspondent of the *San Francisco Bulletin*, Hafen states that the "story, although garbled in chronology and certain data, is an important item." 335–36.

285. Ibid., 337.

286. Carl P. Russell, *Firearms, Traps, & Tools of the Mountain Men* (New York: Alfred A. Knopf, 1967), 17–18.

287. Ibid., 20.

288. Ibid.

289. Ibid., 22–24.

290. Lawrence, "Mexican Trade," 29.

291. Ibid., 29.

292. Ibid., 30–31.

293. Ibid., 32.

294. William J. Snow, "Utah Indians and the Spanish Slave Trade," *Utah Historical Quarterly* 2:81.

295. Ibid., 84.

296. Quoted in ibid., 84–85.

297. Quoted in ibid., 86–87. This law was approved on 7 March 1852.

298. Hafen and Hafen, *Old Spanish Trail*, 203–06.

299. Quoted in ibid., 208.

300. Harvey L. Carter, "Mariano Medina," in Hafen, *Mountain Men,* 247.

301. Ibid., 247–48, fn. 4.

302. Ibid., 248–49.

303. Ibid., 250.

304. Quoted in Janet Lecompte, "Marcelino Baca," in Hafen, *Mountain Men,* 21.

305. Ibid., 22–26.

306. Quoted in Hill, "Spanish and Mexican Exploration," 22–23.

307. A license was granted on 20 September 1850 to Chaves; it was issued by Calhoun and approved by the military commandant at Abiquiú, Brevet Major L.P. Graham. Chaves was granted the right to trade with the Utes in Utah Territory with no mention or restriction of the slave trade. Earlier, in July 1850, thirty licenses were similarly issued to thirty individuals to trade among the Utes. See Records of the Office of Indian Affairs, Record Group No. 75, Records of the New Mexico Superintendency, and Letters Received, National Archives, Washington, D.C.; copies in Center for Southwest Research, Microfilm Collection, University of New Mexico.

308. Quoted in Snow, "Utah Indians," 71.

309. Quoted in Hill, "Spanish and Mexican Exploration," 20.

Bibliography

DOCUMENTARY SOURCES

Albuquerque, New Mexico, United States. University of New Mexico Microfilm. Francisco Trebol Nabarro, governador ynterino y comandante general de este reyno de Nuevo Mexico por el Señor Comandante General Caballero de Croix, *Bando*, 13 September 1778, Spanish Archives of New Mexico (SANM), II, microfilm roll 10, frame 1055; Proceeding (fragment) in a suit against [settlers of Abiquiú] for having traded with the Utes without permission, 3 February 1783, SANM, II, microfilm roll 11, frame 520; Proceedings against Salvador Salazar, Santiago Lucero and Francisco Valverde, 22 April to 9 May 1785, SANM, II, microfilm roll 11, frame 853; Proceso contra Vicente Serna y los demas que expreza por infraciones del comercio del pais de los Yutas gente relados en la conformidad que refiere 920, 31 March to 29 April 1785, SANM, II, microfilm roll 11, frame 837; Proceso contra Marcelino Mansanares y demas que espresa por infracciones del comercio en el pais de los Yutas, y sentenciados como se refiere, 10 April 1785, SANM, II, microfilm roll 11, frame 845; Proceedings against Cristóbal Lovato, et al., Río Arriba, 2 August to 2 September 1797, SANM, II, microfilm roll 14, frame 112; Father José Vela Prada, Custos, to Governor Real Alencaster, Abiquiú, 18 August 1805, SANM, II, microfilm roll 15, frame 780; Governor Real Alencaster to Comandante-General Salcedo, 1 September 1805, SANM, II, microfilm roll 15, frame 810; Proceedings against Miguel Tenorio, et al., Río Arriba, 6 September 1813, SANM, II, microfilm roll 12, frame 783; Ritch Papers, Orders from Albino Pérez, 16 October 1835, roll 2, frame 153; Mexican Archives of New Mexico (MANM) Benjamin Read Papers, roll 24, frame 807; Ritch Papers, Depositions and certificates testifying to the loyalty of Donaciano Vigil in the fight with the insurrectionists in August 1837, MANM, roll 24, frame 169.

Madrid, Spain. Archivo del Servicio Histórico Militar. Diarios de reconocimientos de una parte de la América Septentrional española, 1766. Juan María Antonio Rivera's journals of June 1765 and November 1765 are contained therein.

Madrid, Spain. Real Academia de la Historia. Colección Muñoz, 9/4873. Capitulo 11, Del Principio de la Cristianidad de esta Pimería Progressos y Contradicciones que ha tenido, y estado que al presente tiene.

Madrid, Spain. Real Academia de la Historia. Colección Muñoz. Carta del Padre Fr. Carlos Delgado al Reverendo Padre Comisario General, Fr. Pedro Navarrette, Misión de la Isleta, Junio 18 de 1744.

Madrid, Spain. Real Academia de la Historia. Colección Muñoz. Dictamen del Padre [Alonso de] Posada, Año de 1686.

Mexico City, Mexico. Archivo General de la Nación. Sección Historia, tomo 395, pt. 6, folio 1, numero 161. Diario y derrotero de lo caminando visto, y observando en el discurso de la visita general de presidios situados en las Provincias Internas de Nueva España que de orden de su Magestad executó D. Pedro de Rivera, Brigadier de los Reales Ejércitos, 1736; Archivo Historico de la Nación. Ramo de las Provincias Internas, tomo 47, folio 263. Juan Bautista de Anza, Hoja de Servicios, 1767.

Santa Fe, New Mexico, United States. New Mexico State Archives and Record Center. Spanish Archives of New Mexico. Francisco Cuervo y Valdés, *Bando,* Santa Fe, 5 August 1705, 118; Juan Ignacio Flores Mogollon, *Bando,* Santa Fe, 16 December 1712, 185; Alcalde Mayor of Taos, *Bando,* 9 September 1725, 339; and Juan Domingo Bustamante, *Bando,* Santa Fe, 17 September 1725, 340; Francisco Marín del Valle, *Bando,* 26 November 1754, 530; Proceso contra Juan Baldes, genízaro, May 1762, 548; Prince Papers, Contemporary New Mexicans, J.M. Chaves 4, "A Famous Centenarian, General José María Chaves of New Mexico. An official under three flags"; Prince Papers, J.M. Chaves 14. Rosa Chaves to Governor Prince, Abiquiú, New Mexico, 5 December 1902; Prince Papers, Contemporary New Mexicans, J.M. Chaves 14, Rosa Chaves to Governor Prince, 24 August 1902; Prince Papers, J.M. Chaves 14, "On the Road."

Santa Fe, New Mexico, United States. Archives of the Archdiocese of Santa Fe. General List of Patentes, Patentes 1. Patente de Custos Zavaleta, Santa Fe, 2 July 1700.

Santander, Spain. Archivo Diocesano. Libro de Bautizados, Parroquia Santa María de Treceño, Año 1736 al 1781.

BOOKS

Adams, Eleanor B., ed. *Bishop Tamaron's Visitation to New Mexico, 1760.* Albuquerque: Historical Society of New Mexico, 1954.

———; and Fray Angelico Chávez, eds. and trans. *The Missions of New Mexico, 1776: A Description by Fray Francisco Atanasio Domínguez with Other Contemporary Documents.* Albuquerque: University of New Mexico Press, 1956.

Bancroft, Hubert Howe. *History of California.* Vol. 3. San Francisco: A.L. Bancroft & Company, 1885.

[Benavides, Alonso de]. *Benavides' Memorial of 1630 by Alonso de Benavides.* Edited by Cyprian J. Lynch and translated by Peter P. Forrestal. Washington, D.C.: Academy of American Franciscan History, 1954.

Bolton, Herbert E. *Outpost of Empire: The Story of the Founding of San Francisco.* New York: Alfred A. Knopf, 1931.

————. *Pageant in the Wilderness: The Story of the Escalante Expedition to the Interior Basin, 1776.* Salt Lake City: Utah State Historical Society, 1950.

Briggs, Walter. *Without Noise of Arms: The 1776 Domínguez-Escalante Search for a Route from Santa Fe to Monterey.* Flagstaff: Northland Press, 1976.

Burrus, Ernest J. *Kino and Manje, Explorers of Sonora and Arizona, Their Vision of the Future: A Study of their Expeditions and Plans.* Rome: Jesuit Historical Institute, 1971.

Carroll, Bailey H., and J. Villasana Haggard, eds. and trans. *Three New Mexico Chronicles: The Exposición of Don Pedro Bautista Pino, 1812; the* Ojeada *of Lic. Antonio Barreiro, 1832; and the additions by Don José Agustín de Escudero, 1849.* Albuquerque: The Quivira Society, 1942.

Carter, Harvey L. "Mariano Medina." In Leroy R. Hafen, *Mountain Men and the Fur Trade of the Far West.* Vol. 8. Glendale CA: The Arthur R. Clark Company, 1971.

Chapman, Charles Edward. *Founding of Spanish California: The Northwestward Expansion of New Spain.* New York: Macmillan, 1916.

Coues, Elliott, ed. and trans. *On the Trail of a Spanish Pioneer: The Diary and Itinerary of Francisco Garcés (Missionary Priest) in His Travels through Sonora, Arizona, and California, 1775–1776.* 3 vols. New York: Francis P. Harper, 1900.

Covey, Cyclone. *Cabeza de Vaca's Adventures in the Unknown Interior of America.* Albuquerque: University of New Mexico Press, 1961.

Ebright, Malcom. *Land Grants and Lawsuits in Northern New Mexico.* Albuquerque: University of New Mexico, 1994.

Geiger, O.F.M., Maynard. *Franciscan Missionaries in Hispanic California, 1769–1848.* San Marino: Huntington Library, 1969.

Gregg, Josiah. *Commerce of the Prairies.* Dallas: Southwest Press, 1933.

Hafen, Leroy R. *Mountain Men and the Fur Trade of the Far West.* Vol. 2. Glendale: Arthur H. Clark Company, 1971.

Hafen, Leroy R., and Hafen, Ann W. *Old Spanish Trail, Santa Fé to Los Angeles: With extracts from contemporary records and including diaries of Antonio Armijo and Orville Pratt.* Glendale: Arthur H. Clark Company, 1954.

Hallenbach, Cleve. *Alvar Núñez Cabeza de Vaca: The Journey of the First European to Cross the Continent of North America, 1534–1536.* Glendale: Arthur H. Clark, 1940.

Hammond, George P., and Agapito Rey, trans. *Narratives of the Coronado Expedition, 1540–1542.* Albuquerque: University of New Mexico Press, 1940.

———. trans. *The Rediscovery of New Mexico, 1580–1594.* Albuquerque: University of New Mexico Press, 1966.

Hodge, Frederick Webb, George P. Hammond, and Agapito Rey, trans. *Fray Alonso de Benavides' Revised Memorial of 1634.* Albuquerque: University of New Mexico Press, 1945.

Hordes, Stanley M. "A Sixteenth-century Spanish Campsite in the Tiguex Province: A Historian's Perspective." In Bradley J. Vierra, general editor, *Current Research on the Late Prehistory and Early History of New Mexico.* Albuquerque: New Mexico Archaeological Council, 1992.

John, Elizabeth A.H. *Storms Brewed in Other Men's Worlds.* College Station: Texas A & M Press, 1975.

Jones, Oakah L., Jr., *Pueblo Warriors & Spanish Conquest.* Norman: University of Oklahoma Press, 1966.

Lecompte, Janet. "Antoine Francois ('Baronet') Vasquez." In Leroy Hafen, *Mountain Men and the Fur Trade of the Far West.* Vol. 7. Glendale: Arthur H. Clark Company, 1969.

———. "Marcelino Baca." In Leroy Hafen, *Mountain Men and the Fur Trade of the Far West.* Vol. 3. Glendale: Arthur H. Clark Company, 1966.

Milich, Alicia Ronstadt, trans. *Relaciones by Zarate Salmeron.* Albuquerque: Horn & Wallace Publishers, Inc., 1966.

Oglesby, Richard E. "Manuel Lisa." In Leroy Hafen, *Mountain Men and the Fur Trade of the Far West.* Vol. 5. Glendale: Arthur H. Clark Company, 1966.

Priestley, Herbert I., ed. *A Historical, Political and Natural Description of California by Pedro Fages, Soldier of Spain.* Berkeley: University of California Press, 1937.

——— *Franciscan Explorations in California*, Edited by Lillian Estelle Fisher. Glendale: Arthur H. Clark, 1946.

Russell, Carl P. *Firearms, Traps, & Tools of the Mountain Men.* New York: Alfred A. Knopf, 1967.

Sánchez, Joseph P. *The Río Abajo Frontier, 1540–1692: A History of Early New Mexico.* Albuquerque: Albuquerque Museum History Monogaph Series, 1987, revised second edition, 1996.

———. *Spanish Bluecoats: The Catalonian Volunteers in Northwestern New Spain, 1767–1810.* Albuquerque: University of New Mexico Press, 1990.

———. "Twelve Days in August: The Pueblo Revolt in Santa Fe." In *Santa*

Fe: History of an Ancient City. Edited by David Grant Noble. Santa Fe: School of American Research Press, 1989.

Simmons, Marc. *The Little Lion of the Southwest: A Life of Manuel Antonio Chaves.* Chicago: Swallow Press, Inc., 1973.

————. *Spanish Government in New Mexico.* Albuquerque: University of New Mexico Press, 1968.

Thomas, Alfred Barnaby. *After Coronado: Spanish Exploration Northeast of New Mexico, 1696–1727.* Norman: University of Oklahoma Press, 1935.

————. *Alonso de Posada Report, 1686: A Description of the Area of the Present Southern United States in the Seventeenth Century.* Pensacola: Perdido Bay Press, 1982.

————. *The Plains Indians and New Mexico, 1751–1778.* Albuquerque: University of New Mexico Press, 1940.

Thomas, Alfred Barnaby, trans. and ed. *Forgotten Frontiers: A Study of the Spanish Indian Policy of Don Juan Bautista de Anza, Governor of New Mexico, 1777–1787.* Norman: University of Oklahoma Press, 1932.

Vierra, Bradley J. "A Sixteenth-century Spanish Campsite in the Tiguex Province: An Archaeologist's Perspective." In Bradley J. Vierra, general editor, *Current Research on the Late Prehistory and Early History of New Mexico.* Albuquerque: New Mexico Archaeological Council, 1992.

Warner, Ted J., ed., and Fray Angelico Chávez, trans., *The Domínguez-Escalante Journal: Their Expedition through Colorado, Utah, Arizona, and New Mexico in 1776.* Provo: Brigham University Press, 1977.

ARTICLES

Adams, Eleanor B. "Fray Francisco Atanasio Domínguez and Fray Silvestre Vélez de Escalante." *Utah Historical Quarterly* 44:40–58.

Auerbach, Herbert S., trans. "Father Escalante's Journal, 1776–1777: Newly Translated with Related Documents and Original Maps." *Utah Historical Quarterly* 2:1–142.

Bloom, Lansing B. "New Mexico Under Mexican Administration." *Old Santa Fe* 2:351–365.

Bolton, Herbert E. "In the South San Joaquín Ahead of Garcés." *California Historical Quarterly* 10:211–219.

Burrus, Ernest J., S.J., "Quivira and Teguayo in the Correspondence of Bandelier and Shea with Collet, 1882–1889." *Manuscripta* 11:67–83.

Cutter, Donald C. "Prelude to a Pageant in the Wilderness." *Western Historical Quarterly* 8:4–14.

Hafen, Leroy. "Armijo's Journal." *Huntington Library Quarterly* 11:87–101.

Hill, Joseph J. "Spanish and Mexican Exploration and Trade Northwest from New Mexico into the Great Basin." *Utah Historical Quarterly* 3:4–23.

Lawrence, Eleanor. "Mexican Trade Between Santa Fe and Los Angeles, 1830–1848." *California Historical Society Quarterly* 10:27–39.

Richie, Eleanor. "General Mano Mocha of the Utes and Spanish Policy in Indian Relations." *Colorado Magazine* 9:150–57.

Sánchez, Joseph P. "Año Desgraciado, 1837: The Overthrow of New Mexico's Jefe Político, Albino Pérez." *Atisbos: Journal of Chicano Research* (Summer–Fall 1978):180–91.

Snow, William J. "Utah Indians and Spanish Slave Trade." *Utah Historical Quarterly* 2:68–90.

Tyler, Lyman S. "The Myth of the Lake of Copala and Land of Teguayo." *Utah State Historical Society.* 20:313–29.

Index